Box-Making
Basics

Box-Making Basics

Design, Technique, Projects

David M. Freedman

The Taunton Press

COVER PHOTOS: David M. Freedman
(top left); Sally Ann Photography (top right);
Skot Weidemann (bottom)

The Taunton Press
Inspiration for hands-on living®

Printed in the United States of America
10 9 8 7 6

A FINE WOODWORKING Book

FINE WOODWORKING® is a trademark of The Taunton Press, Inc.,
registered in the U.S. Patent and Trademark Office.

The Taunton Press, Inc., 63 South Main Street, PO Box 5506,
Newtown, CT 06470-5506
e-mail: tp@taunton.com

Distributed by Publishers Group West

Library of Congress Cataloging-in-Publication Data

Freedman, David M.
        Box-making basics : design, technique, projects / David M. Freedman.
            p.   cm.
        Includes index.
        ISBN 1-56158-123-2
        1. Woodwork.   2. Wooden boxes.   3. Box making.   I. Title.
    TT200.F74   1997   96-51096
    745.593 — dc21   CIP

To Harriet Kohn, my beloved and eternal companion

Acknowledgments

For their encouragement, I would like to thank Gerry Freedman, Bob and Deenie Kohn, Eugene Watson, Ernie Wright, and David Friedman, Jr.

For their help, I'd also like to thank Jean Oseth of Akuba Studios and Gene Wengert, extension specialist in wood processing at the Department of Forestry, University of Wisconsin at Madison.

Thanks also to Neil and Suzanne McGinn, Helen Albert, Rick Peters, Tom McKenna, and Billaud duSavl.

Contents

Introduction

The popularity of wooden boxes never seems to diminish. They combine the resplendence of nature with human craftsmanship and creative spirit. At the same time, wooden boxes are useful. In their simplest forms, they're relatively easy to construct, inexpensive to acquire, yet limitless in their variety.

I made my first hardwood box about 13 years ago. It was a modest little box of walnut, with surface-mounted butt hinges. I cut the finger joints by hand, and you could tell. But I sanded everything flush, finished the box with oil, and gave it to a cousin as a gift. She seemed thrilled with the box, and her reaction was worth every minute I spent making it.

After years of practice and experimenting with design, I now sell boxes at craft fairs and art galleries for prices ranging from $30 to $300. It's gratifying when people come into my booth at a fair and caress the boxes and say, "Boy, I wish I could do work like that." And I always answer, "You can; all it takes is patience."

This book is divided into six chapters. The opening chapter is an introduction to the fundamentals of box making. Subsequent chapters are in two parts: The first part explains some basic woodworking techniques; the second part is a group of projects that employ those techniques.

For the most part, the projects are presented in order of increasing complexity, from very simple boxes suitable for the beginner to more sophisticated pieces for experienced woodworkers. So start at the beginning, or wherever you feel comfortable, and you'll learn something new in each succeeding chapter.

With some power tools (such as a table saw, a router, and a variable-speed drill for starters) and a little patience, you can make most of the boxes shown in this book, even if you've never made anything like them before. With practice and an adventurous spirit, you can create original designs that are prized for their beauty, as well as for the storage function they serve. I believe that we all have, somewhere within us, the creative drive and design sense needed to produce fine crafts or art; it's just a matter of setting it free and having the patience to grow.

A word about safety

Like any other form of woodworking, box making requires strict attention to safety in the workshop. Every time you buy a new power tool, read the manual before you plug in the machine. Keep your shop uncluttered (as much as humanly possible), and sweep the floor often so that you won't slip. Wear eye and ear protection, and use a dust mask or respirator when necessary.

Use high-quality blades, bits, knives, and chisels, and keep them sharp so that you won't have to apply undue pressure to make them cut. Keep a supply of push sticks and featherboards handy for feeding wood into blades and bits. Stay alert to possible hazards at all times; don't work when tired, distracted, or under the influence of medication. If woodworking becomes tedious or aggravating, take a break or quit for the day.

Be ecologically sensitive

If you use rain-forest woods, such as mahogany and rosewood, please take some time to acquaint yourself with the ecological issues associated with harvesting such species. Some suppliers practice sustainable-yield forest management, others don't. A good source of information is The Good Wood Alliance (289 College St., Burlington, VT 05401; 802-862-4448) or the forestry department at your nearest university.

1 BASICS OF BOX MAKING

Elements of Good Design

The design of boxes is highly subjective. I can tell you what I think about it and what designs have been successful for me, but you will ultimately develop and express your own design sensibilities. Your sense of design will mature over time as you gain more box-making experience. And once you've gained confidence in your own design sense, experiment and have some fun.

To help you get started on box design, I recommend that you look at what other craftspeople have done. Next time you see some interesting boxes in a gallery or at an art fair—or, for that matter, small containers of any kind anywhere—look closely and see if you can determine what makes some attractive and others awkward-looking.

Two of the main decisions you'll have to make when designing your own boxes involve dimensions and wood selection. But you also must pay attention to wood movement and to the grain pattern. To create pleasing designs, you'll have to keep all of these things in mind. Let's look at dimensions first.

Dimensioning a Box

When you set out to design an original box, you have total freedom to establish the dimensions of the box. Sometimes that freedom can be daunting. Your choices are infinite. Where do you start? When figuring a box's dimensions, you should consider two things: function and proportion.

FUNCTION

Your first consideration in the design of a box should be its function. What are you going to keep in the box? Or is the box decorative, with no intended function or mission other than to bring visual pleasure to its owner? If you design a box to hold specific objects, obviously it must be large enough for those objects.

For instance, a pencil box should be around 8½ in. long and not more than a few inches wide. A stationery box (made of ½-in. stock) should be around 12¼ in. by 10¼ in. by 1⅞ in. if it is to hold full-size letterhead. But a box for jewelry, or a box you make simply to showcase a spectacular piece of wood, can be just about any size.

PROPORTION

Once you know the function of the box, you should think about proportion next. Your mind naturally distinguishes between well-proportioned and ill-proportioned objects, and the sight of something that seems ill-proportioned can give you a feeling of displeasure, perhaps on a subconscious level.

You might want to begin by considering some of the proportions that have been used repeatedly throughout the centuries by architects, builders, and designers alike. Called classical or traditional proportions, these include the double cube, the root-of-two box, the 1:2:3 box, and the golden rectangle (see the drawing on the facing page). When in doubt, start with one of these or a slight variation thereof.

When thinking about proportion, you should also consider the thickness of the wood you're planning on using. In general, I recommend using thinner stock for a small box and thicker stock for a larger box, depending on the box's use. A very small box made of ⅝-in. stock will look bulky and clumsy, while a large box made of thin stock may not be sturdy enough for repeated use, although it may look elegant or delicate.

The rule of thumb that I use is if the perimeter of the box is 30 in. or greater, use ½-in. stock; if the perimeter is less than 30 in., use ⅜-in. stock. I've made exceptions, of course, and other woodworkers follow different guidelines altogether. You'll have to trust your own eye and judgment.

Selecting Wood

Okay, you know the function of the box and have a design that you think is well proportioned. Now you have to select the wood. I've made boxes out of a dozen or more species, and I have personal favorites. But I wouldn't try to tell you which species are best or what kind of wood you should use to make your box—it's a matter of personal taste. As you work with wood, you'll develop your own favorites, based on such factors as cost, hardness, texture, workability, how much the wood swells and shrinks seasonally, and maybe even where and how a species is harvested (for more on preparing stock, see pp. 12-16).

SPECIES

You certainly don't have to use expensive, exotic wood with sensational figure to make a fine box. A box made of an inexpensive, plain wood can be just as pleasing as one made with exotic wood, as long as it is well proportioned and well crafted. As a matter of fact, some people prefer the understated elegance of plain-figured domestic hardwoods.

If you choose to combine two or more species in one project, you should consider a couple of factors: visual contrast and wood movement. Contrasting light and dark woods (such as maple and walnut) can create a dramatic look. Less contrast (cherry and walnut, for example) will give a subtle, more traditional look. It's also a good idea to choose two species with similar rates of seasonal movement so that they will shrink and expand equally.

The strategy I use most often to select wood is to first decide on the look I'm after. Let's say I want a medium to dark wood with a fairly plain grain pattern. Walnut, butternut, and mahogany all fit this bill. But which to choose? To help in the decision-making process, I next look at the properties of the different species: cost, hardness, texture, workability, and wood movement. The chart on p. 6 shows the most important properties of various wood species that box makers commonly use.

Cost Lumber prices vary from year to year and from region to region, according to supply and demand. The price of maple is naturally higher on the West Coast than in its native eastern region, and redwood is likewise more expensive back East. Wood imported from other continents can be very expensive. Since you don't need large pieces of wood to make boxes, consider buying lumber in the lower grades (such as No. 1 common) and cutting around the defects. Or see if your lumberyard sells "shorts." Either of these options can save you a lot of money.

Hardness The botanical definitions of "hardwood" and "softwood" don't always relate to the actual hardness of a species, which is its ability to resist denting and scratching.

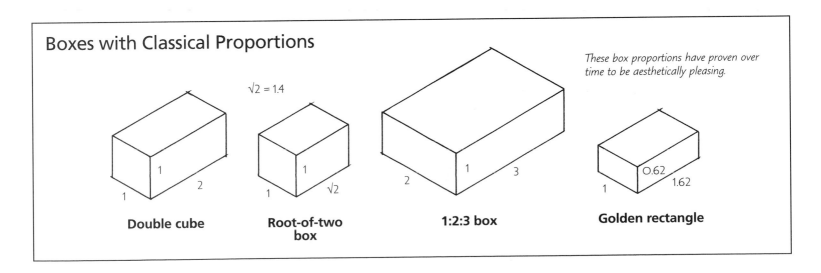

Boxes with Classical Proportions

√2 = 1.4

These box proportions have proven over time to be aesthetically pleasing.

Double cube

Root-of-two box

1:2:3 box

Golden rectangle

Hardwoods come from deciduous trees with leaves. They have relatively thick cell walls and small cell cavities. Some hardwoods may actually seem soft, such as balsa and basswood, but they're still designated as hardwoods.

Softwoods come from needle-bearing conifers (evergreens). They have relatively thin cell walls and large cell cavities. Some softwoods are quite hard and sturdy—southern yellow pine being one of them.

If you expect your box to be handled frequently—opened and closed, picked up and set down—then the hardness of the wood is important to minimize scratches and dents. Some softer woods are easily dented with a fingernail, even if the wood has a couple of coats of finish on it.

Note also that hardwoods are easier to polish to a high luster after sanding and finishing. Softwoods can wind up with a fuzzy surface after being sanded, which makes it hard to achieve a smooth, lustrous finish. Moreover, softwoods generally don't take penetrating oil finishes well because the rate of absorption varies throughout a board, yielding a blotchy look. For strength and a better finish, I recommend building boxes out of hardwood.

Texture Although texture may seem unimportant, it sends an unspoken message about the function and quality of a piece every time it's handled.

Woods with a fine or closely spaced cell structure (such as birch, cherry, and maple) provide a smooth, unbroken surface. Coarse or

WOOD CHARACTERISTICS

Species	Cost	Hardness	Texture	Workability	Tangential movement
Ash, black	medium	medium	coarse	low	high
Ash, white	medium	high	coarse	low	medium
Aspen	low	low	fine	high	low-medium
Basswood	low	low	fine	high	high
Beech	low	high	fine	low	high
Birch	low	medium-high	fine	low	medium-high
Butternut	high	low-medium	coarse	high	low-medium
Cherry	medium	medium	fine	medium-high	medium
Ebony	very high	high	fine	low	low-medium
Elm, rock	low	high	coarse	low	medium-high
Hickory	low	high	coarse	low	high
Koa	high	high	fine	high	medium
Mahogany, Honduras	high	medium	medium	high	very low
Mahogany, Philippine	low	medium	medium-coarse	high	medium
Maple, hard	medium	high	fine	low	high
Maple, soft	low	medium	fine	medium	medium
Oak, red	medium	high	coarse	medium	medium
Oak, white	medium	high	coarse	low	medium
Padauk, African	high	high	coarse	medium	low
Pecan	low	high	coarse	low	high
Rosewood	very high	high	fine	low	low
Sycamore	low-medium	medium	fine	low	medium
Tupelo	low	medium	fine	low	medium
Walnut	medium-high	medium	medium-coarse	high	medium
Yellow-poplar	low	low	fine	medium	medium

Three Directions of Wood Movement

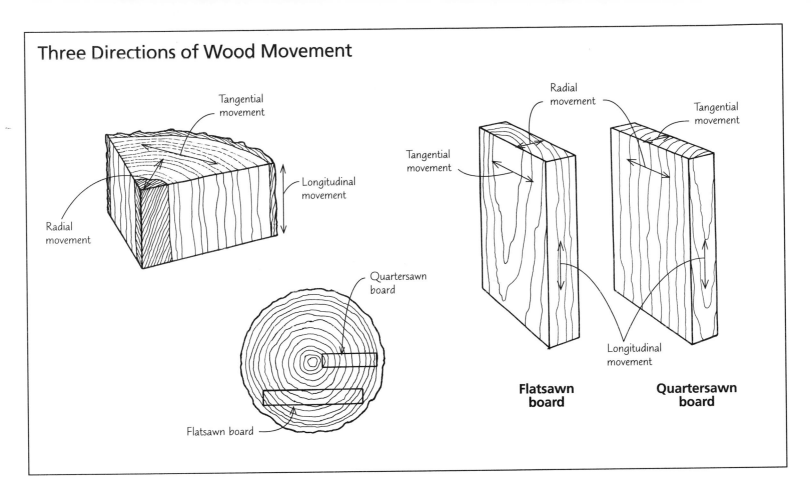

Tangential movement

Radial movement

Longitudinal movement

Quartersawn board

Flatsawn board

Radial movement

Tangential movement

Tangential movement

Longitudinal movement

Flatsawn board

Quartersawn board

open grain appears in wood that has large cells spaced farther apart, such as oak and ash. These woods offer a rich texture that breaks up the surface.

Workability For beginning woodworkers, workability should be a major factor in deciding which wood to select for a project. Highly workable wood is comparatively easy to cut, shape, drill, and carve with hand tools. Very hard woods, such as white ash, hickory, and hard maple, are not only difficult to work but also can dull non-carbide blades and bits quickly.

Wood movement Wood shrinkage and swelling, in response to changes in humidity, is greatest across the grain, or tangentially. But different species have different rates of tangential movement (see the chart on the facing page). Rosewood and mahogany, for example, move very little in response to climatic changes, while hard maple and white oak move more than most species. Depending on where you live, wood movement can have a dramatic, often devastating impact on your boxes. As a rule, for larger boxes I try to use woods that are the most stable.

But all wood shrinks and expands. So no matter which species you choose, you'll need to pay attention to how the wood will move—before you construct the box—because movement continues even after your box is finished. In a log or a board, shrinking and swelling are measured in three different directions: longitudinally, radially, and tangentially (see the drawing above).

The least movement occurs in the longitudinal direction, or along the lines of the grain. For most species, after a board is kiln-dried, longitudinal movement is insignificant.

Movement from the center of a log to the bark is radial movement. It can be 50 times the amount of longitudinal movement, given an equal change in moisture content.

The greatest movement occurs in the tangential direction, or perpendicular to radial movement. Tangential movement can be double the amount of radial movement.

Don't Use Nails or Screws

When humidity increases with warm weather, wood expands and moves. Due to that movement, screws and nails driven into the wood are pulled and tugged until they tear the wood fibers around them. When the wood shrinks again in dry weather, screws or nails can loosen. Over the years, a screw can work its way out of a joint unless you tighten it periodically (there's not much you can do when the nail falls out, except drive in another). Even if you tighten the screw or drive another nail, the joint will weaken without other methods of bonding, such as glue.

So forget about those nails and screws and concentrate on making well-crafted wood joints. The combination of a tight, well-mated woodworking joint and modern glues creates a bond that is stronger than that achieved with nails or screws.

Minimizing Cup on Large Panels

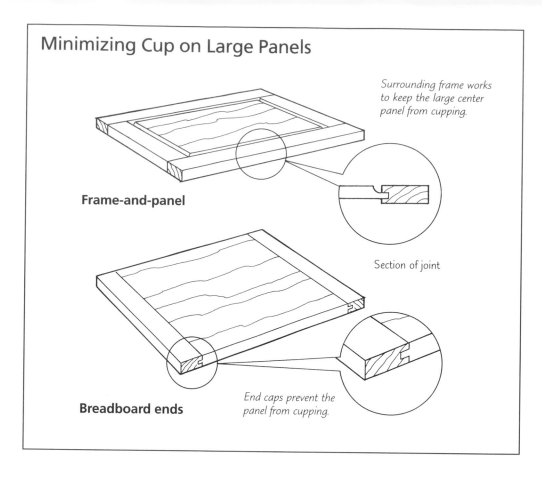

Frame-and-panel

Surrounding frame works to keep the large center panel from cupping.

Section of joint

Breadboard ends

End caps prevent the panel from cupping.

Orienting Grain to Minimize Joint Stress

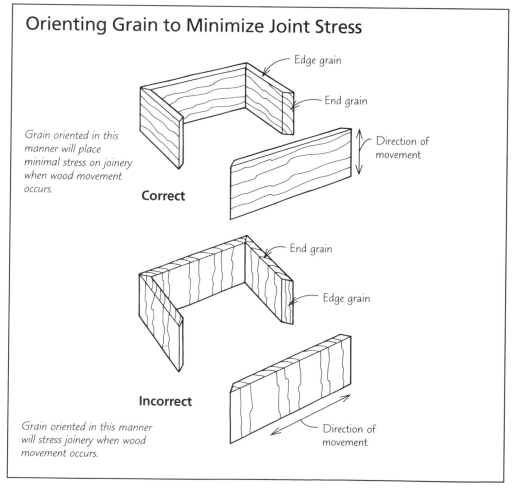

Edge grain

End grain

Grain oriented in this manner will place minimal stress on joinery when wood movement occurs.

Direction of movement

Correct

End grain

Edge grain

Incorrect

Grain oriented in this manner will stress joinery when wood movement occurs.

Direction of movement

Limiting Wood Movement

You can reduce movement by applying a finish, which partially closes the wood's pores and lowers its rate of moisture absorption and evaporation. But you can never stop wood movement totally, no matter how many coats of finish you apply. Fortunately, woodworkers over the ages have developed ways of coping with wood movement.

WARP

There are two broad categories of wood movement: the expected shrinking and swelling that naturally occurs in an organic material, and the undesired distortion of a piece, called warp. Warp is a misleading term because it actually encompasses four different defects: bow, cup, twist, and crook (see the drawing on p. 13). Of these four, cup is the most common problem for box makers, especially when working with wide, flatsawn boards, such as those used for a top or bottom of a box.

You can restrain cup mechanically with certain construction methods—for example, frame-and-panels or breadboard ends (see the top drawing at left). Both methods are stable, attractive, and not difficult to make. The surrounding frame of a frame-and-panel lid or door works to keep the large center panel from cupping. Likewise, breadboard ends do the same thing. Another way to minimize cup is to assemble a large panel from strips. Narrow strips glued together edge-to-edge with alternating end-grain patterns tend to balance out any movement that does occur.

SHRINKING AND SWELLING

Although it's desirable to restrain warp, you should never try to restrain shrinking and swelling mechanically, unless you want your box to self-destruct after a few years. Restraining the wood's natural movement will create stresses that lead to joint failure, splitting, and distortion.

Since you can't defeat shrinking and swelling, you'll have to work with them. When you design a box, or make a joint, try to anticipate the ways that movement will affect the finished product and then let the movement happen in such a way that it doesn't create stress (see the bottom drawing at left). The methods you choose will depend on the box you are making.

However, you can get around the problem of shrinking and swelling of solid wood by using man-made sheet goods such as plywood, which is available in nominal thicknesses

Working with Burls, Spalted Wood, and Wild Grain

What some people view as grotesque distortions of nature, others recognize as its most spectacular creations. At many lumberyards and even a few cabinet shops, burled and spalted woods are routinely discarded or burned. More and more, though, suppliers and woodworkers—and consumers, too—are learning to appreciate the savage beauty of these aberrations (and, of course, prices are going up with the demand).

Burls are wartlike growths, or bulges, on tree trunks, branches, and roots. Burls can grow on just about any species of tree, and they usually have to do with healing injuries to the tree—sort of like scabs. The grain pattern in burl wood is distorted, sometimes severely, and in root burls you'll sometimes find gray and blue tones from minerals seeping into the wood.

Spalting is caused by decay. As a felled tree lies in the forest, it soaks up moisture from the ground and attracts fungus and microorganisms that feed on the decaying organic matter. The invasion of microorganisms discolors and distorts the grain pattern—and ultimately disintegrates the wood fibers—until the wood becomes soft and worthless. But if harvested and dried before the decaying process is too advanced, the wood—although weakened considerably—is still strong enough to use.

Normal wood can develop wild grain patterns, too, especially around large knots or in crotches where branches diverge. The patterns can be attractive or downright ugly.

Burls, spalted woods, and wild grain are more difficult to work with than normal wood. They must be dried slowly and carefully, or they'll check, split, and crack. Their behavior in the shop is unpredictable. When you dimension any wood with these "defects," cut the stock oversize and sticker the boards a few days longer than usual, and then thickness them on a wide-belt sander. Don't use a thickness planer: Because of the irregular grain, the knives of a planer tend to gouge or even shatter the workpiece. If you don't have a thickness sander, your local cabinet shop might sand it for you for a nominal fee.

A few warnings

Dust from spalted wood can cause severe allergic reactions in some people and may produce symptoms similar to emphysema. Wear a respirator and provide adequate ventilation.

Be careful when cutting into root burls because they may contain rocks and dirt. And when you're sanding spalted wood, go very lightly over the cream-colored soft spots because they'll abrade much quicker than you would expect.

These soft spots will also soak up penetrating finishes faster than other areas, resulting in dramatic darkening of the color. If you want to preserve the colors in spalted wood, use lacquer or clear varnish.

The grain distortions and black streaks in this piece of burled maple made it perfect for the lid of a box.

The overlay lid panel of this necklace box is bookmatched spalted maple.

Achieving a Continuous Grain Pattern

Three-corner match

1. Start with a board that's as long as the box's perimeter, plus three saw kerfs, plus 1 in. for error. Mark the lengths of each side and label the joints.

2. Miter-cut the pieces to length.

3. Align matching labels, then assemble. One corner (D-D) will not match, so make sure that corner is on the back of the box.

down to ⅛ in., with various hardwood veneers on the outside. Plywood is made of thin layers of wood with alternating grain direction, so movement is negligible. Box makers commonly use plywood for bottom panels, as well as for lid panels when frame-and-panel construction is employed.

Tempered hardboard (such as Masonite), which is another stable, man-made material, can be used in your project. It has no grain orientation at all (it also comes in precise thicknesses down to ⅛ in.). However, the appearance of hardboard leaves something to be desired, so you'll have to incorporate veneer into your design.

Continuous Grain Pattern

If you examine really fine wood boxes, you'll find that in most cases the grain pattern is continuous all around the box's perimeter. The best woodworkers take care to match the grain at each corner. Beginners may tend to overlook this detail because it requires extra planning and care, but this attention to detail can make the difference between a simply functional wood box and a finely crafted one.

Achieving a continuous grain pattern is critical in boxes with miter joints because there is no end grain showing to interrupt the continuity around the corners. In boxes with butt joints, dovetail joints, or other joints, where end grain does interrupt the pattern, achieving continuous grain is not as critical.

To achieve a continuous grain pattern, all four sides of a box should be cut from the same board. Different boards of the same species—even if they're from the same tree—can vary significantly in both color and grain pattern. To make the grain continuous around a box, you can simply use straight-grained stock, or you can try to match the corners.

THREE-CORNER MATCH

If you're working with stock that has a wavy or irregular grain pattern, the quickest way to achieve continuous grain is to crosscut all four carcase pieces consecutively from one piece of dimensioned stock (already cut to final width). Number the ends in pencil or chalk so that you'll remember the order in which they are to be assembled (see the drawing above). You'll have a perfect match at three corners, so make sure the fourth, unmatched corner is in back or in the least-conspicuous place. If you plan ahead, you can even make the fourth corner appear fairly well matched.

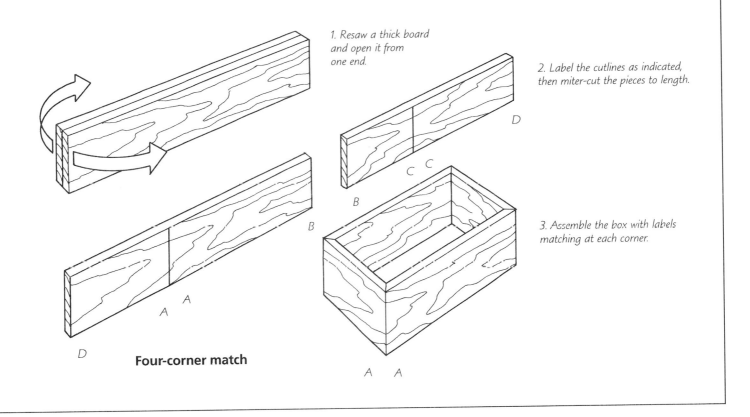

1. Resaw a thick board and open it from one end.

2. Label the cutlines as indicated, then miter-cut the pieces to length.

3. Assemble the box with labels matching at each corner.

Four-corner match

FOUR-CORNER MATCH

The four-corner match (see the photo at right), is elegant and labor-intensive. When you resaw a board (slice it in half like a bagel), the freshly exposed surfaces are mirror images of one another (this is known as a bookmatch). These freshly exposed surfaces become the outside of the box, and the pieces are lined up, as shown in the drawing above, to achieve a perfect continuous grain pattern on all four corners. Of course, you have to start with a board that's more than twice as thick as the final stock thickness and a little longer than one side plus one end of the box. Mark each piece before cutting the miters so that you'll remember the order of assembly.

I realize that going to the trouble of achieving a continuous grain pattern may seem unnecessary or even excessive. But I can't emphasize enough how it's the subtle things that combine to create a good design and a beautiful box—one that will be both used and cherished.

A four-corner match will achieve a perfect continuous grain pattern.

Selecting Wood and Preparing Stock

For a wood box to appear well proportioned, it must be made out of thin lumber (½ in. to ⅜ in. thick). The thin stock gives the box a light or delicate look, not one that is heavy or klunky. Interior parts, such as dividers and trays, are often made from stock that's ¼ in. thick or less (referred to as "micro-lumber").

There are two basic strategies for obtaining thin lumber: You can buy it already dimensioned, also called four-square or surfaced four sides (S4S), or you can buy rough lumber and dimension it yourself.

Dimensioned Lumber

Beginning woodworkers should buy lumber that is already dimensioned and surfaced. That means the boards are planed to their final thickness, smooth on both faces (see the drawing below), and have at least one edge ripped straight, square, and smooth (jointed). You can buy dimensioned thin lumber and micro-lumber at some specialty lumber dealers, woodworking stores, and craft supply outlets, as well as through various woodworking catalogs.

LUMBERYARDS

When you shop for dimensioned lumber, do business with a reputable dealer that sells boards properly kiln-dried to around 6% to 8% moisture content. It's also important, especially for beginners, to choose a dealer that will take the time to give you advice on how to select the appropriate boards for your project. If you're not familiar with dealers in your area, ask an experienced woodworker or professional cabinetmaker to recommend one.

You should look for boards that are as straight as possible, with little or no warp (see the drawing on the facing page). A crooked board can be straightened fairly easily on the table saw (see the drawing on p. 14). But don't buy a board if it's cupped, twisted, or bowed because these defects cannot be fixed easily.

It's also good practice to buy around 20% more lumber than you think you'll need. This way you'll have extra to account for defects and the occasional mistake.

MAIL ORDER

Don't hesitate to buy lumber through a reputable mail-order catalog company, especially if the nearest lumber dealer is a long drive. Before I bought a bandsaw and started dimensioning my own lumber, I had good luck purchasing lumber through mail-order companies. A reputable catalog company will allow you to return or exchange boards that don't meet your expectations and will replace (at its expense) any defective boards. However, dimensioned lumber is expensive, and catalog orders often take a week or two to fill, so you have to plan ahead.

Rough Lumber

I prefer to buy rough lumber, which comes in thicknesses of 1 in. or more, and dimension it in my shop because it affords me greater control to select and match grain.

Also, dimensioned lumber is expensive in terms of cost per board foot. (To figure the amount of board feet in a piece of lumber, multiply the piece's thickness by its width, then by its length—in inches. Then divide that number by 12. One board foot can take on many shapes, as you can see in the drawing on p. 15.) I once calculated that I pay 20% to 50% less for rough lumber, depending on the species and quantity I need. And by dimensioning lumber carefully, you can practically eliminate warp, and your stock will be as true as it can be (straight, flat, and square). For those of you who do want to dimension your own boards, you'll need a bandsaw, a jointer, a thickness planer, and a table saw. If you buy and use a lot of lumber, it's easy to justify the cost of this equipment.

BUY THICK STOCK

Since you'll be resawing your rough stock into thinner boards (more about this later), you need to buy rough stock at least twice as thick as the final thickness needed, plus ¼ in. The extra ¼ in. is for the width of the bandsaw kerf (about 1/16 in.), plus the material that you plane off each face to get it smooth. For example, a rough 5/4 board (1¼ in. thick) will yield two ½-in. boards with smooth faces. I've found, however, that some boards will warp so much after they are resawn that I'll have to do

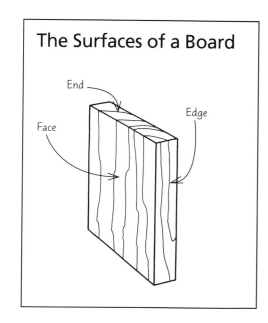

The Surfaces of a Board

End

Edge

Face

Common Types of Warp

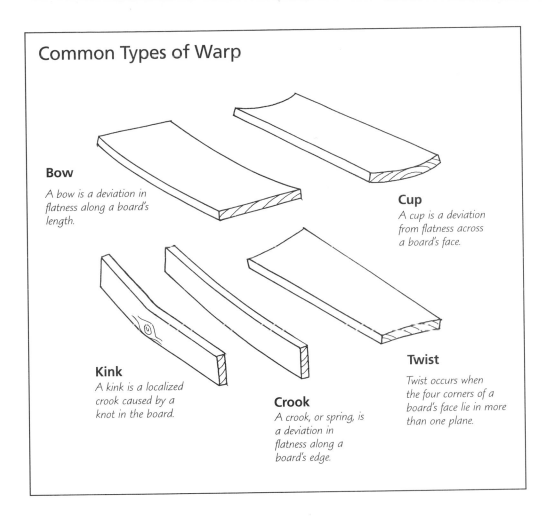

Bow

A bow is a deviation in flatness along a board's length.

Cup

A cup is a deviation from flatness across a board's face.

Kink

A kink is a localized crook caused by a knot in the board.

Crook

A crook, or spring, is a deviation in flatness along a board's edge.

Twist

Twist occurs when the four corners of a board's face lie in more than one plane.

Working with Severely Warped Boards

When a board is resawn, each resawn piece will dry and shrink. As I said previously, this shrinkage occurs unevenly throughout the board, depending on the orientation of the growth rings and grain pattern.

Most of the time, this shrinkage is not a problem. But occasionally you'll get a board that bows drastically after resawing, due to the release of internal stress and tension. If you can't bear to consign the board to the fireplace, here's how to fix it.

Resaw all remaining boards from the same stock a little thicker (an extra 1/16 in. to 1/8 in.), if possible. Don't bother stickering; let the resawn boards sit overnight so the freshly cut faces can dry.

Cut the boards into shorter lengths, according to the dimensions needed for your project. The shorter the board, the less stock you'll need to remove on the jointer to flatten it.

If the resulting pieces are long enough (consult your jointer's manual for minimum length, typically 12 in.), joint the concave face and one edge, then rip the other edge parallel to the first on the table saw. If the boards are too short for the jointer, flatten the concave face on a belt sander and joint both edges on the table saw.

Thickness each board in a planer, with the flat side down. If the board is too short to run through the thickness planer, flatten the convex edge and thickness the stock on the table saw. Then rip the board to final width. Use featherboards and push sticks to keep the board against the fence and to prevent kickback, as well as to keep your fingers away from the blade.

Straightening a Crooked Edge

For short boards, place the concave edge against the table saw's fence and rip the opposite edge straight.

Straightedge tacked to board

Fence

For long boards, tack a straightedge to the board and hold the straightedge against the rip fence.

a lot of planing to get them flat, and I'll lose too much thickness in the process. So I often buy 6/4 hardwood (1½ in. thick), which usually yields two ½-in. boards, and perhaps a slice of ⅛-in. micro-lumber.

To save wear and tear on your planer blades, you might see if the dealer will plane each face lightly but not smooth: just enough to remove gross surface irregularities and residual dirt.

When you bring the boards home, let them acclimate to your workshop environment before resawing them (for more on storing lumber in your shop, see the sidebar below). Even if you're in a big hurry, let them sit at least a few days in the shop. You want the majority of the movement to occur before you start dimensioning a board.

CUT TO ROUGH LENGTH AND WIDTH
For box making, where most dimensions are short (as opposed to furniture and cabinet making), a crooked board may be acceptable—as long as it's not bowed or cupped—because it can be straightened easily. First, crosscut the board into shorter lengths, if your plan permits. Place the concave edge of any crooked piece against the table saw's fence and rip the opposite edge straight (see the drawing at left).

A long board will require a bit more work, however. Start by attaching a straight length of wood or a metal straightedge to one edge of the board and rip the opposite edge. Then remove the straightedge, turn over the board, and rip the other edge, with the straightened edge against the fence.

Storing Lumber

Once you purchase your lumber, stack it flat up off the floor or on a shelf in your shop for a couple of weeks—or at least a few days for micro-lumber—before you start building your project. This will allow the wood to acclimate to its new environment.

If you cut open a board that hasn't adjusted to the climate in your shop, the freshly cut surface will absorb or lose moisture until it achieves equilibrium with the air, resulting in movement. And if you use two different boards with varying moisture content in the same project, they could move in conflicting ways and ruin the most painstakingly formed joinery. There's nothing more frustrating than trying to join two pieces of warped wood. Straight boards allow you to make strong, attractive joints.

If you live in a region that has wide humidity swings, especially if your shop is in a basement or an unheated garage, keep a humidistat in your shop to monitor humidity levels. Extreme changes in humidity can cause lumber to swell, shrink, warp, split, and just plain misbehave. Run a dehumidifier when the humidity gets extremely high, and run a humidifier if your shop gets extremely dry. (A dehumidifier will also help keep your tools from rusting.)

If your boards are free from warp, crosscut them into manageable lengths before planing and cut off any loose knots. The shorter the boards, the easier they are to handle. But be sure you cut them long enough for your project; if your box dimensions are 6 in. by 8 in., for example, you'll need a board that's at least 29 in. long (the perimeter plus an extra inch for saw kerfs). Leave the board longer still if your planer "snipes" the board's ends, in which case you'll have to trim off a couple of inches at each end. Most planers require a board to be at least 14 in. long to run it through; check your manual to be sure.

When the boards are cut to their rough lengths, cut them to manageable widths on the bandsaw. This will not only make them easier to handle, but will also reduce any cupping that has already occurred and therefore will require less planing.

JOINT FACE AND EDGES

Plane one face of each board flat on the jointer. If a board is wider than the jointer, use a thickness planer.

Joint the edges of the boards, holding the flat face against the fence. Jointing will also square the face to the edge. Cut with the grain, not against it. Cutting against the grain tends to create a chipped, rough surface. However, if it's not possible to cut with the grain (for instance, if you've planed only one face and can't get the grain direction to cooperate), take light passes on the jointer to minimize chipping.

RESAW ON THE BANDSAW

Resaw each board on the bandsaw with the jointed edge down and the planed face against the rip fence. Use the widest blade your saw will allow (in most cases ½ in.). I get best results from a hook-tooth blade with three teeth per inch.

Attach a high auxiliary fence to the standard fence and make sure the boards bear fully against the high fence, so you can keep them perfectly vertical throughout the cut. Feed each board into the blade slowly and steadily; it shouldn't take much effort, only patience. Remember to leave a little extra thickness on each board because you'll still have to thickness it.

Some wood movement is to be expected when resawing a board in the shop. No matter how carefully a board has been kiln-dried, there will always be slightly more moisture left in the interior than near the surface. So, when

you resaw a board and expose a new face, the newly exposed surface will dry and shrink slightly. And if the opposite surface has already dried and will not shrink much further, the conflicting movement will warp the board slightly over the course of a few days.

Moisture is not the only cause of warp after resawing. Internal tensions were built up in the board while it was a living tree. Ripping a board can relieve that tension, resulting in unexpected movement. Wood that moves like this is often referred to as reaction wood. The movement will occur during or immediately after cutting. You cannot prevent or predict warp due to internal tension. If the wood warps severely, see the sidebar on p. 13.

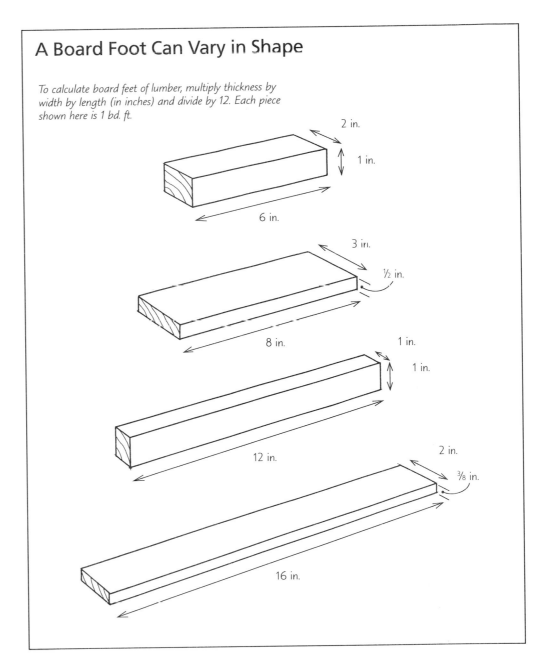

A Board Foot Can Vary in Shape

To calculate board feet of lumber, multiply thickness by width by length (in inches) and divide by 12. Each piece shown here is 1 bd. ft.

Stickering Boards

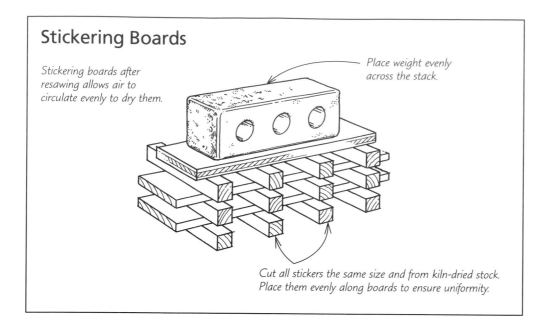

Stickering boards after resawing allows air to circulate evenly to dry them.

Place weight evenly across the stack.

Cut all stickers the same size and from kiln-dried stock. Place them evenly along boards to ensure uniformity.

STICKER ALL BOARDS

After resawing, sticker the boards and let them sit in the shop for a few days (see the drawing above). Stickering allows the air to flow evenly across both faces of the stock so the wood can adjust uniformly to the shop environment. Cut the stickers from scraps of kiln-dried lumber of equal thickness, and spread them consistently across each board (keep them vertically aligned). Place the stack where there is good air circulation and put a heavy board or other evenly distributed weight on top of the stack.

After a few days, remove the stickers. You may find that the freshly exposed face of each board is a bit concave, as the loss of moisture caused it to shrink relative to the smooth face. If so, joint this rough face flat, taking care

not to put too much downward pressure on the middle of the board as it passes across the knives.

PLANE TO THICKNESS

Plane the boards to final thickness. If you need boards that are less than 3/8 in. thick, consult your machine's manual for the safest way to plane thin boards. Running a too-thin board through the planer may cause the wood to split or shatter.

Check the edges with a straightedge to see if they've become a bit crooked as a result of all this cutting and planing. If so, joint the edges again. After this step, the boards are ready to be cut to final widths and lengths.

Finishing

Before delving into the techniques of box construction, I want to say a few words about finishing. Although there are purists who like the look and feel of wood in its unfinished, natural state, I don't recommend purism when it comes to wood boxes. A finish protects the wood, beautifies it, and makes it pleasant to touch.

A wood box is going to be handled often, so it will collect dust, grime, and oils from your fingers, which can discolor the wood. By applying a coat or two of finish to your box, you can prevent dirt from working its way into the grain. And a finish also makes it easier to clean off any dirt that accumulates on the surface.

Most finishes add a satiny luster or a gloss to the surface, which people find attractive. Some finishes, especially penetrating Danish oils, accentuate the natural grain patterns and color variations in wood. And I've found that adding a thin coat of paste wax on top of a couple of coats of Danish oil creates a look of magnificent depth and richness.

Preparing the Surface

Achieving a quality finish begins with proper surface preparation. This consists of patching major blemishes, sanding out scratches and small blemishes, and easing the edges.

PATCH MAJOR BLEMISHES

You should start by filling or fixing any major blemishes that can't be removed by sanding. Get rid of errant patches of glue by scraping with a cabinet scraper or chisel. Fill major chip-outs, holes, or cracks with wood putty. You can buy commercial putty (which comes in a wide variety of hues and tones) or make your own by mixing fine sawdust and white glue into a thick paste.

If you make your own putty, use sawdust from the same board that you used for your box to achieve a good color match. And avoid mixing too high a proportion of glue to dust, or your finish won't penetrate the filled spot adequately. Allow plenty of time for the putty to dry before sanding the surface.

If your box was dented during the building process, don't fret. Raising a dent is easier than you might expect (see the drawing at right). First, place a drop or two of water on the dent. After the water soaks in, lay a damp cloth over the dent and apply heat with a clothes iron or

the tip of a soldering iron for several seconds. The combination of heat and water will generate steam, which causes the wood fibers to swell, lifting the dent. Repeat this procedure if necessary. Let the surface dry thoroughly before proceeding.

SAND SMALL BLEMISHES

The first step in sanding is to determine which sandpaper grit to start with. If you can easily see small scratches or subtle planer marks (which look like a series of scallops) on the wood surface with your naked eye, you probably should start with a medium-grit paper, such as 120 or 150. If you see major scratches, chips, saw marks, or obvious planer marks, you might have to start with coarser 100-grit or even 80-grit sandpaper. With a little practice you'll learn to "read" the wood surface and select the appropriate grit.

I like to sand with a commercial sanding block made of rubber or cork. It's a good idea to tap the block against the bench often to

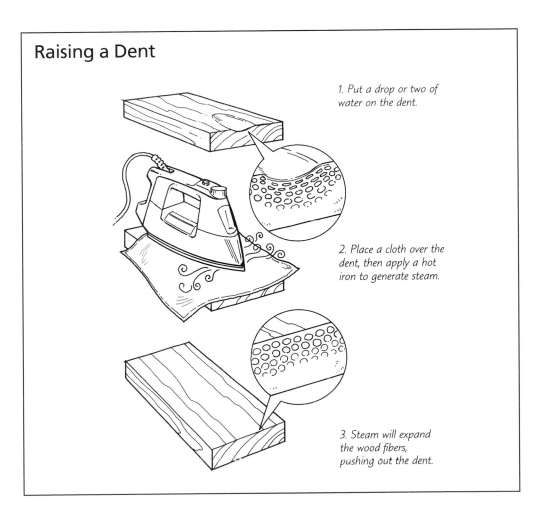

Raising a Dent

1. Put a drop or two of water on the dent.

2. Place a cloth over the dent, then apply a hot iron to generate steam.

3. Steam will expand the wood fibers, pushing out the dent.

dislodge sawdust that will eventually clog the sandpaper. Be sure to change the sandpaper as soon as it becomes dull, to prevent the sandpaper from burnishing the wood surface. (Burnishing the wood makes it impervious to penetrating finishes.)

When you no longer see any scratches or blemishes, hold the wood up to a bright light so that the light reflects off the wood at a low angle, as shown in the drawing below. This will allow you to see even the tiniest scratches and imperfections. Even these minute blemishes will be readily visible after the first coat of finish, so don't stop sanding with your first grit until they're all erased. If your first sanding grit doesn't seem to be effective, switch to coarser grit and try again.

Never skip a grit when you're sanding by hand. If you start with 80 grit, for example, work your way up through 100, 120, 150, and 180. When you're using power sanders, though, you may skip one grade each time you switch because power sanders abrade stock more aggressively.

Between grits, vacuum or brush the wood and your workbench thoroughly to remove the loose grits; otherwise, you'll just continue to rub those coarser grits into the wood when you switch to finer sandpaper, which defeats your purpose.

How high you progress in grits of sandpaper depends on what kind of finish you intend to use. If you plan to finish your box with a penetrating finish, such as oil, you can stop after 180 grit. There are two exceptions to this rule. First, for coarse-grained wood, such as oak or butternut, you can stop after sanding with 150-grit paper. Second, if you have a surface with a wild grain pattern (such as curly, burl, or spalted wood) or a marquetry panel, you'll need to sand a little more, finishing with 220-grit paper. Use a swirling motion, preferably with a random-orbit sander.

On the other hand, if you plan to apply a surface film, such as varnish or lacquer, you should progress through 320-grit or higher, depending on what's recommended by the manufacturer of the finishing product you use.

EASE THE EDGES AND CLEAN THE SURFACE
When you reach 180 grit, ease, or round over slightly, the box's sharp corners and edges. Easing makes corners and edges not only more comfortable to touch, but also less likely to collect dents, dings, and chips. Another reason for easing is that sharp corners and edges

When to Use Hand Planes and Scrapers

You can plane your wood by hand or use a scraper to achieve a smooth surface free of discernible imperfections. This will save you a lot of time because you can skip all the coarse and medium sanding grits. But you may still need to sand lightly with fine sandpaper before applying a finish.

Some woodworkers claim they get best results by going directly from planing or scraping to finishing, without sanding at all. But I've found that metal plane irons and scrapers—though they are a pleasure to use—often leave raised wood fibers on the surface. To check for these raised fibers, drag a soft cloth in both directions along the grain and see if the cloth gets snagged. If it does, scuff those areas lightly with 180-grit sandpaper before finishing.

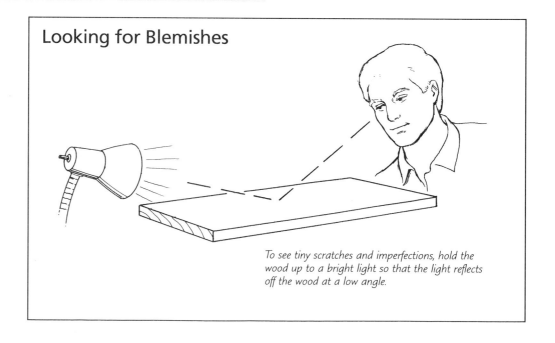

Looking for Blemishes

To see tiny scratches and imperfections, hold the wood up to a bright light so that the light reflects off the wood at a low angle.

What Is Danish Oil?

Danish oil is really a hybrid of oil and varnish. The oil in Danish oil is either linseed oil or tung oil or both. These natural oils can be wiped or brushed on wood, and they penetrate into the wood pores—in contrast to varnish and lacquer, which merely coat the wood's surface. Once oil and varnish are blended, however, the resulting substance is no longer oil and varnish, chemically speaking. It's a penetrating varnish that can be wiped on. But Danish oil is not the same thing as "wiping varnish." The latter is simply varnish thinned with mineral spirits so it can be wiped instead of brushed.

Danish oil comes in various color tints, but I prefer the "natural" color, which actually has a slight amber tint. Newer water-based Danish oils (see the sidebar on p. 20) can be almost clear, but they produce a duller sheen and are much less moisture-resistant than real oil blends.

A note of caution about Danish oil: It's extremely flammable. In fact, rags that are saturated with some brands of Danish oil can combust spontaneously under certain conditions. So read the product literature and labels carefully, and follow instructions on how to dispose of oily rags and brushes. Keep a fire extinguisher handy, and ventilate the room in which you do your finishing.

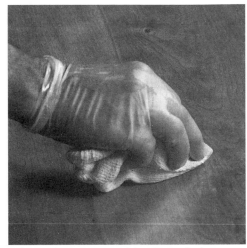

When wiping on Danish oil, work the rag into all corners and gaps. Work quickly and remove excess oil, which will leave lumps on the surface when it dries.

don't hold surface finishes (lacquer, varnish, and paste wax) very well.

I've found that using 180 grit gives a subtle, elegant easing. If you prefer a more blunt roundover, you can use 150 grit. But proceed cautiously at first—sharp corners can wear away very quickly.

Finally, to prepare the box for finishing, thoroughly vacuum and/or brush away all the dust from the wood surfaces. A horsehair brush works best for this.

Finishing with Oil

Most oil finishes add an amber tint to the wood's natural color, which can be pleasing in the case of medium and dark woods such as cherry or walnut. However, this darkening effect may be troublesome if you want to preserve the natural color of lighter woods, such as maple, sycamore, or aspen—in which case you can use lacquer or clear, water-based varnish (for more on water-based finishes, see the sidebar on p. 20). I recommend applying a coat of finish to a piece of scrap from your box project to test the color first.

I prefer to finish my boxes with Danish oil because it's very easy to apply, and it enhances the natural beauty of the wood. Whereas some lacquers and varnishes tend to leave the surface feeling hard, glossy, and plastic, Danish oil gives the wood a softer, more natural feeling. And you don't need fine brushes or fancy spray equipment to apply it (for more on Danish oil, see the sidebar above).

APPLY IT, THEN WIPE IT

Danish oil can be brushed or wiped on. You can pour the finish on the box and spread it. Or you can dunk the box in a tub of finish. Whichever way you do it, the goal is to let the oil soak into all the wood surfaces, inside and out. If you notice, after five minutes or so, that some areas of the wood surface (especially end grain, wavy grain, burls, and spalted wood, which soak up moisture quickly) are drying out, apply more finish to those areas.

The label on the product will advise you on how long to leave the finish on—to allow it to soak into the wood—before wiping off the excess. In any case, if the finish starts to get tacky, wipe it off immediately and vigorously.

Some woodworkers sand the wood with 220-grit wet/dry sandpaper while the oil is still wet, before wiping off the excess. This is supposed to fill the pores and remaining minor surface defects to provide a smoother finished surface with a deeper luster. I've tried this many times and have never noticed any improvement. So I don't bother with this step any more.

When it's time to wipe off the finish, work quickly and remove the bulk of the excess oil with a soft cotton rag. Then work the rag into all the little corners and gaps. The object is to get *all* the excess oil off every inch of the surface. Any remaining excess oil will dry, leaving glossy lumps on the surface, and you'll have to sand vigorously with very-fine sandpaper to mat down that gloss.

Even after you thoroughly wipe off the excess once, some oil may bleed back out of the wood pores up to several hours later. Such bleeding occurs especially around loose joints, such as where the bottom panel of a box is inserted into its grooves. To minimize bleedout at loose joints, I insert strips of paper into the joint. The paper soaks up much of the oil, so the bleeding is kept to a minimum.

Even with this extra step, however, you'll still have to inspect the project every two hours or so and wipe off any oil that bleeds out. I usually apply oil finishes in the morning, so I can keep an eye on the project all day.

ALLOW EACH COAT TO DRY

Most Danish oils dry in a day or so. After the first coat dries, you can apply a second coat. Because it's crucial that each coat dry thoroughly before adding another, I usually wait two days—or twice as long as the label suggests—before applying the next coat.

After each coat of finish dries (including the final coat), you should rub down the whole box with an ultrafine, abrasive nylon pad.

These pads are available in most hardware stores and building supply centers.

The rub down accomplishes three things. First, it knocks off dust that got stuck to the surface while the last coat was drying. Second, it scuffs any dried, glossy droplets formed as a result of bleedout so that the next coat will adhere nicely. And third, it smooths out any grain that was raised by the first application (called whiskering), which typically shows up on oak and thin veneer.

Once you've rubbed down the box, brush and/or vacuum the surface free of dust, and you're ready for the next coat.

The first coat of Danish oil does a good job of sealing the wood pores so that moisture exchange with the air is minimized. But the first coat doesn't really leave much of a sheen on the surface: The second coat does that. Two coats are normally sufficient, unless you are looking for a slightly higher sheen, which a third coat will provide. But after the third coat, additional applications add little incremental protection or sheen. I rarely apply more than two or three coats of Danish oil before polishing.

Water-Based Oils

There are an increasing number of water-based oils on the market, including penetrating finishes that you wipe on like Danish oil. Two examples are Amity Aqua Oil and Hydrocote Danish Oil. Both come in clear, natural, and tinted versions.

Water-based oils dry quickly and clean up fairly easily with soap and water—plus they're less toxic and less flammable than tung oil, linseed oil, and solvent-based finishes. But before choosing a water-based oil for any of your projects, it's important to know the problems associated with this type of finish.

First of all, water-based oils do not penetrate as deeply as traditional oil finishes, so they don't enhance the wood's natural grain pattern as well. And they don't achieve the richness and depth that real oil finishes can.

Before applying the finish, you must wipe the box with a damp cloth and let it dry for at least an hour. This will raise

the grain on most species. That means the severed wood fibers on the surface will swell from the moisture and stick up like tiny whiskers. You can't see them, but you can feel them.

The raised grain can be sanded away with 220-grit sandpaper. But don't sand more than necessary to make the surface smooth again, or you'll expose new fibers that will be raised when you apply the water-based finish.

Another problem with water-based oils is that you need to raise the grain. Still another problem is that it's hard to apply water-based oils without getting bubbles or foam on the surface. You have to wipe off the excess quickly to prevent the bubbles from drying into little nibs.

Between coats, sand with successively finer sandpaper, starting with 320-grit paper and concluding with 600 grit, followed by an ultrafine abrasive pad.

Over the years, a Danish-oil finish can deteriorate as a result of frequent exposure to sunlight or excessive heat, prolonged contact with water, or heavy wear and tear. If the surface starts to look dull, worn, or dry, you can rejuvenate it simply by applying another coat of Danish oil. Or you can clean the surface with furniture polish or "lemon oil," both of which contain solvents that help remove dust and grime.

Polishing with Wax

Danish oil alone gives a very presentable finish. But polishing a box with a coat of wax can create a deeper luster. I use either paste wax or beeswax. Paste wax is harder than beeswax and therefore offers some protection from scratches. Beeswax is softer and offers very little in the way of protection, but it's easier to buff by hand.

Paste wax comes in both light and dark versions. I use dark paste wax for walnut and mahogany, and the light paste wax for cherry and maple. If your project has contrasting light and dark woods, it's better to use beeswax, which dries relatively clear.

One coat of wax is all you may need. The key to achieving a good polish is to apply a very thin, even coat of wax on the surface and then wipe it off as soon as it dries (usually around 10 minutes). If you wait too long to wipe, the wax will become hard to buff by hand, and you'll end up with a streaky surface. If that happens, simply apply another thin coat of wax. The second coat will dissolve the first coat. (In fact, paste wax will dissolve any uncured Danish oil, too, so be sure to let the oil dry thoroughly before waxing.)

When you wipe the wax off, do so vigorously. The mild heat generated by buffing will give the wax coat a richer luster.

I never wax the bottom of a box. But as a final touch, when the box is completely finished, I apply self-stick felt disks (available at craft supply stores) to the four corners of the box's bottom, so that it won't scratch the tabletop, dresser, or shelf where it's ultimately displayed.

MAINTAINING THE POLISH

You can't use furniture polish or "lemon oil" to clean wax because the solvents in those products will dissolve the wax and smear it. The best way to clean a waxed surface is to wipe it with a soft cloth dampened with water (or mild soap and water).

If you really need a total face-lift, remove the wax with mineral spirits, apply a coat of Danish oil, let it cure, and then add a new coat of wax. You'd be amazed at how great a worn-out, old box can look after such a face-lift.

2 MITERED BOXES WITH ONE-PIECE LIDS

Techniques

For beginning box makers, I recommend using miter joinery. Miters are fairly easy to cut, and assembling a box with mitered corners is a breeze. Miter joints are clean, because they don't show any end grain, and with miter joints you can cut full-length grooves for the bottom panel.

However, miter joints are relatively weak because there is no mechanical method of holding the joint together, as with dovetail or finger joints. Fortunately, miter joints can be strengthened with keys (see pp. 28-30), which also add a decorative touch to the box.

Cutting Miters

In addition to decorative keys, there are two other factors that will affect the strength of a miter joint: the fit of the joint and the glue you use (for more on glues for box making, see the sidebar below).

Glues for Box Making

The most commonly used adhesives in box making—yellow and white glues—are in the polyvinyl acetate (PVA) family. These glues are popular because they are nontoxic, inexpensive, and simple to use. And because they're water based, they're easy to clean up.

Yellow glue (also called aliphatic resin) is stronger than white glue, resists moisture better, and is easier to sand. These qualities make yellow glue the most useful all-purpose woodworking adhesive. Sometimes labeled woodworking glue or carpenter's glue, it also comes in a chocolate brown color, which I use for gluing walnut and other dark woods. Yellow glue is sufficient for most of your box-making projects.

Yellow glue has an open assembly time of about five minutes—that's how long you can leave the glue spread on the open joints before the glue starts to set. That means you have to assemble the box in less than five minutes to ensure good glue joints. Yellow glue sets in 30 minutes, so leave joints clamped or taped together for at least that long. You should also let yellow glue cure for 24 hours before handling the assembly or applying stress to the joints.

White PVA glue is commonly known as craft or hobby glue. It has an open time of about six to eight minutes, and it sets in about an hour. But white glue is not as strong as yellow glue, has lower initial tack, and tends to clog sandpaper more than yellow glue. White glue is really best for working with paper and fabric.

Most PVA glues have a shelf life of about a year. After that, they start to get stringy or curdled and are less effective. I always mark the date on a new bottle when I purchase it, and replace it when it's a year old.

When joining wood with PVA glues, mated surfaces must be smooth and in full contact with each other. PVAs are not gap-filling glues and will not bond rough surfaces well at all. If you need a glue with gap-filling properties, use epoxy. For complex boxes, you may need a glue with a longer open assembly time: Hide glue has a 10-minute open time; plastic resin glue has a 15-minute open assembly time.

The secret to a good fit—one without gaps—is a smooth cut and an accurate setup. To get a smooth cut with little or no tearout, I recommend using a high-quality crosscut sawblade with at least 60 teeth (on a 10-in. blade). As to the setup, it will depend on which method you choose to cut the miters. The two methods I use most often are to cut them on the table saw or on the miter saw.

TABLE SAW

Setting the table-saw's blade angle to cut accurate 45° miters is a process of adjusting, testing, and readjusting.

Start by setting the blade angle to 45°. Don't rely on the table-saw's blade-angle scale—this scale is notoriously inaccurate. Instead, check the angle with a 45-45-90 drafting triangle. Once you're confident that the blade is set to 45°, set the miter gauge to 90°. Now make a test cut on two pieces, place them on a flat surface, and check the fit, as shown in the left drawing below. If there is a gap, readjust the blade angle and make another test cut.

Once you've got the blade angle and miter gauge set up, fasten a wooden auxiliary fence to the miter gauge, as shown in the right drawing below. An auxiliary fence will provide

a backing surface to prevent tearout when crosscutting. It will also allow you to set stop blocks to ensure that pieces are cut to equal length.

Cut a small chamfer on the inside corner of the stop block so that sawdust does not build up and cause inaccurate cuts. Clamp the stop block to the auxiliary fence at the correct distance (measure from the blade to the stop block). Test-cut a piece of scrap to ensure accuracy and adjust if necessary. Cut the front and back pieces of the box to length first, and then reset the stop and cut the two side pieces.

MITER SAW

You can avoid the hassle of setting up the table saw for miter cuts by using a quality miter saw. A miter saw (or chopsaw) allows you to set the blade angle to a precise 45° in just a few seconds. However, unless you own a sliding compound miter saw, you are limited to using stock around 3 in. wide (that is, your box carcase can be no taller than 3 in.).

Before cutting, attach an auxiliary fence to the miter saw, with a "bed" that eliminates tearout at the end of the cut (see the photo on p. 24). Also, to ensure accurate repeat cuts, clamp a stop block to the fence. Then simply place each carcase piece on the bed with its

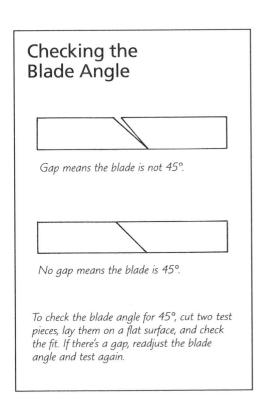

Checking the Blade Angle

Gap means the blade is not 45°.

No gap means the blade is 45°.

To check the blade angle for 45°, cut two test pieces, lay them on a flat surface, and check the fit. If there's a gap, readjust the blade angle and test again.

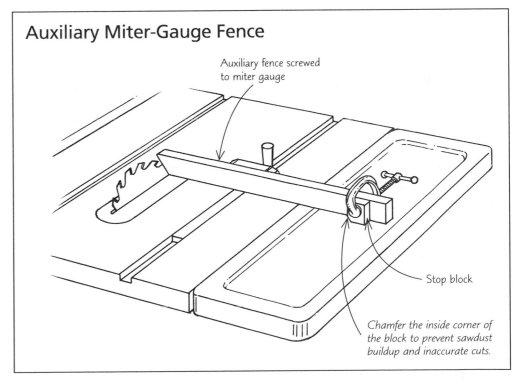

Auxiliary Miter-Gauge Fence

Auxiliary fence screwed to miter gauge

Stop block

Chamfer the inside corner of the block to prevent sawdust buildup and inaccurate cuts.

outside face against the fence, and make the cut. It's also a good idea to cut a test piece first to be sure the setup is accurate.

To eliminate tearout, attach an auxiliary fence and bed to the miter saw. To ensure accurate repeat cuts, clamp a stop block to the auxiliary fence.

Cutting Grooves for the Bottom Panel

Once you've cut the miters, the next step is to cut grooves in each piece to accept a bottom panel. With a miter joint, these grooves can be cut on a table saw the full length of each piece.

I prefer to cut the grooves in the sides before cutting to length. This makes sense for two reasons: First, if you're making more than one box, you'll save time by running long stock through the saw rather than many smaller pieces. Second, if you're making a very small box, it's easier and safer to run a longer piece through the blade than four very short pieces.

The width and depth of the grooves, as well as the distance between the grooves and the bottom of the box, are dictated by whether you're making a large box or a small one. The drawing below shows two types of grooves and gives general guidelines for setting the dimensions of the grooves. I think

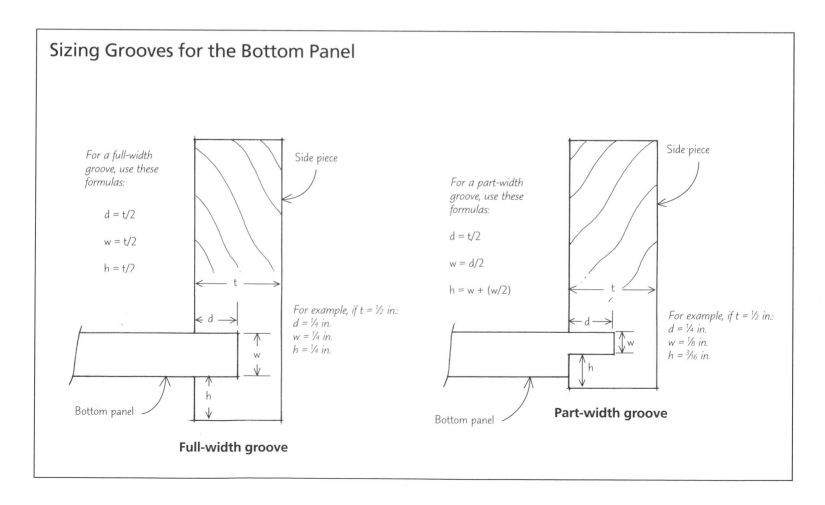

Sizing Grooves for the Bottom Panel

For a full-width groove, use these formulas:

$d = t/2$

$w = t/2$

$h = t/2$

Side piece

For example, if t = ½ in.:
$d = ¼$ in.
$w = ¼$ in.
$h = ¼$ in.

Bottom panel

Full-width groove

For a part-width groove, use these formulas:

$d = t/2$

$w = d/2$

$h = w + (w/2)$

Side piece

For example, if t = ½ in.:
$d = ¼$ in.
$w = ⅛$ in.
$h = 3/16$ in.

Bottom panel

Part-width groove

the easiest way to cut the grooves is on the table saw. However, some woodworkers prefer to use a router table with a ⅛-in. or ¼-in. straight bit. Either machine works well.

Note that for boxes with very thin sides (¼ in. or less), cutting a groove halfway through the side may weaken the box too much. An alternative is to glue a bottom directly to the carcase without grooves, but this only works for small boxes that are less than a few inches wide.

To cut grooves on the table saw, first measure and make pencil marks to indicate where the groove is to be cut on the workpiece. You can either cut the groove in a single pass with a dado blade or take multiple passes with a standard blade. If you're using a rip blade or combination blade with raker teeth, you'll cut a flat-bottomed groove. But if you have only an alternate-top-bevel (ATB) blade, you'll have to cut a slightly deeper groove to compensate for the resulting peak in the bottom of the groove (see the drawing at right).

After marking the workpiece, line up your pencil marks with the sawblade and position the rip fence to cut the groove.

Next set the blade height. Use a scrap piece to test the depth of the cut, make adjustments if necessary, and then groove the workpiece. When making repeated cuts to reach the desired groove width, don't try to cut too much at once. Instead, "sneak up" on the proper width gradually with successive, light cuts. After each cut, test the fit of the panel. It should fit snug, but not too tight.

Making the Bottom Panel

I don't know any modern-day box makers who use solid-wood bottoms, but I imagine there are still a few out there. Even for a quasi-purist like me, plywood is difficult to resist when it comes to making bottoms for boxes, drawers, and trays.

PLYWOOD VS. SOLID WOOD

A solid-wood bottom will shrink and expand with changes in humidity, so you have to let it "float" in its grooves—that is, give it room to move—and not glue it in place (usually a gap of 1⁄16 in. is sufficient, but you may need more if the box is large). Plywood, on the other hand, is so stable that you can cut it almost big enough to fill the grooves completely, and you can glue it in place, which adds strength to the box assembly.

Measure the thickness of your plywood carefully before you cut the grooves. The plywood's actual thickness is a bit thinner than its stated (nominal) thickness. For example, most plywood that's nominally ⅛ in. thick is actually closer to 3⁄32 in.—too thin to be a heavy-duty box bottom. Hardboard (or Masonite), on the other hand, comes in precise thicknesses, but you'll have to laminate veneer to it (or line the interior with suede or velvet) unless you don't mind the dull-brown, synthetic look of a hardboard bottom.

In general, the bottom of a small box—one with a perimeter less than 20 in.—can be ⅛-in. plywood, unless it's going to hold heavy objects. For large boxes, use ¼-in. plywood. For medium-size boxes (those with perimeters between 20 in. and 36 in.), you may create intermediate-size (around 3⁄16 in.) plywood by laminating veneer to ⅛-in. hardboard panels.

CALCULATE THE PANEL'S DIMENSIONS

To determine the dimensions of a plywood or hardboard bottom panel, simply measure the grooves from end to end. Then subtract about 1⁄32 in. from each measurement.

Why subtract the 1⁄32 in. instead of cutting the panel to fill the grooves completely? After all, filling the grooves with the bottom would let you square up the carcase perfectly as you assemble it. If you can achieve that sort of perfection, be my guest! However, it's extremely difficult and time-consuming to measure and cut the bottom to such small tolerances. You're going to be off a hair 9 times out of 10. You don't want the bottom panel to be too big because the mitered corners would not close completely. So, it's best to make the bottom panel a hair too small. (You'll learn another method for squaring up the carcase later in this chapter.)

After you cut the bottom to its final dimensions, ease the corners and sharp edges lightly to make it easier to slide the panel into the grooves during assembly.

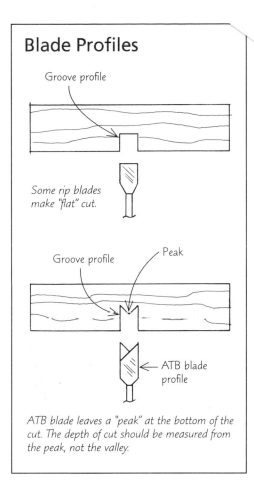

Blade Profiles

Groove profile

Some rip blades make "flat" cut.

Peak

Groove profile

ATB blade profile

ATB blade leaves a "peak" at the bottom of the cut. The depth of cut should be measured from the peak, not the valley.

Assembling the Box

Assembling the box is the most exciting step. It's where you start to see the box take form and where all your meticulous planning and preparation pay off. First, however, you should take a few minutes to final-sand some of the surfaces that will be hard to reach after the box is assembled.

SAND THE INSIDE FACES

It's always tempting to postpone sanding as long as possible and get on with assembling your box. But if you've ever tried to sand the inside of an assembled box, you'll understand why it's imperative to sand now.

For solid-wood pieces, like the sides, start with 120-grit sandpaper (for rough surfaces with scalloped planer marks) or 150-grit sandpaper (for fairly smooth surfaces) and finish with 180 grit. For plywood pieces, like the bottom, you can usually start with 180 grit, unless you have serious scratches to eliminate. Always sand with the direction of the grain. Note that if you're going to finish your box with lacquer or straight varnish, you may want to sand up to 220 grit, or even 320 grit.

A PRELIMINARY FINISH?

Some woodworkers finish the sides and bottom panel before assembling them. There's one advantage: When you assemble the carcase, any glue that squeezes out will not adhere to (or soak into) a surface that has a finish on it, so you can easily chisel off any glue squeeze-out when it dries. If you glue up before finishing, any glue that soaks into the wood and dries will not allow the finish to penetrate.

However, you must be extremely careful not to get finish on the miters or in the grooves. If you do, glue will not adhere, and your joints will be weak. Some woodworkers cover these areas with masking tape before they apply the preliminary finish. However, I've found that masking tape often leaves adhesive residue on the surfaces—even on the adjacent surfaces that you want to apply the finish to. This residue can discolor a finish or inhibit the glue bond.

In my opinion, the disadvantages and advantages of preliminary finishing cancel each other out, and I'd rather wait until the box is assembled to finish it. On those rare occasions when I do apply a preliminary finish, I use a small, fine brush and carefully avoid the joints, rather than covering them with masking tape.

Small, flat glue brushes with moderately stiff bristles will apply the glue thoroughly and evenly. They are available at art-supply or craft stores.

DRY-FIT THE PIECES

Once you have all your pieces cut to size, with the grooves cut and the inside faces sanded, you're ready to assemble the box. First, make a dry run. Assemble the four sides and bottom panel without glue to make sure everything fits. Use rubber bands to hold the assembly together.

Check with a square to make sure each of the carcase's four corners are 90°, with no protruding edges. The bottom panel should slip readily into its grooves. The top edges of the sides should be flush, so that if you put the box upside-down on a flat surface, it won't rock from corner to corner. If the dry assembly fails any of these tests, you should go back and fix the problem—by planing, sanding, or trimming—before you glue up.

APPLY THE GLUE

Gluing up a box with mitered corners is simple. The surfaces to be glued must be dry and free of dust. Use a vacuum with a brush attachment. If your shop is dusty, move to a different room for glue-up.

To apply the glue thoroughly and evenly, use a small, flat glue brush with moderately stiff bristles, which you can buy at art-supply or craft stores (see the photo at left). Place a piece of waxed paper on the surface of your workbench to protect it from the glue.

Miters first Lay the four sides on a flat surface, outside faces up, with the sharp miter corners touching, as shown in the top drawing on the facing page. Be sure to line the sides up in the proper sequence. To keep the top edges properly aligned, butt them up against a straight edge, such as the rip fence on a table saw. Then tape the three joints as shown. Keep the tape smooth and unwrinkled and the miter corners touching as you apply the tape.

Flip the row of taped sides over and check to see that the grooves are lined up. Then brush the glue onto the miters. From this point on, you'll have to work quickly and efficiently to get the box assembled before the glue starts to set—you'll have about five minutes if you're using yellow glue (see the sidebar on p. 22).

Put a thin film of glue onto each miter surface. Be sure to get the brush down into the corners where the miters meet. At the same time, avoid spreading glue on the inside surface of the box.

Because the miters are cut into end grain, which is porous, the wood will absorb the glue quickly. If the first miter surface you spread glue on looks nearly dry (not glossy) after you put glue on all the miters, go back and put a second thin film of glue on one surface of each pair.

Grooves second If you're using plywood for the bottom panel, the next step is to put glue in the grooves (as I mentioned earlier, you should not use glue if the bottom panel is solid wood). When you finish brushing on the glue, drop your brush into a cup of water, which will prevent the glue from drying on the bristles.

ASSEMBLE THE PIECES
After applying the glue, insert the bottom panel into one of the longer grooves. Grab the two ends of the row and gently pull the two free miters together and "roll up" the pieces, as shown in the drawing below. The tape will pull taut at the three joint lines. When the pieces are rolled up and adjusted to achieve a flush rim around the carcase top, put masking tape on the last miter joint. Then put two or three rubber bands around the whole box to keep everything secure.

The bottom panel will keep the whole assembly nearly square. But you should still check for squareness and fine-tune if

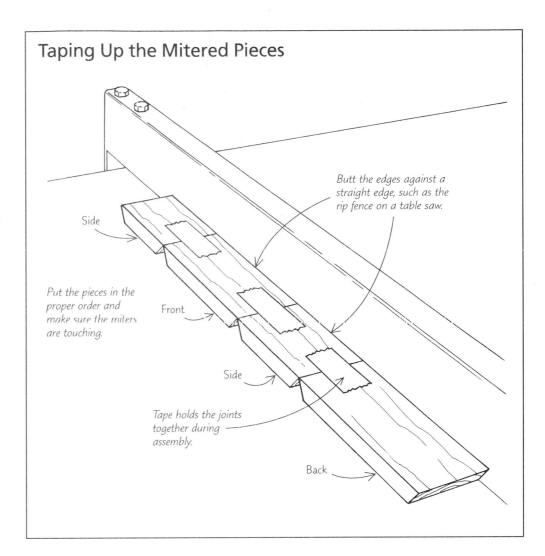

Taping Up the Mitered Pieces

Butt the edges against a straight edge, such as the rip fence on a table saw.

Side

Put the pieces in the proper order and make sure the miters are touching.

Front

Side

Tape holds the joints together during assembly.

Back

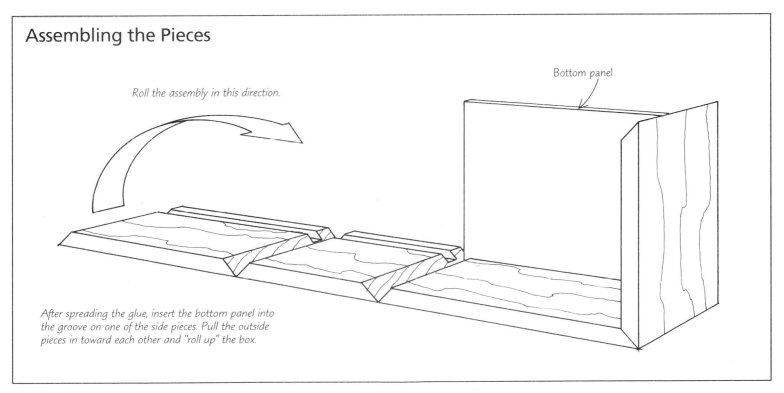

Assembling the Pieces

Roll the assembly in this direction.

Bottom panel

After spreading the glue, insert the bottom panel into the groove on one of the side pieces. Pull the outside pieces in toward each other and "roll up" the box.

necessary. The best way to do this is to measure the two diagonals, which should be equal if the box is a rectangle. If not, simply apply a little pressure to the longer diagonal with your hands and recheck the measurements.

DEAL WITH SQUEEZE-OUT

When you assemble the box, you should see tiny beads of glue squeeze-out at each joint. If you don't see any, you may have "starved" the joint of glue.

If you accidentally dripped some glue onto an exposed surface, now is the time to get rid of it and any squeeze-out. One option is to take a wet rag and wipe off the excess glue immediately. Another option is to let the glue dry for an hour and then, when it's slightly hard but not yet cured, pare it off with a sharp chisel.

LET THE GLUE CURE

Now let the assembled, squared-up box sit undisturbed while the glue cures. If in doubt about how long the glue takes to cure, follow the instructions on the glue bottle; to be on the safe side, I let the box sit overnight before working on it.

Remove the tape as soon as the glue cures. Some brands of tape leave an adhesive residue if you wait too long to remove it. The residue can be removed with acetone or lacquer

thinner, but you must be extra careful not to let the solvent seep into the joint and weaken the glue bond.

Reinforcing Miter Joints with Keys

At this point you can use the box as it is, but I prefer to reinforce the miter joints. Keys (also called corner keys or cross-splines) and splines (sometimes called loose tongues) are two methods commonly used to reinforce miter joints. I prefer keys because they work better than splines and are easier to make.

One problem with splines is that you rely on end grain for strength (see the drawing below left). Also, the slots for splines must be cut into end grain on the table saw or router table, which is difficult to do accurately. I use splines only to reinforce miter joints when I don't want to interrupt or deface the grain pattern on the box sides.

Keys are stronger than splines because a long-grain surface is glued to another long-grain surface. Also, the key slots are fairly simple to cut. Finally, keys are more decorative than splines.

You can make key stock of contrasting wood (maple keys on a walnut box, for example) to call attention to them; use complementary wood (such as cherry keys on a walnut box) for an understated effect; or use same-species wood to make the keys

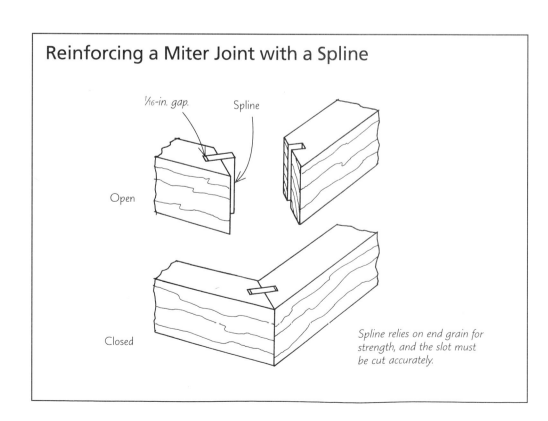

Reinforcing a Miter Joint with a Spline

1/16-in. gap.

Spline

Open

Closed

Spline relies on end grain for strength, and the slot must be cut accurately.

Strong, attractive keys can be made from laminations of contrasting woods.

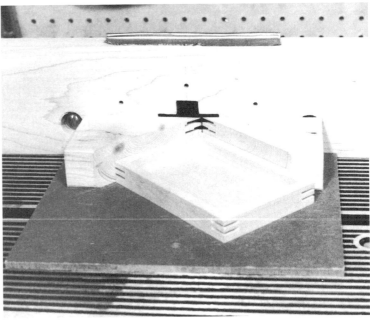

This carriage jig makes cutting key slots easy on the table saw. It consists of two 2x4s, each mitered at 45°, which are glued or screwed to a piece of ¾-in. plywood.

When cutting slots with a slot cutter on the router table, use a carriage jig made of two 2x4s, mitered at 45° and screwed or glued to a piece of plywood or hardboard.

inconspicuous. Key stock can also be a lamination of contrasting species. A properly glued-up lamination provides strong reinforcement for the miter joint, and it's also very attractive (see the photo on the facing page).

POSITION THE KEYS

The position of the keys is important. For carcases up to 2 in. in height, I recommend at least two keys per miter joint: one key near the top and one near the bottom. If the box is taller than 2 in., add a key in the middle or install two near the top and two near the bottom. You can get artistic with the size and spacing of your keys, but just remember that the more keys you install and the more evenly spaced they are, the stronger the joint will be. On the other hand, sometimes just a few keys offer a more elegant look.

One other thing about positioning the keys: If you have a lid panel built into the carcase (see pp. 46-48), be sure not to cut a slot into the panel and install keys that restrict the panel's movement.

CUT THE KEY SLOTS

Once you've determined the size and position of the keys, you're ready to cut the slots, make the keys, and install them. You can do this on the table saw or router table. Either way, you should use a carriage jig.

Table saw To make cutting key slots easy, make a simple jig for your table saw. Cut two 2x4s, each mitered at 45°, and glue or screw them to a piece of ¾-in. plywood, as shown in the left photo above (I also added a handle for safety).

Set the height of the blade. The deeper the slot, and the deeper you insert the keys, the stronger the joint will be. But you don't want to cut the slot so deep that the keys protrude inside the box. I just eyeball the depth, but I make test cuts using stock the same thickness as the carcase sides.

Next, position the box to cut a slot in the correct location along the joint line. You can do this by adjusting the fence or by placing spacer blocks between the box and the jig. When you adjust the fence, be sure you're not going to cut into any screws that may be holding the carriage jig together.

Now cut the slots. Rotate the carcase 90° between cuts. If you flip the carcase around, you'll be able to cut four more slots the same distance from the opposite edge for a symmetrical look. Or you can adjust the fence to cut slots anywhere along the joint line.

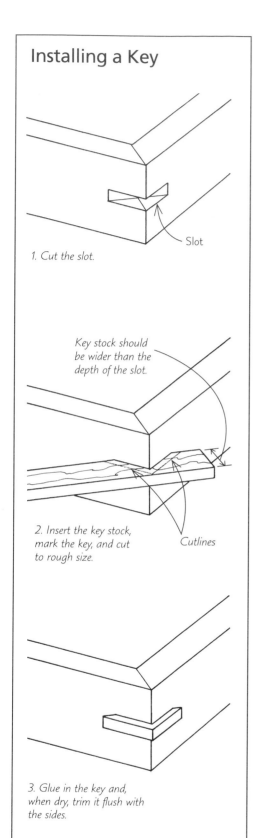

Installing a Key

Slot

1. Cut the slot.

Key stock should be wider than the depth of the slot.

Cutlines

2. Insert the key stock, mark the key, and cut to rough size.

3. Glue in the key and, when dry, trim it flush with the sides.

Router table For small boxes, I prefer to use a slot cutter with my router table because the box lies down horizontally during the operation, rather than sticking up vertically, which makes it easier to hold the box steady during the cut. Slot-cutter bits come in a wide range of sizes, including ³⁄₃₂ in., ⅛ in., ⁵⁄₃₂ in., and larger.

The carriage jig I made for this operation is simple. It consists of two pieces of 2x4, mitered at 45° and screwed or glued to a piece of plywood or hardboard (see the photo at right on p. 29). I prefer to use hardboard because the jig slides along the table more easily.

To use this jig, adjust the router-table fence to set the depth of cut and adjust the height of the cutter to locate the slots along the joint line.

CUT THE KEYS

Once you've cut the slots for the keys, you can cut the keys to fit. I usually make my keys ⅛ in. thick, and occasionally ³⁄₃₂ in. for small boxes and trays.

The key should slide into the slot with slight friction. You're going to apply glue to both the slot and the key, so the final fit will be tighter than a dry test-fit. Don't use too much force trying to insert the key into the slot, because at this point the miter joint is still weak—too much stress now could break it apart.

You can buy some species of wood in ⅛-in. thicknesses at hobby shops and building-supply stores, including basswood, aspen, and oak. Several other species (including exotics) are available in ⅛-in. thicknesses through some woodworking catalogs and retail stores.

If you're dimensioning your own key stock, there are two methods of achieving the right thickness. One is to rip a long strip from the edge of a ¾-in. board and then plane or sand it down to the thickness you need (you probably won't rip it to the perfect thickness the first time). The second method is to build up your key stock by laminating veneers and/or very thin strips together. The width of the key stock should be oversized. If your slot depth is ⅝ in., for example, the key stock should be at least ¾ in. wide.

Make sure the key stock has two straight, parallel edges and try to cut all the keys from one length of stock. Insert one edge of the key stock in a slot and draw cutlines for an oversized key (see the drawing at left). Turn the stock around and insert the other edge into a key, and mark off another oversized key. Work your way along the stock until you've marked off as many keys as there are slots, plus one or two extra in case of mistakes. Keep in mind that the grain direction of the key must be perpendicular to the miter-joint line.

Cut the keys apart with a small backsaw or a Japanese *dozuki* saw. Test-fit each key, and sand if necessary to ensure a smooth fit.

GLUE THE KEYS IN PLACE

Now you're ready to glue up. Using a small brush, spread a thin film of glue in the slot and on both faces of the first key. Insert the key in the slot firmly, rocking it back and forth gently to force the excess glue out. You should see some squeeze-out, especially at each end of the slot.

After you've glued the remaining keys in place, let the glue dry overnight before you trim and sand the keys flush with the carcase. There's a good reason to wait that long. The moisture in glue causes the area around each key to swell slightly. After it dries, the area shrinks back to its original dimensions. If you sand the keys while they're still swollen, they'll dry and shrink, forming a depression.

Trim the keys almost flush. I like to use a flush-cutting handsaw—the Japanese version is called a *kugihiki*. This type of saw has teeth with no set, which lets you trim keys flush without scratching the surrounding surface. Because the grain of the keys runs perpendicular to the joint line, it's easy to chip out the corner of the key. To avoid doing that, saw a kerf into the corner of the key first, and then trim the keys from the opposite direction. You can also trim the keys on a bandsaw or by hand with a chisel.

Finally, sand the keys flush with the sides of the box.

Projects

BOX WITH A SLAB LID

A box with a slab lid is about as elementary as you can get, but even the simplest box can be done artfully. Thanks to its massive base and rich materials, the box shown here is both strong and attractive.

You can use almost any material for a box lid, and it doesn't necessarily have to be wood. I used a slab of "Chinese writing rock" (geologists call it porphyry) from a rock shop to make the lid for the box shown at right. I paid the shop about $15 to cut a slab to size and polish it. I made a similar box lid with a slab of spalted maple burl (see the photo below). With a little imagination, you can come up with more exciting ideas for lids, such as wood carvings, ceramics, acrylic, or pewter.

For this box, the lid should stand proud of the carcase rim but not be too prominent. If you use wood for the lid, remember that it's going to move slightly over the years. For this reason, this type of box shouldn't be more than 4 in. or 5 in. in length. If you're using a rock slab or other hard material for the lid, make sure that you have it cut to final

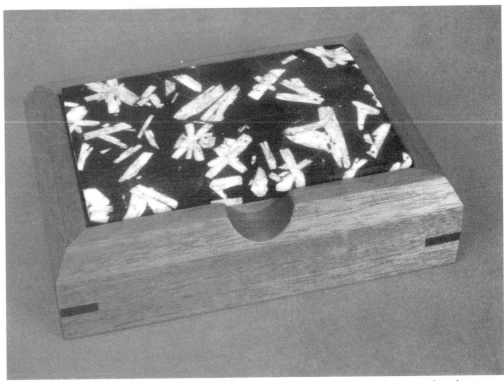

This mahogany box has a slab lid made of "Chinese writing rock" (called porphyry).

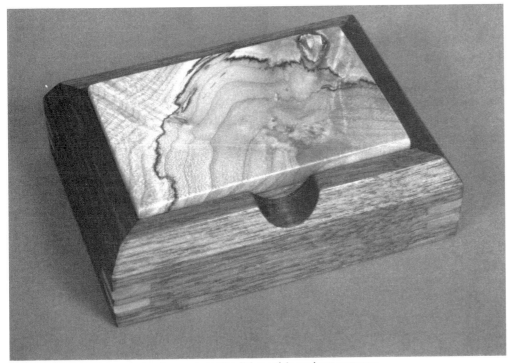

A slab of spalted maple burl serves as the lid on this walnut carcase.

Box with a Slab Lid

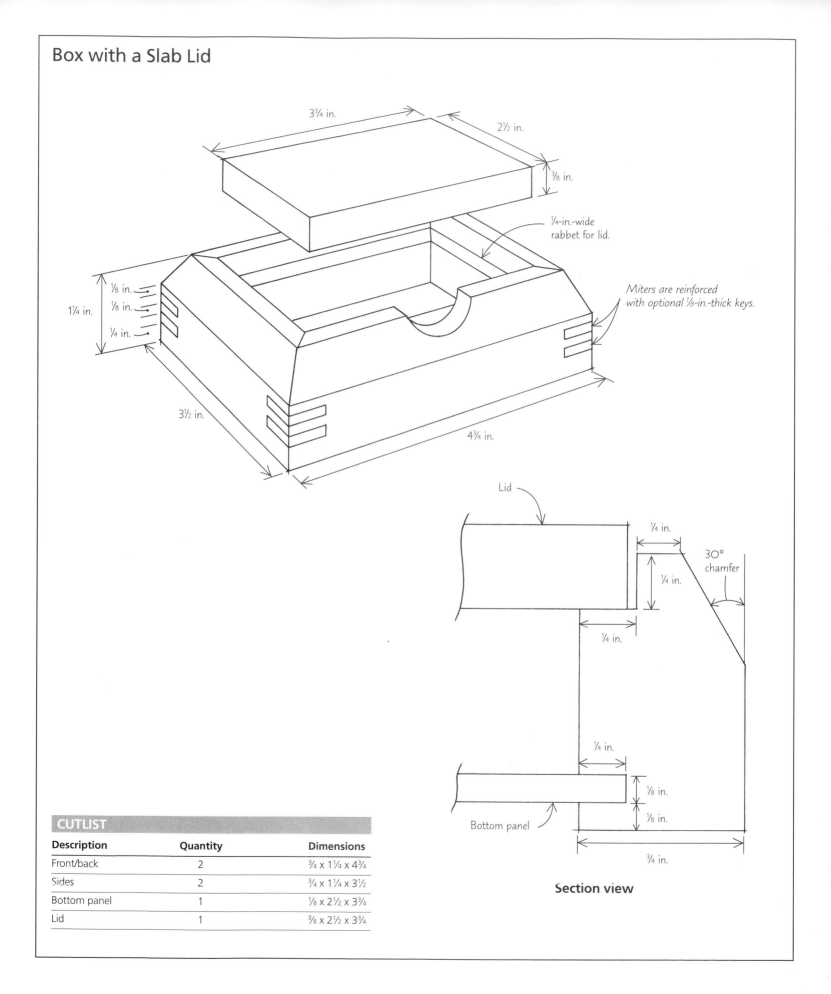

3¾ in.

2½ in.

⅜ in.

¼-in.-wide rabbet for lid.

⅛ in.
⅛ in.
¼ in.
1¼ in.

Miters are reinforced with optional ⅛-in.-thick keys.

3½ in.

4¾ in.

Lid

¼ in.

30° chamfer

¼ in.

¼ in.

¼ in.

⅛ in.

⅛ in.

Bottom panel

¾ in.

Section view

CUTLIST

Description	Quantity	Dimensions
Front/back	2	¾ x 1¼ x 4¾
Sides	2	¾ x 1¼ x 3½
Bottom panel	1	⅛ x 2½ x 3¾
Lid	1	⅜ x 2½ x 3¾

dimensions before you plan the carcase dimensions. You can't trim a rock slab (at least not easily) to fit inside the carcase's rim, but you can adjust the size of the rim to accommodate the slab.

To achieve a massive appearance, I used ¾-in.-thick stock for the box carcase instead of thin lumber. You can find ¾-in.-thick "shorts" at almost any hardwood lumber dealer for reasonable prices.

You can use the dimensions given in the drawing on the facing page, or you can adapt the box's dimensions to fit the size of whatever lid you have in mind. I have included a cutlist with the drawing. Refer to the Techniques section of this chapter (pp. 22-30) for detailed instructions on how to cut miter joints, assemble the carcase, and install keys to reinforce the joints.

Making the Carcase

1. Cut a ¾-in.-thick board at least 17 in. long for the front, back, and sides to a final width of 1¼ in. Don't cut the four pieces to length yet.

2. Cut a ⅛-in.-wide, ¼-in.-deep groove for the bottom panel along the inside face of the board.

3. On the same face, cut a ¼-in. by ¼-in. rabbet to create the ledge for the lid (see the photo above right).

4. Miter-cut the front and back pieces (4¾ in.) and the sides (3½ in.) to length.

5. To create a thumb relief on the front piece, drill a recess with a ¾-in. Forstner bit (see the drawing at right). To do this, clamp the workpiece to the drill-press table along with a scrap piece that's the same thickness as the workpiece. The scrap piece will keep the bit from wandering as you begin drilling. Set the depth stop to drill only ½ in. deep, leaving the ¼-in. ledge intact.

6. Cut 30° chamfers on the outside faces of all four sides. If you do this on the table saw, angle the blade away from the rip fence for safety. If you cut the chamfers on the router table (which will give you smoother chamfers), use a zero-clearance auxiliary fence to prevent the workpiece from dipping into the throat surrounding the bit.

7. Sand the inside faces, finishing with 150-grit sandpaper. Round over the inside edge of the rim somewhat to allow easy entry for the lid. Sand the ledge and the sharp edges along the top and bottom, finishing with 180-grit paper.

8. Cut a ⅛-in.-thick plywood bottom panel to just less than 2½ in. by 3¾ in. and sand it with 180-grit sandpaper.

The lid sits on a ¼-in. ledge rabbeted on the inside faces of the carcase pieces. The thumb relief on the front is created on the drill press.

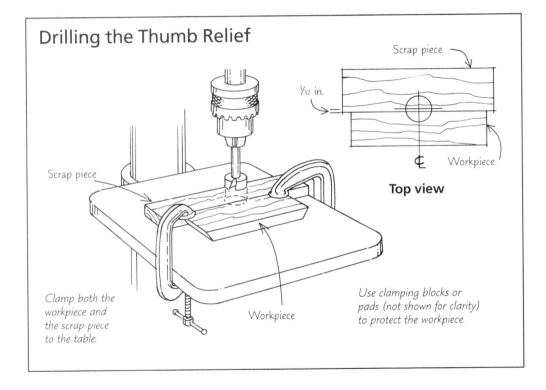

Drilling the Thumb Relief

Scrap piece

³⁄₃₂ in.

Top view

Workpiece

Scrap piece

Clamp both the workpiece and the scrap piece to the table.

Workpiece

Use clamping blocks or pads (not shown for clarity) to protect the workpiece.

9. Dry-assemble the carcase to check that everything fits well.

10. Glue up the carcase and let it dry overnight (for more on gluing up a mitered box, see pp. 26-28). Then sand the top and bottom edges flush.

11. Cut the slots for the reinforcing keys. You need only one key per miter joint because of the relatively large glue surface in each joint (you could probably get by without keys). But you can use two keys per joint for a decorative effect if desired (for more on making and installing keys, see pp. 28-30).

12. Make the keys, glue them into the slots, and allow to dry overnight. Then trim the keys flush with the sides. Final-sand the carcase with 180-grit sandpaper.

Installing the Lid

If you've made your lid out of something other than wood, check the fit now. Hopefully, your careful planning will have paid off, and the lid will slide in with virtually no gap. However, if the fit is too tight, you can widen the rabbets in the carcase sides slightly with sandpaper. If you've designed a box with a wood slab lid, here's how to make it:

1. The lid should be about ⅜ in. thick. Check the inside dimensions of the carcase rim (it should be close to 2½ in. by 3¾ in.) and cut the lid to a hair less than that.

2. Test-fit the lid. Trim it until there's about a ¹⁄₃₂-in. gap or less between each side of the lid and the rim to allow for wood movement.

3. Final-sand the lid with 180-grit sandpaper (or 220 grit for burl), gently rounding off all sharp corners and edges.

Finishing

1. Apply a finish to the carcase and lid. If you're using Danish oil, I recommend two coats on the carcase. If your lid is made of wood, apply at least four coats on it to minimize movement. Also apply an extra coat or two around the ledge, because it's going to be subject to a lot of wear as the lid is removed and replaced repeatedly (for more on finishing, see pp. 17-21).

If you're using a rock lid, for even greater protection against wear wait until the oil cures (ideally a few days) and apply a few coats of polyurethane varnish around the ledge. Rub the lid after each coat of varnish dries with an ultrafine abrasive pad to remove the gloss.

2. For a final touch, apply self-stick felt disks to the bottom in the four corners.

BEVELED BOX WITH A RABBETED LID

The most prominent feature of this maple box is the knotted lid.

There are many ways to build a box without hinges. In the previous project, the lid rested on a ledge rabbeted into the carcase. With this project the process is reversed: The rabbets are cut in the lid instead of in the carcase.

Geometrically speaking, this box, which I call the "pointless pyramid," is a radically truncated pyramid with a rectangular base. The box sides are beveled 5° away from perpendicular. (Keep the bevel slight, or the box may slip out of your grasp when you pick it up.)

The box shown at left is made of maple. Its most prominent feature is the knot in the top. Most knots are ugly and end up in the fireplace. However, I found this one rather charming, in its own grotesque way, and so I designed a box around it. Of course, don't feel that you need a knot in the lid for the box to be attractive: You can use a piece of nicely figured wood to make one.

You can use the dimensions given in the drawing on the facing page and in the instructions, or you can adapt the box's dimensions to fit the lid you have in mind. A cutlist is included with the drawing. Begin with the carcase.

Beveled Box with a Rabbeted Lid

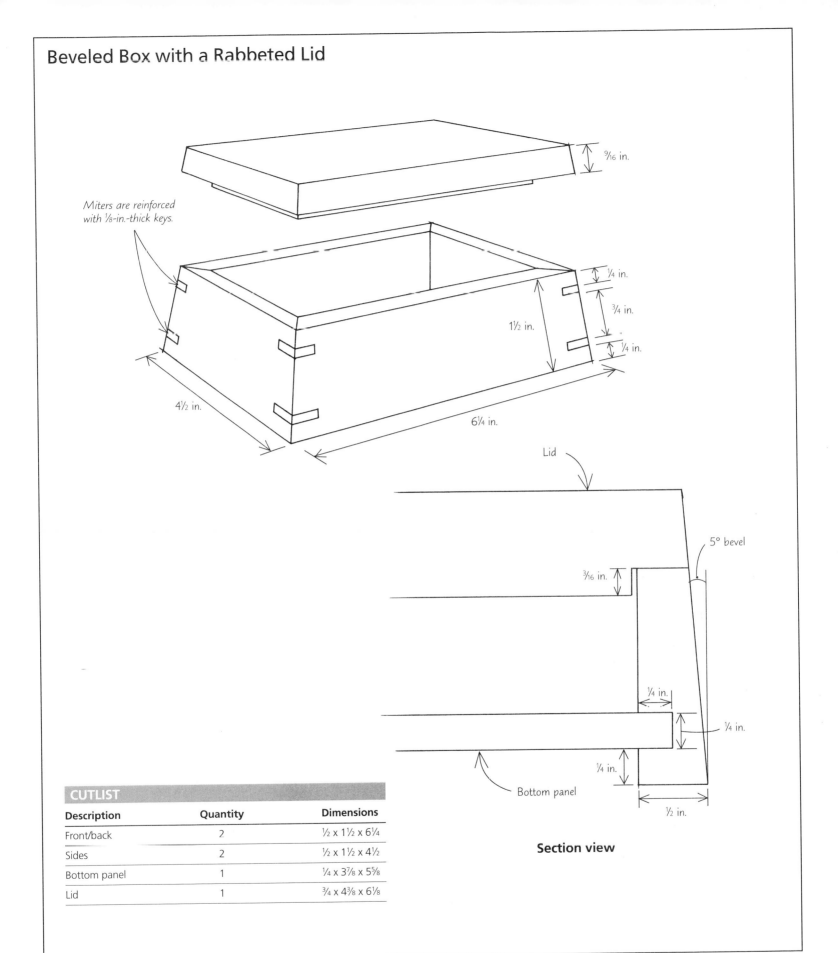

Miters are reinforced with ⅛-in.-thick keys.

9⁄16 in.

¼ in.

¾ in.

¼ in.

1½ in.

4½ in.

6¼ in.

Lid

5° bevel

3⁄16 in.

¼ in.

¼ in.

¼ in.

Bottom panel

½ in.

Section view

CUTLIST		
Description	**Quantity**	**Dimensions**
Front/back	2	½ x 1½ x 6¼
Sides	2	½ x 1½ x 4½
Bottom panel	1	¼ x 3⅞ x 5⅝
Lid	1	¾ x 4⅜ x 6⅛

Rabbeting the lid allows it to sit snug in the box carcase.

Making the Carcase

1. Cut a ½-in.-thick, 1½-in.-wide, 22-in.-long board to width for the front, back, and sides.
2. Cut a ¼-in. groove for the bottom panel along the inside face of the board.
3. Miter-cut the carcase pieces to length. Do not bevel the sides until after the carcase is assembled and the lid is fitted to it.
4. Cut a piece of ¼-in. plywood for the bottom panel.
5. Sand the inside surfaces and bottom panel, finishing with 180-grit paper.
6. Assemble the carcase as described on pp. 26-28, and reinforce the miter joints with keys. The keys for this maple box are ⅛-in.-thick maple. You can use contrasting keys as a design element, but high contrast attracts attention, and I wanted to keep the spotlight on the wonderful knot in the lid. With the carcase assembled, make the slab lid.

Making the Lid

1. Cut the lid stock to the dimensions shown in the cutlist on p. 35. (The lid's finished dimensions will be slightly smaller after the bevels are cut.)
2. Using the router table and a straight or rabbeting bit, cut ³⁄₁₆-in.-deep rabbets around the underside of the lid (see the photo above). The rabbet will be at least ⅜ in. wide, but sneak up to the final width gradually, checking to see how the lid fits into the carcase after

each pass. You want a very tight fit so that when you cut the 5° bevel on the sides, the lid will not shift with respect to the carcase. You can widen the rabbets slightly later to allow easier lid removal and replacement.

If you accidentally cut the rabbets too wide and there is plenty of play between the lid and the carcase, use masking tape to shim out the rabbet shoulders to ensure a tight fit when you cut the 5° bevel.

Cutting the Bevels

1. With the lid in place on the box, set up the table saw to cut the bevels. You'll need to use a combination blade because the beveling operation involves crosscutting the ends of the lid as well as ripping the sides. Set the blade angle to 5°. The blade height should be about 2½ in. on the perpendicular.
2. Bevel the two 4½-in. sides first. This way, when you bevel the front and back, you'll be able to remove any tearout that occurred when the sides were beveled. Tape the lid to the carcase, applying masking tape on the front and back only. Use the miter gauge with an auxiliary fence and a stop block to push the box through the blade.
3. Remove the masking tape from the front and back, and then tape the two sides closed. Bevel the front and back of the box using the rip fence. With the bevels cut, now's the time to add some finishing touches.

Finishing

1. Remove the masking tape and sand the four sides smooth, with the lid still set tight in the carcase. When you get to 180 grit, ease the four corners. To retain the box's crisp, sharp, angular look, refrain from rounding off the corners too much.
2. Remove the lid from the carcase. If necessary, widen the lid rabbets slightly on the router table so that the lid will fit down easily onto the box.
3. Fine-sand the lid and the carcase individually.
4. Apply the finish. I wanted to preserve the light maple color of this box, so I applied three coats of a water-based, penetrating finish.

The interesting feature of this pen-and-pencil box is the lever-action lid. Looking at the top when the box is closed, it's hard to figure out how to open it, other than turning it upside down. The secret is underneath the lid, where a pair of fulcrums lets you push down on either end of the lid to tilt up the other end (see the photo at right).

Follow the dimensions given in the drawing on p. 38 and in the instructions, or adapt the box's design to your needs. A cutlist is included with the drawing.

Making the Carcase

1. Cut a ¼-in.-thick, 1½-in.-wide, 25-in. long piece of stock for the front, back, and side pieces.
2. Rout the ¼-in.-deep by ⅛-in.-wide rabbets to form a ledge for the lid, and then cut the ⅛-in. by ⅛-in. grooves for the bottom panel.
3. Miter-cut the carcase pieces to length.
4. Sand the inside surfaces with 180-grit paper (remember to ease the sharp edges on both sides of the rabbet).
5. Cut the bottom panel and sand it, finishing with 180-grit paper.
6. Assemble the carcase and bottom (see pp. 26-28). Take extra care to ensure that the box is square at each corner.
7. Install the keys (for more on making and installing keys, see pp. 28-30). When the glue has cured, trim and sand the keys flush. Then make the lid.

Making the Lid

1. Measure the inside dimensions of the carcase at the top.
2. Cut the lid to fit with a gap of less than 1/64 in. Set the lid into the ledge. (You'll have to turn the box upside down to remove the lid.)
3. Now you can cut the rabbets on the underside of the lid to form the fulcrums. To do this, use a ½-in. straight bit or rabbeting bit in the router table, set the bit height to ⅛ in. (the rabbet depth), and set the fence to allow a ³⁄₁₆-in.-wide rabbet (see Option 1 in the detail drawing on p. 38).
4. First rout a rabbet in each end of the lid. Use a rectangular guide block to push the lid past the bit. This keeps the lid perpendicular to the fence and minimizes tearout (see the drawing at right). If necessary, clamp a zero-clearance

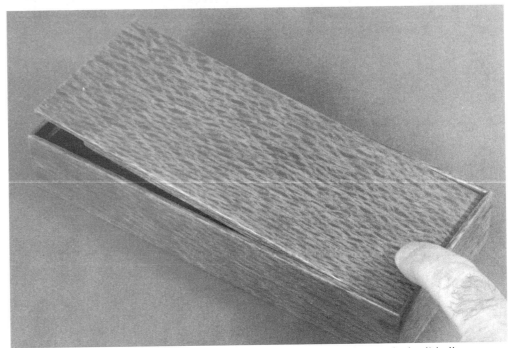

This lacewood box has a lever-action lid. A pair of fulcrums underneath the lid allows you to push down on one end of the lid to tilt up the other end.

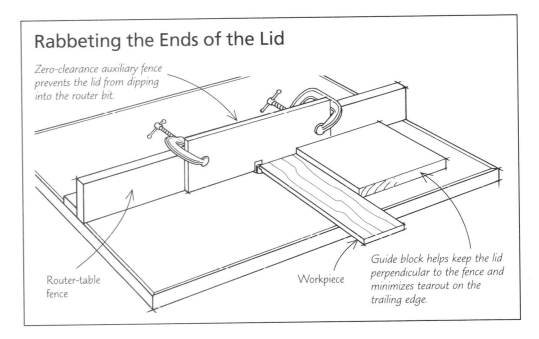

Rabbeting the Ends of the Lid

Zero-clearance auxiliary fence prevents the lid from dipping into the router bit.

Router-table fence

Workpiece

Guide block helps keep the lid perpendicular to the fence and minimizes tearout on the trailing edge.

auxiliary fence to the router-table fence to prevent the lid from dipping into the bit.
5. Next clamp a stop block to the fence, ⅞ in. from the center of the bit, on the right side of the fence (see the left drawing on p. 39). With the lid's edge against the fence, climb-cut

Lever-Action Pen-and-Pencil Box

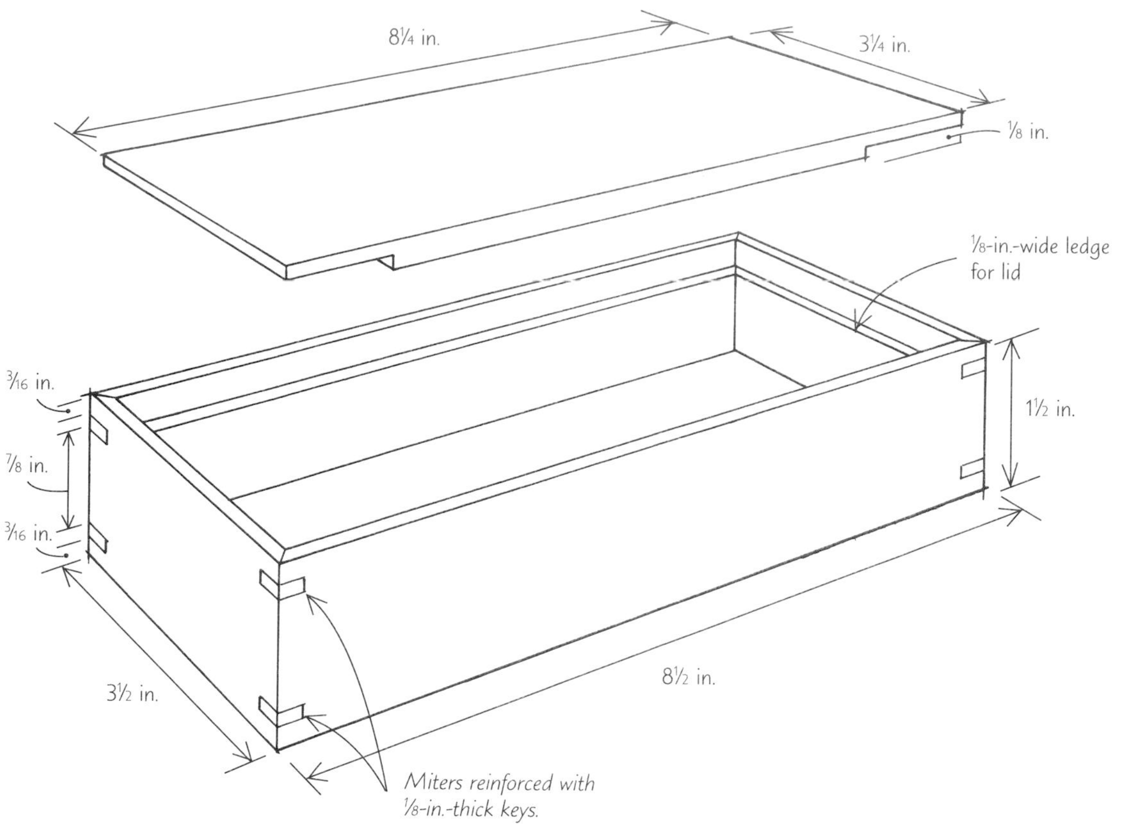

8¼ in.
3¼ in.
⅛ in.
⅛-in.-wide ledge for lid
3⁄16 in.
⅞ in.
3⁄16 in.
1½ in.
3½ in.
8½ in.
Miters reinforced with ⅛-in.-thick keys.

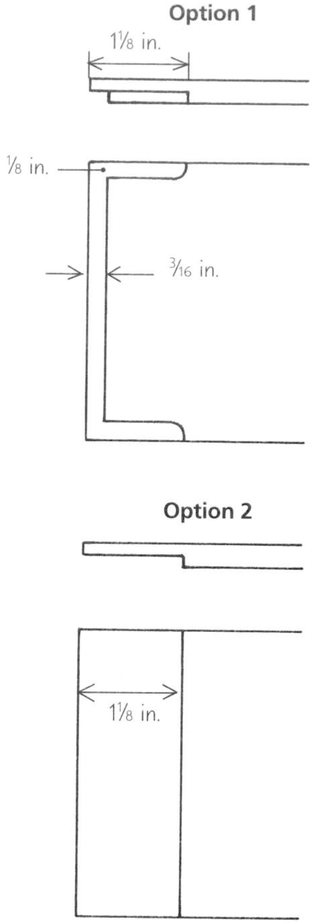

Option 1
1⅛ in.
⅛ in.
3⁄16 in.
Option 2
1⅛ in.

Bottom view of lid

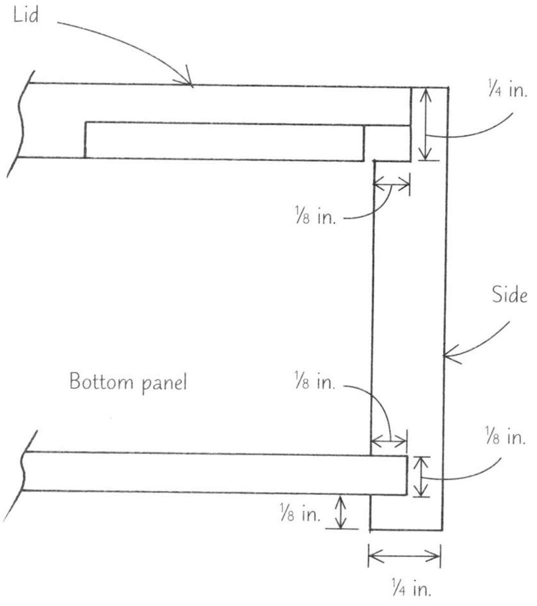

Lid
¼ in.
⅛ in.
Side
Bottom panel
⅛ in.
⅛ in.
⅛ in.
¼ in.

Section view of carcase

CUTLIST		
Description	**Quantity**	**Dimensions**
Front/back	2	¼ x 1½ x 8½
Sides	2	¼ x 1½ x 3½
Bottom panel	1	⅛ x 3¼ x 8¼
Lid	1	¼ x 3¼ x 8¼

Climb-Cutting Stopped Rabbets

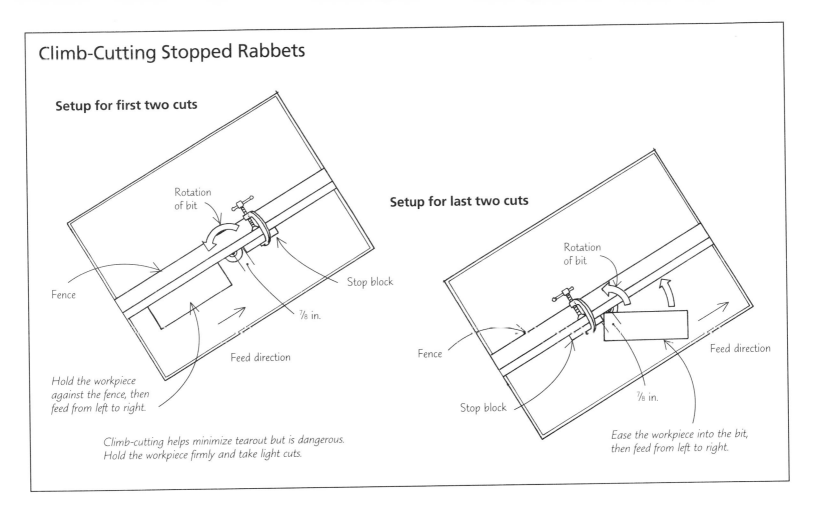

Setup for first two cuts

Rotation of bit

Fence

Stop block

7/8 in.

Feed direction

Hold the workpiece against the fence, then feed from left to right.

Climb-cutting helps minimize tearout but is dangerous. Hold the workpiece firmly and take light cuts.

Setup for last two cuts

Rotation of bit

Fence

Stop block

7/8 in.

Feed direction

Ease the workpiece into the bit, then feed from left to right.

(working from left to right) a rabbet on opposite corners of the lid. Climb-cutting (also called back-routing) helps minimize tearout but is dangerous because it tends to pull the workpiece faster than you want it to go. Maintain a firm grip on the workpiece and take light passes. (Climb-cutting should be avoided on narrow stock.)

6. Switch the stop block to the left side, again 7/8 in. from the bit's center, and rout the other two rabbets (see the right drawing above). To reduce tearout, start with the lid over at the stop on the left side, ease the lid into the bit, and feed from left to right again. I recommend practicing this cut on pieces of scrap.

You can avoid these time-consuming router-table setups by simply cutting a 1 1/8-in.-wide rabbet on the underside of the lid all the way across each end (see Option 2 in the detail drawing on the facing page). Install a dado-blade set on the table saw and use a backing board to prevent tearout. The result will be less attractive, in my opinion, but the fulcrum mechanism will work just as well.

7. Once you've routed the rabbets, the lid's underside should look like the one in the photo at right. Place the lid on the box and test the lever action. If you push one end down, the other end should tilt up just enough to grab it and remove it. Now you're ready to finish the box.

Finishing

1. Sand the box, finishing with 180-grit paper.
2. For the lacewood box shown here, I applied three coats of a water-based finish that preserves the delicate grain pattern. I sanded between coats with successively finer sandpaper (starting with 320 grit and finishing with 600 grit). Then I added a fourth coat to the lid only, to help minimize warp, and polished it with an ultrafine abrasive pad.

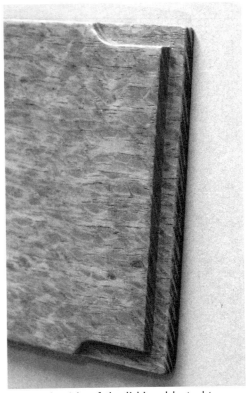

The underside of the lid is rabbeted to form fulcrums.

3 BOXES WITH DECORATIVE LIDS

Techniques

The lid is usually the most prominent feature of a box, so it's important that it be attractive and/or interesting, if not dramatic. The lid also needs to be constructed in such a way that it will not noticeably warp or otherwise distort.

Each project in the previous chapter has a one-piece lid. This type of lid is fine for small or plain boxes. But when the box gets larger or when you're after a more distinctive look, you can build a lid out of two or more pieces of wood, sometimes incorporating plywood or other sheet materials.

Assembling Lid Panels

The two most common ways to assemble a stable lid panel are to glue boards edge-to-edge or to make a frame-and-panel lid.

Edge-gluing two or three boards together to make the lid takes some time and preparation, but it's not difficult. You can shape the edges (with roundovers or chamfers, for example) for a decorative effect, and you don't have to frame the panel if you orient the end grain correctly—although frames (or breadboard ends) do add stability.

MAKING GLUED-UP LID PANELS

Woodworkers who make cabinets and tables spend a lot of time gluing up wide door panels and tabletops out of narrower boards. Sometimes they join several boards edge-to-edge at once, and they use specialized clamping equipment and elaborate stands and accessories that keep glued-up surfaces flat and properly aligned.

In box making, even if you're making large boxes with wide lid panels, you rarely need to glue up more than two or three boards edge-to-edge to attain the desired width. And the equipment and accessories are much simpler. But the same principles apply for selecting, arranging, and squaring up the boards (keeping in mind the goal of achieving an attractive, flat panel).

Wood selection is key Be selective in your choice of boards for a glued-up lid panel. Choose boards of the same species, preferably from the same log, so that you can match the color and grain pattern. If you want to join different species, let them acclimate in your shop so they at least have the same moisture content.

I prefer not to mix plainsawn and quartersawn boards in the lid panel, because I find contrasting grain patterns unappealing. In general, plainsawn boards have an attractive surface figure, while quartersawn boards provide maximum stability.

Boards of the same width joined together are usually more attractive than joined boards of varying widths. Once you've chosen the wood, you can start laying out the pieces.

Pay attention to grain orientation
There are a couple of reasons to be particular in arranging the boards for glue-up. The first is to avoid cupping, and the second is to avoid tearout.

To avoid cupping, flip the adjoining boards so that the end grain alternates (see the drawing on the facing page). Orienting the grain in this manner balances out any minor cupping, retaining the overall flatness of the panel.

You may prefer to arrange the boards to show the best faces and matching grain patterns. However, if doing so prevents you from alternating the end grain, stabilize the panel by framing it or by using breadboard ends (see p. 8).

When assembling a panel of glued-up boards, you'll need to plane the surface to even it up. To avoid tearout during planing, arrange the boards so that their grain lies in the same direction so you can plane with the grain. Draw arrows on the boards to indicate the grain direction so that you'll know in which direction to plane.

Try to arrange the boards so that the grain pattern of one piece merges nicely with that of the next. When you've finally got all your boards arranged in order, number each board on the face so you'll remember which board fits where. Once you've got the grain pattern you want, mark the joints to help you align the pieces later during glue-up (I draw a triangle on them).

Make sure the edges are square The edges of each board must be square and smooth to achieve a good glue joint. Rip the boards on the table saw using a high-quality sawblade. If necessary, make a pass or two on the jointer to square and smooth the edges further.

It's also important that the boards be the same thickness before joining them. And because they will be planed or sanded after glue-up, start with boards 1/64 in. to 1/32 in. thicker than the final dimension.

If you like, you can use short splines, biscuits, or dowels to help align the boards during glue-up, but use the minimum number necessary (usually two) to maintain proper alignment.

Glue-up is simple Gluing up a box lid is much easier than making a large cabinet door or tabletop. In many cases, assuming the edges are nicely jointed, you can get by with rubber bands instead of clamps. Here's how to get a good edge-to-edge joint:
1. Make a dry run. Test-fit all the parts to make sure your rubber bands or clamps are the right size—you'll have to work quickly and efficiently after spreading the glue.
2. When you're ready for glue-up, place a sheet of plastic or waxed paper on the bench or table to catch any glue squeeze-out. Spread

Laying Out Boards for Glue-Up

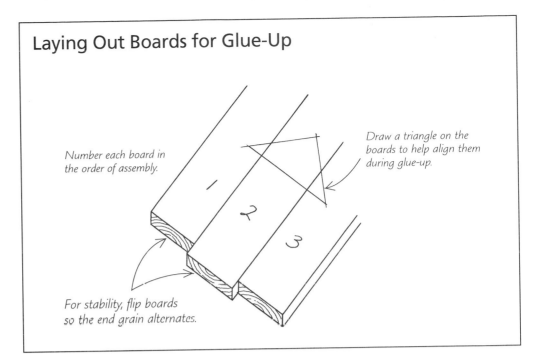

Number each board in the order of assembly.

Draw a triangle on the boards to help align them during glue-up.

For stability, flip boards so the end grain alternates.

yellow glue evenly and thoroughly on both mating surfaces with a stiff brush.
3. If the panel is fairly small and fits together nicely, stretch a couple of pieces of masking tape across the joint lines (not along the joint) on both sides of the panel, to keep the boards from shifting position. Then secure the assembly with strong rubber bands or clamps every few inches. (If you're using clamps, place scrap wood between the clamp and the boards to protect the lid panel.)

Check to make sure the joints are flush, and adjust them if necessary. When using rubber bands, make sure they are flat, not twisted, so that the panel doesn't rack when it is set on a flat surface to dry.

You should see some glue squeeze-out. If you don't, add clamping pressure (by hand if you're using rubber bands for clamps) until you see a small, fairly continuous bead of glue along the joint line.
4. Place the assembly on a flat surface and leave it undisturbed for several hours, preferably overnight, before you remove the rubber bands or clamps. Then carefully scrape off the excess glue.
5. Wait a couple of days, if possible, before you plane or sand the panel to its final thickness. If you plane or sand while the joints are swollen (from the water in the glue), then later when the joints shrink, you'll be left with depressed joint lines. By the way, I don't like to run a glued-up panel through a thickness

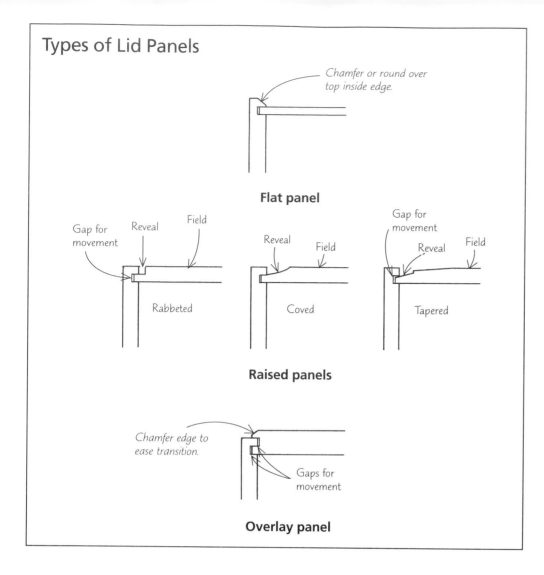

Types of Lid Panels

Flat panel

Chamfer or round over top inside edge.

Raised panels

Rabbeted

Gap for movement — Reveal — Field

Coved

Reveal — Field

Tapered

Gap for movement — Reveal — Field

Overlay panel

Chamfer edge to ease transition.

Gaps for movement

The flat panel is the easiest to install in the carcase, because the grooves are as wide as the panel's thickness, and the panel can simply "float" in its grooves.

To ease the transition from carcase to panel, I like to round over or chamfer the carcase's top inside edge. I usually seal the panel with a coat of finish before assembling the box.

Raised panels A raised panel is a variation of the flat panel. The difference is that a raised lid panel has shaped edges; a flat panel does not.

You can't use plywood if you want to make a raised panel, because it involves shaping the edges, and the striations will be highly visible. If you're working with a solid or glued-up panel, however, there are three basic raised-panel profiles to choose from: rabbeted, coved, and tapered. The choice is mainly a matter of personal taste and what tools you have.

A raised panel has two elements: the reveal and the field. The reveal is the portion of the panel that sits below the top edge of the carcase. The field is the interior portion of the panel and is usually nearly flush with the top of the carcase.

Overlay panels What makes overlay panels different from the other two styles is that both the carcase and the lid panel are grooved. The joint is known as an interlocking double-groove joint. It's very simple to cut, once you have your table saw set up correctly. Here's how to do it:

1. Chamfer or round over the top outside edge of the lid panel to create a pleasing transition.
2. Adjust the fence so that the width of the blade and the fence's distance from the blade are equal. For instance, with a 1/8-in.-thick sawblade, the rip fence should be 1/8 in. from the blade. Set the blade height to half the thickness of the carcase stock.
3. Take two straight, square pieces of scrap and cut grooves in their edges. Remember to cut the groove about 1/16 in. deeper than needed to allow for wood movement. Then try to interlock the two scrap pieces. If the joint is too tight (or the pieces don't interlock at all), move the fence a little closer to the blade. If the joint is too loose, move the fence farther from the blade. Continue cutting the test pieces until they fit together just right. Also, check the depth of the cut to make sure it's accurate. (If you use this joint often, save the

---

planer because the cured glue is very hard and nicks the planer knives. So I take my panels to a local cabinet shop and pay the owner to run them through his wide-belt sander, which can thickness the panel to precise dimensions.

Once your glued-up lid panel is thicknessed, you can cut it to its final dimensions. Here again, you can shape the edges as desired.

TYPES OF LID PANELS

In addition to simply placing the panel on top as described in the previous chapter, there are three basic ways to incorporate the panel into your box: as a flat panel, a raised panel, or an overlay panel (see the drawing above).

Flat panels The flat panel is the easiest lid panel to make. Though a flat panel can be made of solid wood, it's most often plywood. The disadvantage of this type of panel is that it's quite plain.

scraps from your final setting and use them to set the fence next time.)

4. Cut grooves in the four edges of the lid panel, with the bottom face against the fence. Then cut grooves in the four sides of the carcase, with the top edge against the fence.

5. Test the fit of the pieces. If the fit is too tight, wrap 100-grit sandpaper around a metal ruler and sand lightly inside the grooves. It shouldn't take much sanding.

MAKING PLYWOOD LID PANELS

Using plywood for the lid panel is an option that offers the greatest stability. Plywood with attractive hardwood veneer is widely available in nominal thicknesses of 1/8 in., 1/4 in., and thicker. Or you can laminate exotic and spectacular wood veneers to tempered hardboard.

The main disadvantage of plywood or hardboard is that you'll need to hide the edges. One way to do this is to capture the panel in grooves cut near the top edge of the carcase—the same way a bottom panel is installed in the carcase. Another option is to build a frame around the panel. Regardless of which method you choose, making a plywood panel is simple.

If you buy a sheet of hardwood plywood and cut a lid panel to the proper dimensions, all you have to do is fine-sand and it's ready to go. But be careful not to sand through the thin veneer layer. If you select your plywood sheet with care, avoiding those with too many scratches or other surface blemishes, you won't need to sand much at all.

Be sure to buy plywood with two "show sides" so that you'll see an attractive surface when you open the box as well as when the lid is closed.

Where to buy veneer In some retail stores, you can find attractive hardwood plywood with face veneers such as oak, ash, maple, walnut, cherry, mahogany, and birch. But you won't find any really dramatic stuff. For drama, you'll have to buy a substrate—plywood or hardboard—and veneer each surface of it.

You can buy a wide array of domestic and exotic veneers, including flamboyant burls, at specialty woodworking stores and through some catalogs. You can also buy them in flitches, or "books," of consecutive sheets. The flitches are stacked in the same sequence in

Flattening Veneer

Some wood species, and burls especially, warp and wrinkle considerably as they dry after they're sliced into veneer. To achieve good adhesion to the substrate, it's important that the veneer you use be flat. Flattening a sheet of wrinkled or warped veneer is simple. Here's how:

1. Using a brush or sponge, coat both sides of the veneer with water. If the wrinkles are severe, use a mixture of six parts water, one part glycerin (available in drug stores), and one part white PVA glue. The glycerin helps soften the veneer and prevents cracking, while the glue stiffens the veneer after it dries to help keep it flat. (If you plan to finish the box with lacquer or varnish, you can use more glue in the sizing mixture. Danish oil won't penetrate when there's too much glue, however.)

2. Sandwich the veneer between two sheets of flat, 3/4-in. plywood. First, though, lay a sheet of waxed paper on the bottom piece of plywood, and a layer of brown Kraft paper (a grocery bag without ink is fine) over that. Then place the veneer on the Kraft paper. Follow that with another layer of Kraft paper, waxed paper, and the top piece of plywood. The Kraft paper will slowly absorb the veneer's moisture, and the waxed paper will keep the moisture out of the plywood. Place weights on top of the sandwich to form a press (see the drawing below).

3. Let the sandwich sit for 24 hours and then check the veneer. If it's still wrinkled, dampen the veneer again and add more weight.

4. If the veneer is flat but still damp, remove the damp Kraft paper and replace it with dry paper. Then put the sandwich back together. Check it again every few hours. When the veneer is flat and dry, it's ready for use. (Keep the veneer sheet stored between the plywood pieces, under pressure, until you're ready to use it.)

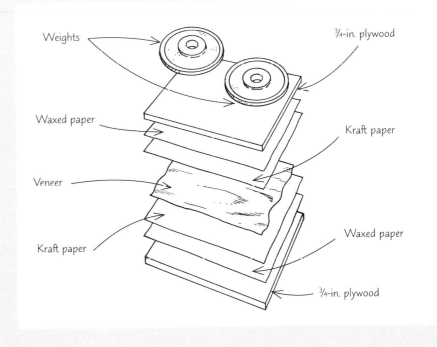

Weights

3/4-in. plywood

Waxed paper

Kraft paper

Veneer

Waxed paper

Kraft paper

3/4-in. plywood

which they were cut from the log, so any two consecutive sheets are almost identical, which lets you match both faces of a panel.

The easiest kind of veneer I've found to work with is backed veneer, which is an ultra-thin slice of wood (typically $\frac{1}{64}$ in. thick) that is bonded to a paper backing and commonly sold in rolls. However, you are limited in your selection of backed veneer. A wider selection of species is available in veneers sold without backing, typically $\frac{1}{28}$ in. to $\frac{1}{40}$ in. thick.

How to apply veneer Veneering a lid panel is so quick and easy that you might find yourself hooked on it. For best results, veneer one face of the substrate at a time, and then do the opposite face. I use contact cement because it's quick, permanent, and doesn't require clamps. Be sure to read the safety instructions on the container and use adequate ventilation. Here are the steps I follow to veneer a lid panel:

Jazzing Up a Lid

Though there are many elegant boxes with simple, undecorated, solid-wood lids, don't feel that your box has to be plain. Be creative and decorate the lid to your tastes. It can be a lot of fun, and it adds your signature to the box. Here are some of the ways you can jazz up a lid.

BOOKMATCHING

The two halves of a bookmatched panel are mirror images of each other. Burls, spalted wood, and wood with wild grain produce some spectacular bookmatches (see the photo at left below).

A bookmatched panel is made by resawing a thick board, and then opening the two halves like a book. You can match the grain pattern by gluing the halves edge-to-edge or even end-to-end. You may have to shift the halves a bit to preserve the match, since you lost at least $\frac{1}{16}$ in. of wood when you sawed the board in half. Note that a bookmatched panel shouldn't be planed by machine after glue-up because the grain of the two halves lies in opposite directions.

LAMINATING

If you're building a lid from edge-glued boards and the grain pattern doesn't quite match, you can offset the problem by laminating thin strips of contrasting wood between the boards to create stripes (see the photo at right below). The laminated strips will draw attention away from poorly matched boards in a panel.

INLAYING

Inlays in a lid can create stunning effects and are a great way to add creativity to your boxes. Inlays are created by cutting grooves into the lid and then inserting strips of wood into the grooves. By using a circle-cutting jig on the router, you can even cut radiused (curved) grooves and bend the inlays to fit.

When you press an inlay into a groove, draw an arrow in pencil next to the inlay, indicating which direction to plane or chisel off any protruding part.

You can use a contrasting wood for the inlay, like that shown in the top left photo on the facing page, or you can use metal inlays. I've seen boxes with inlays of brass, pewter, and copper.

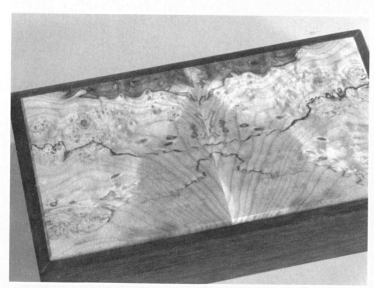

This spectacular lid is made from bookmatched spalted maple.

These laminated lid panels are decorated with contrasting veneer strips and laminated dowel plugs.

1. Cut the veneer sheets (one for each side of the panel) oversized by an inch or so on each dimension. Use a utility knife and a metal straightedge to guide the cut.

2. If the veneer is wavy or wrinkled, moisten each sheet and press it between plywood boards until it's perfectly flat (for more on flattening veneer, see the sidebar on p. 43). If your veneer is an oily species, such as rosewood or teak, wipe it first with acetone or lacquer thinner before applying adhesive, and let it dry for 30 minutes.

3. Cut the substrate to its final dimensions, or slightly oversized. For a small panel (less than 30 sq. in.) you can use ⅛-in. hardboard. For larger panels, use ¼-in. hardboard or plywood. If you use plywood, orient the grain of your veneer so that it's perpendicular to the plywood's face grain for stability.

4. Coat both surfaces—the substrate and the underside of the veneer—with contact

INTARSIA

Intarsia is an advanced woodworking technique. Once mastered, the skill can turn an ordinary box into a sculpted work of art. Intarsia is the process of assembling a mosaic, or picture puzzle, and gluing the pieces to a substrate. What makes intarsia different from a mosaic is that the pieces are sculpted and three dimensional.

The walnut box shown in the photo at right below, made by Kim Hoppenrath of Stevens Point, Wisconsin, features an intarsia lid. (No stains or dyes were used in the process.)

MARQUETRY

Marquetry is the use of contrasting veneers to create a picture or design inset in a substrate. The design need not be complicated to create a beautiful lid (see the bottom left photo below). To create a marquetry lid, cut the veneer using a utility knife (or a fretsaw with a special marquetry blade), and then lay the pieces out, like a puzzle, into a pattern or picture. Tape the pieces together on the face and glue the picture down to a substrate.

The soft-maple lid (top left) features radiused inlays of cherry and straight inlays of mahogany and walnut.

There are many pieces to the intarsia lid (above): sumac (the hill), goncalo alves (the sky), and bocote (the tree trunks); the leaves are Brazilian satinwood, padauk, and pernambuco.

The marquetry design (left) features walnut and cherry veneers.

cement. If the veneer has no paper backing, apply a second coat of cement, since the first coat has probably soaked into the wood. Keep dirt and dust off the surface.

5. When the cement is slightly tacky to the touch, but not dry, position the veneer on the substrate. But be careful: The disadvantage of contact cement is that once the surfaces touch, they bond instantly and permanently, and you can't adjust them. So you have to position the veneer right the first time.

The best way to do this is to cover the substrate with a sheet of waxed paper. Then place the veneer on top and align it just right. Slowly slide the waxed paper out from under the veneer, pressing down and smoothing the veneer from the center to the edges with a small roller.

6. As soon as you finish one side of the panel, flip it over and trim the overhanging veneer, using a sharp utility knife.

7. If you discover air pockets on the surface, fix them now so that they don't cause trouble later. Slit the veneer with the grain, using a utility knife to let the air out, and then press the veneer flat to the substrate so it will bond. If there's a bump caused by a particle,

try to pry it out without marring the surrounding surface. Then veneer the opposite face.

8. If your panel is oversized, don't saw it to final dimensions yet; wait until you build the frame or box carcase.

9. Sand the panel with fine sandpaper. For burls and wild grain patterns, use a random-orbit sander. Here again, be careful not to sand through the veneer.

Assembling Carcase-and-Panel Boxes

In Chapter 2, I showed you how to assemble a carcase with the bottom panel captured in grooves in the box's sides, with the lid built separately. Now I'll show you how to assemble a box with an integral lid, where the lid is captured in grooves cut near the carcase's top edge (I call it carcase-and-panel construction). The result is a closed, six-sided box (see the drawing below). After the box is assembled, the lid is separated by sawing the assembly in two on the table saw or bandsaw.

There are two advantages to constructing a box in this manner. First, the lid and the carcase will always be perfectly matched and mated. Second, carcase-and-panel construction is an easy way to frame a lid panel, whether it's solid wood or plywood.

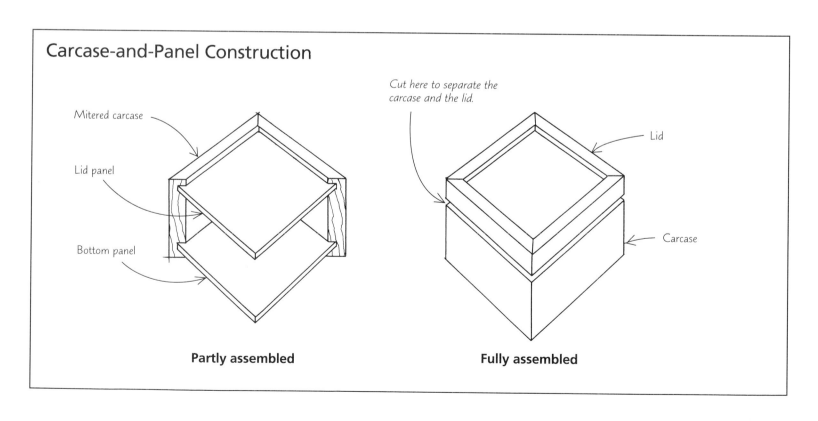

Carcase-and-Panel Construction

Mitered carcase

Lid panel

Bottom panel

Cut here to separate the carcase and the lid.

Lid

Carcase

Partly assembled

Fully assembled

LID-PANEL DIMENSIONS

When figuring the dimensions of the lid panel, remember to allow for wood movement. You can calculate the lid panel's dimensions once you know the dimensions of the whole box. You just need to remember a simple formula (which assumes that the grooves are cut half as deep as the carcase thickness).

Start by measuring the length and width of the carcase. Then subtract the thickness of the carcase stock and $1/16$ in. for wood movement. For example, if your box is 4 in. by 6 in. and the carcase stock is $3/8$ in. thick, the panel will be $3\frac{9}{16}$ in. by $5\frac{9}{16}$ in. This formula allows the panel $1/32$ in. of movement in each direction. For a larger panel (36 sq. in. or more), allow more room (about $1/8$ in. for every 12 in. of width).

If you fail to leave a gap for wood movement, or if you glue the panel in place, the force of the movement will eventually break apart the carcase. However, to keep the lid panel from shifting, spot-glue the panel to the frame at both ends (see the drawing at right). Spot gluing allows you to direct wood movement from those two points.

ASSEMBLING THE BOX

To assemble a carcase-and-panel box, simply follow the procedures for gluing up a mitered box (see Chapter 2). However, because the lid is included in the assembly, you've got to be careful in the preparation and construction.

Finish the lid panel Before assembling the box, apply at least one coat of finish to the lid panel. This way, when movement occurs, you won't see an unfinished area that had previously been concealed by the frame. Just remember not to apply finish to the two spots where you intend to spot-glue the panel to the frame.

Dry-fit the pieces As with any box assembly, it's important to make a dry run to ensure a good fit all around. The lid panel should not be too tight in the grooves; otherwise, you won't be able to adjust its position after assembly.

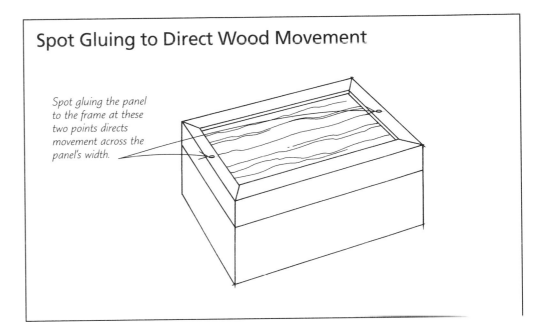

Spot Gluing to Direct Wood Movement

Spot gluing the panel to the frame at these two points directs movement across the panel's width.

If you're using a raised panel, check to make sure that the reveal is equal around the field; if not, trim back the wider shoulders of the field. In the case of an overlay panel, you'll need to measure the distance between the edges of the lid panel and the box sides, and then adjust the panel during assembly to equalize those distances.

Reinforce with care Before you cut slots and install keys to reinforce the box, think carefully about where you want to separate the lid from the box. Normally you want to saw the box apart no less than $5/8$ in. from the top edge of the carcase. On very small boxes, you can reduce that distance to as little as $1/2$ in. If you plan to install hinges, remember that the separated lid frame must be deep enough to hold hinge screws.

Allow $3/16$ in. to $1/8$ in. for the saw kerf (depending on the width of your sawblade) at the separation line when positioning the lower keys. I consider three keys on each miter joint to be the minimum, one above the separation line and two below.

Finally, ease the sharp mitered corners before separating the lid and carcase, rather than after, so that the lid and carcase will blend nicely.

Separating the Lid and Carcase

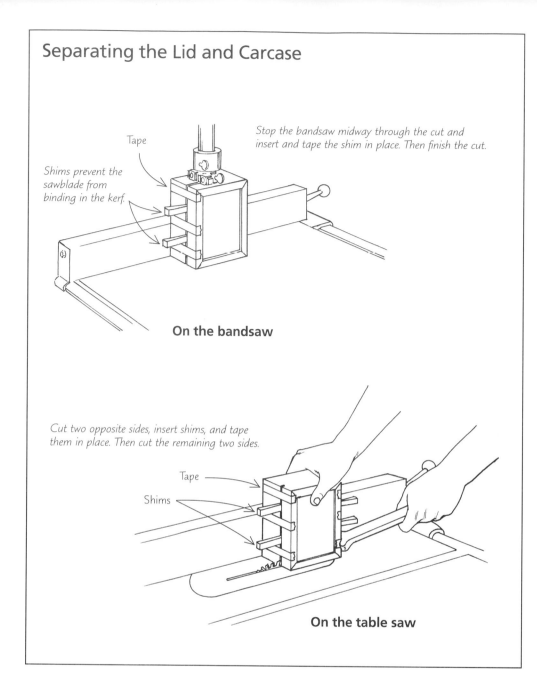

Shims prevent the sawblade from binding in the kerf.

Tape

Stop the bandsaw midway through the cut and insert and tape the shim in place. Then finish the cut.

On the bandsaw

Cut two opposite sides, insert shims, and tape them in place. Then cut the remaining two sides.

Tape

Shims

On the table saw

SEPARATING THE LID AND CARCASE

You can saw the box apart on a table saw or on a bandsaw. Use whatever machine you're most comfortable with.

The bandsaw's blade is thinner, so it'll make a smaller kerf; but it leaves a rough surface. However, the operation can be accomplished in one pass. The table-saw blade makes a bigger kerf (even if you're using a thin-kerf blade) but leaves a smoother surface. And it will take four passes—one for each side of the box. With either machine, you'll need a high enough fence to stabilize the box during the cut.

This procedure is a bit tricky because you have to shim one or more kerfs to keep the box from closing while cutting. If the box closes, it will pinch the sawblade, resulting in rough cuts, burned edges, and/or kickback.

On the bandsaw, stop the saw in the middle of the cut and insert shims in the leading end (see the top drawing at left). On the table saw, cut two opposite sides first, shim both kerfs, and then cut the other two sides (see the bottom drawing at left). With either method, the shims should be the same thickness as the sawblade; tape the shims in place so that they won't drop out.

If you're cutting the box apart on the table saw, there is an alternative to using shims. Set the blade height to about 1/64 in. less than the thickness of the carcase stock. When you cut the kerf, the blade won't go all the way through the carcase, so the lid will still be attached by a thin membrane of wood, which you can slice through with a utility knife. Then plane or sand off the remaining membrane.

Once the box is cut apart, plane or sand the newly exposed edges smooth. I normally use a stationary belt sander for starters, and then sand each edge with the grain using 180-grit sandpaper and ease the sharp inside edges.

After separating the lid from the carcase, you must provide a means of keeping the lid on the carcase. There are two ways to do this: You can install inserts (also called false sides), or you can use hinges (see chapters 4, 5, and 6).

Holding Lids with Inserts

Inserts keep the lid of the box in place. I use inserts only on small boxes. To use inserts on a larger box would require the user to lift the lid off the box with two hands and set it down somewhere, typically on a dresser or desktop. I don't know about you, but neither my dresser nor my desk has much extra space for a large lid. So for large boxes, use hinges.

I make my inserts out of micro-lumber, typically 1/8 in. thick. This stock is available in a wide variety of woods, including exotic species (for more on micro-lumber, see p. 12).

There are two styles of inserts: two-piece end inserts and four-piece mitered inserts (see the drawing at right on the facing page). Both are installed with their grain direction parallel to the carcase's, so they expand and shrink with the carcase.

TWO-PIECE END INSERTS

Two-piece end inserts are installed in both ends of the box (across the width). They're easy to make and install. Here's how:

1. Start with ⅛-in.-thick stock: You can use the same species as the box carcase or choose a contrasting species. Sand the stock with 180-grit paper at this point because it will be more difficult to sand when it's cut into smaller pieces.

2. The inserts should protrude ⅛ in. above the rim of the carcase, so measure the interior height of the box and add ⅛ in. Then rip the stock to that width.

3. Measure the interior width of the box to determine the length of each insert. Set a stop on the miter-gauge fence to ensure that each insert will be the same length. To prevent tearout, attach an extra-long auxiliary fence to the miter gauge. The fence should extend past the blade to support the workpiece on both sides of the sawblade (see the drawing below). It's critical that you avoid cutting the pieces too short, so crosscut the pieces a hair oversized.

4. If necessary, chisel away any glue squeeze-out from the inside corners of the box. Little beads of glue in the corners can keep the inserts from seating properly.

5. Try fitting the inserts into the box. They should be a friction fit. If they're too tight, trim them a little at a time until they fit perfectly. Place a slip of paper (or a playing card) between the stop and the workpiece. The paper will act as a shim. Make the cut, test-fit again, and, if necessary, add another shim. When the fit is just right, the inserts will slide into the box with some friction and will stay in place on their own.

6. When the inserts fit well, ease the top edges and corners with 180-grit sandpaper. Sand only the top ⅛ in. that stands proud of the box; don't round over the bottoms of the inserts.

7. Place the inserts inside the box and fit the lid over them. If the lid goes on smoothly, you can stop sanding. If you feel resistance when the lid goes on, ease the corners a little more and test-fit the lid again.

8. When everything fits, glue the inserts into the box and clamp them with one or two spring clamps until the glue dries.

FOUR-PIECE MITERED INSERTS

Four-piece mitered inserts actually form a bottomless box within a box. I don't use them for very small boxes because they reduce the interior space too much. The inserts need not be the same species as the carcase; in fact, I often use an accent wood, particularly

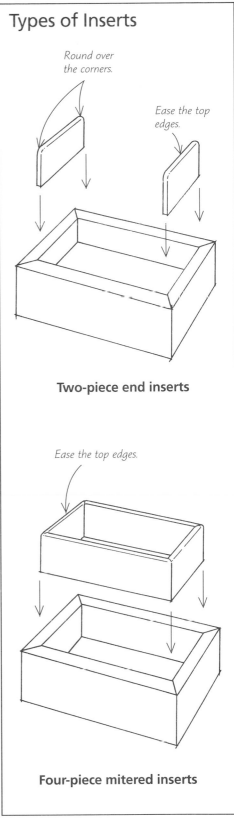

Types of Inserts

Round over the corners.

Ease the top edges.

Two-piece end inserts

Ease the top edges.

Four-piece mitered inserts

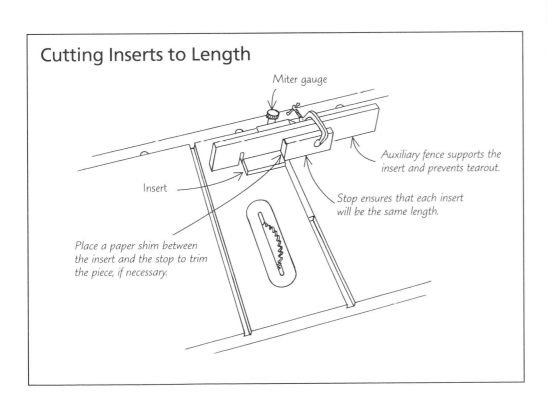

Cutting Inserts to Length

Miter gauge

Insert

Auxiliary fence supports the insert and prevents tearout.

Stop ensures that each insert will be the same length.

Place a paper shim between the insert and the stop to trim the piece, if necessary.

Built-in Inserts

You can make a box with built-in inserts so that you don't have to miter-cut, fit, and glue extra pieces into the box's interior after the lid is separated from the box. The technique entails cutting mating rabbets in the lid and carcase that let the two components fit together just like a box with four-piece mitered inserts. The disadvantage of this method is that you lose the continuous grain match on the exterior of the box.

The rabbets in the lid are inside rabbets, while the rabbets in the carcase are outside rabbets. The drawings below show you the basic steps for creating the mating rabbets.

one that I've used as keys, lid inlays, or interior dividers.

The procedure for cutting and installing four-piece inserts is similar to that for the end inserts. The only difference is that you'll be cutting 45° miters instead of 90° crosscuts. Be sure to sand the faces of the inserts to at least 180 grit before cutting the miters. If you sand after cutting the miters, you might ruin the tight fit.

As long as the four pieces fit tightly together at the corners, you do not need to glue them in place. Again, cut the inserts a tad long to begin with and sneak up on the final length, test-fitting as you go.

A challenging alternative to two-piece end inserts and four-piece mitered inserts is to make built-in inserts, as explained in the sidebar at left.

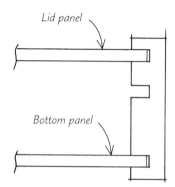

Step 1
Mill three grooves in each carcase piece: one for the lid panel (A), one for the lid rabbet (B), and one for the bottom panel (C).

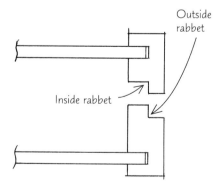

Lid panel

Bottom panel

Step 2
Assemble the box with the four carcase pieces, the lid panel, and the bottom panel.

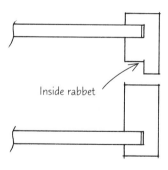

Inside rabbet

Step 3
Separate the lid at the lower edge of the middle groove, which creates the inside rabbet.

Outside rabbet

Inside rabbet

Step 4
Cut a rabbet on the top edge of the carcase to create the outside rabbet, which mates with the inside rabbet.

Projects

KEEPER BOX WITH END INSERTS

This box's *raison d'être* (reason for being) is to showcase the lid panel, which has madrone-burl veneer laminated to both faces of a ⅛-in. piece of hardboard (see the photo at right). I purchased consecutive slices of the veneer so that I could match the panel's faces almost perfectly. You can save time, of course, by using common hardwood plywood for the panel. But then, what's the *raison d'être?*

You can use the dimensions given in the drawing on p. 52 and in the instructions, or you can adapt the box's dimensions and materials to fit your own needs. A cutlist is included with the drawing. Refer to the Techniques section in this chapter (pp. 40-50) for instructions on how to make the lid and the inserts used to hold the lid in place.

Making the Lid

1. Cut the lid and bottom panels first. Then veneer the panels (for more on veneering, see pp. 43-46).
2. Fine-sand the panels to 220 grit. Be careful not to sand through the veneer.
3. Apply a preliminary finish. With veneer, I recommend Danish oil to enhance the grain pattern (Danish oil will really bring out the grain with burl veneer). When the finish is dry, rub the panel lightly with an ultrafine abrasive pad to prepare it for the next coat of finish, which will be applied after the box is assembled.

Making the Carcase

1. Rip the carcase stock to a width of 1⅞ in. (⅛ in. oversized to allow for the saw kerf when separating the lid). Before you crosscut the carcase pieces to length, cut the grooves for the bottom and lid panels and rout a chamfer in what will become the lid frame (see the section drawing on p. 52). Then miter-cut the front, back, and sides to their final lengths (for more on mitering, see pp. 22-24).
2. Fine-sand the inside faces and top edges of the carcase pieces, and then glue up the box.
3. Laminate keys to reinforce the box. For this box, I laminated rosewood to maple veneer, which creates a high-contrast accent. If you don't want to bother with lamination or don't like the high contrast, use a solid wood for the

The lid panel, veneered with madrone burl, is the centerpiece of this box.

keys that complements the burl in the lid (see pp. 28-30 for more on making keys).
4. Cut the slots for the keys and install them. Then sand the keys flush to the sides of the box and ease the four corners.
5. Separate the lid from the carcase using either the bandsaw or the table saw (see p. 48). Sand the newly exposed edges, but don't ease the inside edges until the two inserts are installed.

Finishing Touches

1. Cut the two end inserts (to learn how to make inserts, see pp. 48-50). Round over the top edges and corners with 180-grit sandpaper and glue the inserts in place (see the photo at right). Then ease the carcase's top inside edges.
2. Finish with two coats of Danish oil, and then polish the outside (for more on finishing, see pp. 17-21).

End inserts, made of ⅛-in.-thick microlumber, hold the lid in place.

Keeper Box with End Inserts

Chamfer the inside edge.

5/16 in.

1/8 in.

9/16 in.

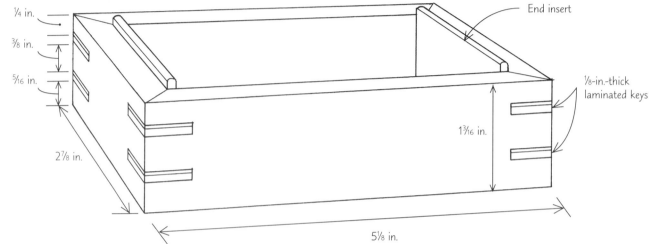

1/4 in.

3/8 in.

5/16 in.

End insert

1/8-in.-thick laminated keys

2 7/8 in.

1 3/16 in.

5 1/8 in.

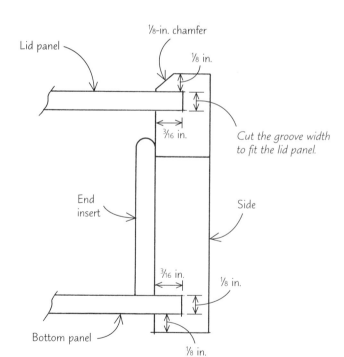

Lid panel

1/8-in. chamfer

1/8 in.

3/16 in.

Cut the groove width to fit the lid panel.

End insert

Side

3/16 in.

1/8 in.

Bottom panel

1/8 in.

Section view

CUTLIST

Description	Quantity	Dimensions
Front/back	2	3/8 x 1 7/8 x 5 1/8
Sides	2	3/8 x 1 7/8 x 2 7/8
Bottom panel	1	1/8 x 2 3/8 x 4 5/8
Lid panel*	1	1/8 x 2 3/8 x 4 5/8
End inserts	2	1/8 x 1 7/8 x 2 1/8

*Thickness depends on thickness of veneer.

Here are two boxes with subtle design differences. For these projects, you'll raise a field in a solid-wood panel and assemble the carcase around it (called carcase-and-panel construction). Unlike the previous project, in which two-piece end inserts keep the lid in place, these boxes employ four-piece mitered inserts.

Each box is designed with a lid panel that complements the frame. One box features a walnut carcase with stepped keys and a goncalo-alves lid panel (see the top photo at right). The other box has a walnut carcase with laminated keys and a maple-burl lid panel (see the bottom photo at right).

Choosing Stock

The most difficult part of making a box with a raised lid panel is finding stock for the panel that's "suitable for framing." Look for any piece of wood that strikes your fancy, for whatever reason—make a statement about what constitutes beauty in your mind. Sometimes searching through the scrap pile (yours or the local hardwood dealer's) will yield pleasant surprises.

As a general rule, you should use ⅜-in.-thick stock for a small keeper box. However, there may be times when the carcase requires more weight. For instance, because the maple-burl lid panel in the box shown at right has such a graceful grain pattern, I felt it needed a richer, weightier frame, so I used ½-in. stock.

Though I chose walnut for the carcases of both boxes shown here, you may choose any other species to contrast or complement the lid-panel stock you select.

Preparing the Parts

You can make the boxes with the dimensions given in the drawings on pages 54 and 55 and in the instructions, or you can adapt the dimensions to suit your specific needs. A cutlist is included with each of the drawings. The assembly process for each box is essentially the same.

1. The dimensions of the carcase depend on the size of the lid panel, so before you crosscut the carcase pieces to length, cut your panel to its final dimensions. (The panel's thickness should be around ¼ in. to ⅜ in.) Sand both faces and all edges, finishing with 180-grit paper.

2. For the box on p. 54, cut the carcase stock to 1⅞ in. wide (oversized to allow for the lid-

Both of these boxes have a lid panel that complements the walnut carcase. The top features a goncalo-alves panel; the bottom box has a maple-burl lid panel.

separation saw kerf); for the box on p. 55, cut the carcase stock to 1½ in. wide. Once you've cut the stock to size, cut grooves for the bottom panel and the lid panel. The lid-panel groove should be at least ⅛ in. wide, as shown in the section drawings, and it must be located down from the top edge so that the panel is recessed after assembly.

(continued on p. 56)

Keeper Box with Stepped Keys and Mitered Inserts

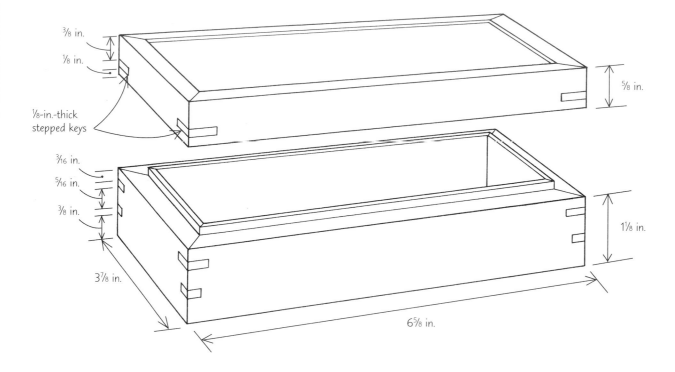

3/8 in.

1/8 in.

1/8-in.-thick stepped keys

5/8 in.

3/16 in.

5/16 in.

3/8 in.

3 7/8 in.

1 1/8 in.

6 5/8 in.

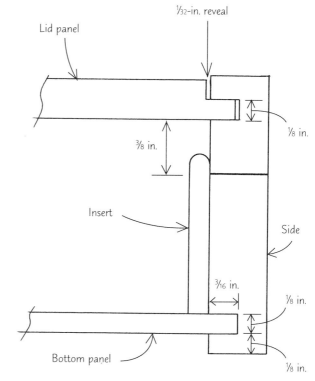

Lid panel

1/32-in. reveal

3/8 in.

1/8 in.

Insert

Side

3/16 in.

1/8 in.

Bottom panel

1/8 in.

Section view

<table>
<tr><td colspan="3">CUTLIST</td></tr>
<tr><th>Description</th><th>Quantity</th><th>Dimensions</th></tr>
<tr><td>Front/back</td><td>2</td><td>3/8 x 1 7/8 x 6 5/8</td></tr>
<tr><td>Sides</td><td>2</td><td>3/8 x 1 7/8 x 3 7/8</td></tr>
<tr><td>Bottom panel</td><td>1</td><td>1/8 x 3 1/2 x 6 1/4</td></tr>
<tr><td>Lid panel</td><td>1</td><td>1/4 x 3 3/8 x 6 1/8</td></tr>
<tr><td>Side inserts</td><td>2</td><td>1/8 x 1 x 3 1/8</td></tr>
<tr><td>Front and back inserts</td><td>2</td><td>1/8 x 1 x 5 7/8</td></tr>
</table>

Keeper Box with Laminated Keys and Mitered Inserts

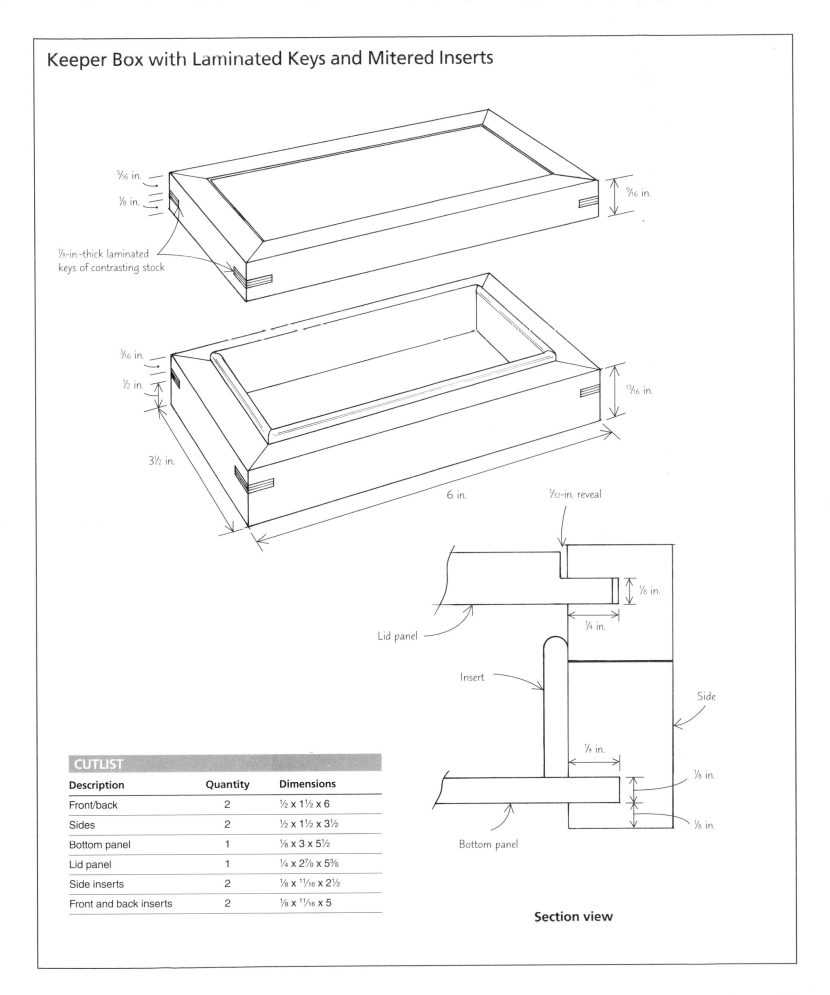

5/16 in.

1/8 in.

1/8-in.-thick laminated keys of contrasting stock

9/16 in.

3/16 in.

1/2 in.

13/16 in.

3 1/2 in.

6 in.

1/32-in. reveal

Lid panel

Insert

1/8 in.

1/4 in.

Side

1/4 in.

1/8 in.

1/8 in.

Bottom panel

Section view

CUTLIST

Description	Quantity	Dimensions
Front/back	2	1/2 x 1 1/2 x 6
Sides	2	1/2 x 1 1/2 x 3 1/2
Bottom panel	1	1/8 x 3 x 5 1/2
Lid panel	1	1/4 x 2 7/8 x 5 3/8
Side inserts	2	1/8 x 11/16 x 2 1/2
Front and back inserts	2	1/8 x 11/16 x 5

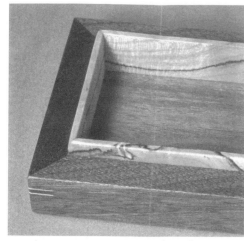

The lids of both boxes are held in place with four-piece mitered inserts made of the same stock as the lid panel.

Raising the Field

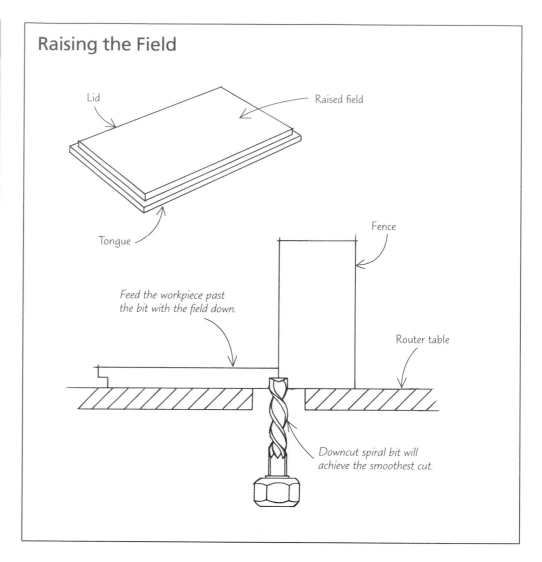

Lid

Raised field

Tongue

Fence

Feed the workpiece past the bit with the field down.

Router table

Downcut spiral bit will achieve the smoothest cut.

3. Cut rabbets around the edges of the lid panel to create a raised field and a tongue that fits into the carcase's grooves, as shown in the drawing above. (This is just one type of raised lid panel. Other types are shown on p. 42.) Start by cutting a narrow, shallow rabbet, and then increase the depth slowly until the tongue fits into the grooves.

Assembling the Box

1. Dry-assemble the entire box and see how well the lid panel fits. If the miter joints don't close (that is, if the raised field is too large), widen the rabbets a little, thereby shrinking the field. Then dry-assemble again and check the fit. Keep widening the rabbets until you have a reveal of 1/32 in. between the raised field and the carcase frame.

When the carcase fits together and you have the reveal you want, clamp the carcase closed with rubber bands (no glue yet) and adjust the panel so that it's centered in the frame. The reveal should be equal all around the panel.

2. With 180- or 220-grit sandpaper, ease the edges around the raised field of the lid panel. Then fine-sand the whole panel and apply a coat of finish, but leave two spots unfinished for spot gluing. When the finish dries, assemble the box (for more on assembling a carcase-and-panel box, see pp. 46-48).

Finishing Touches

1. Reinforce the miter joints with keys. One box uses laminated keys of maple veneer and walnut. To add visual interest to the other box, I stepped the keys, with their depths decreasing from top to bottom (for more on making and installing keys, see pp. 28-30).
2. Cut the box apart to separate the lid and the carcase (see p. 48).
3. Make the inserts (for more on making and installing inserts, see pp. 48-50).
4. Finish and polish the box (for more on finishing, see pp. 17-21).

This hexagonal box has two tiers with built-in inserts to hold the sections in place.

Who says a box has to have four sides to be a box? In fact, there's no limit to the number of sides a box can have. The small keeper box shown above, for example, has six sides and two tiers with built-in inserts. It's a challenging project, but designing and building the box can provide satisfying results.

Designing a Polygonal Box

When designing a polygonal box, the sides do not have to be equal in length. This project, for instance, features an irregular hexagon: Two opposite sides are longer than the other four sides.

To make a polygonal box, you must be able to cut accurate miters (other than 45°) and be able to cut lid and bottom panels to the appropriate polygonal shape.

The tiers of this box were created by adding an extra bottom panel. I didn't want to build a hinged hexagonal box, nor did I want to fit together six mitered inserts for each tier, which would have been tedious. So each tier has built-in inserts created with mating rabbets (for more on built-in inserts, see the sidebar on p. 50). Although the box shown here has two tiers, feel free to create as many tiers as you want—it's easy to do using the mating-rabbets technique.

For the box shown above, I used zebra-wood for the carcase and padauk veneer on the lid panel. Both are relatively coarse-grain woods. I also used padauk for the keys. Of course, you can use any combination of hardwoods that appeals to you.

Preparing the Parts

Use the dimensions given in the drawing on p. 58 and in the instructions, or adapt the dimensions and materials to fit your own needs. A cutlist is included with the drawing.

1. Prepare an oversized rectangular lid panel and two rectangular bottom panels. Veneering the panels in advance will allow you to measure their final thickness so you can later cut accurate grooves inside the carcase. Whether you choose to veneer the panels or use plywood, their final thicknesses should be close to ⅛ in. (for more on making lid panels and veneering, see pp. 40-46).

2. Take a ⅜-in.-thick board, which must be at least 18 in. long, and rip it to a width of 3 in. The finished height of the box will be 2⅜ in. after the mating rabbets are cut (see the section drawing on p. 58).

3. Before cutting the carcase pieces to length, cut all five grooves in the 3-in.-wide board and round over the top edge. If you wait until after you crosscut the pieces, the grooves will be difficult and dangerous to cut because of the

Two-Tiered Hexagonal Keeper Box

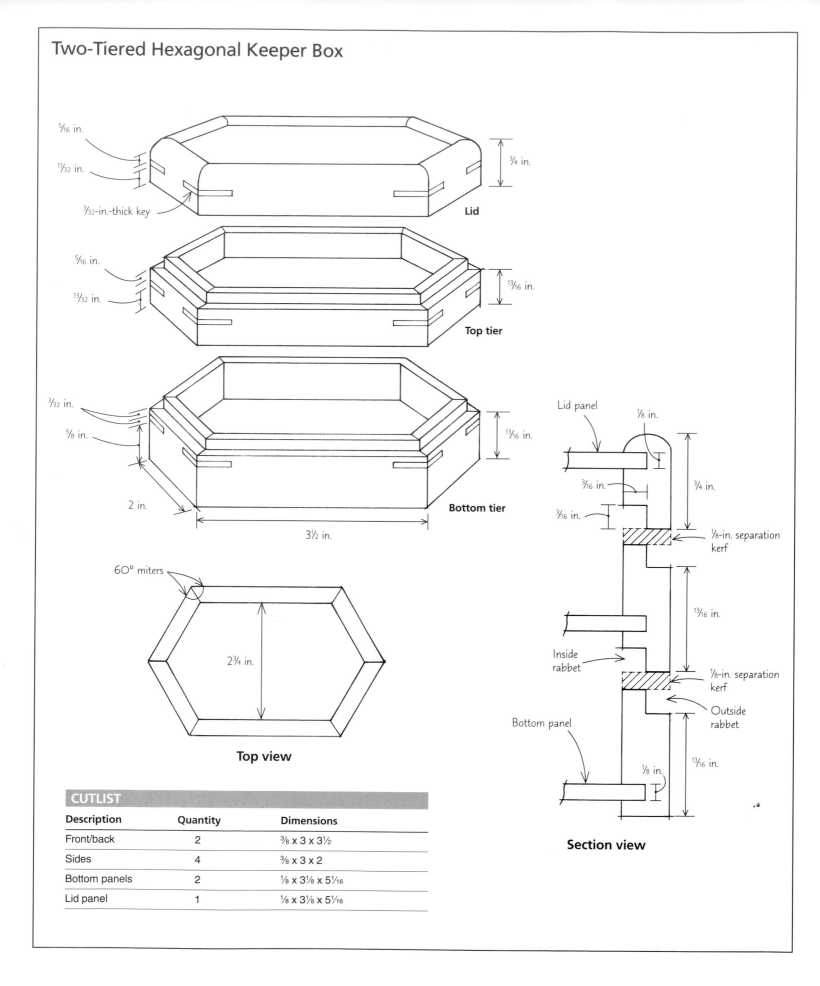

5/16 in.

11/32 in.

3/32-in.-thick key

Lid

3/4 in.

5/16 in.

13/32 in.

Top tier

13/16 in.

3/32 in.

5/8 in.

2 in.

3 1/2 in.

Bottom tier

13/16 in.

60° miters

2 3/4 in.

Top view

Lid panel

1/8 in.

3/16 in.

3/16 in.

3/4 in.

1/8-in. separation kerf

13/16 in.

Inside rabbet

1/8-in. separation kerf

Outside rabbet

Bottom panel

1/8 in.

13/16 in.

Section view

CUTLIST

Description	Quantity	Dimensions
Front/back	2	3/8 x 3 x 3 1/2
Sides	4	3/8 x 3 x 2
Bottom panels	2	1/8 x 3 1/8 x 5 1/16
Lid panel	1	1/8 x 3 1/8 x 5 1/16

short length of the side pieces (some are only 2 in. long). The grooves should all be ³/₁₆ in. deep (half the thickness of the stock), but their width will depend on the thickness of the panel stock.

4. After milling the grooves and rounding over the carcase stock, lay out the sides of the box on the 18-in. board (see the top drawing at right). Make each piece about ⅛ in. overlong to allow for the miters, which will be cut later. Be sure to label each piece so that you can assemble them in order later. Then cut the pieces to length.

You'll have a leftover piece a couple of inches long (I called it the "index"). Keep this piece handy! It's an accurate record of where the ³/₁₆-in. mating-rabbet grooves are cut, so you can use it as an index for cutting the tiers apart after the box is assembled and reinforced with keys.

5. Cut the twelve 60° miters and dry-assemble the side pieces.

While the carcase is banded together, trace the inside of the hexagon onto the lid panel and the bottom panels. Then draw a parallel line a little less than ³/₁₆ in. outside of each of the traced lines. This line will give you the dimensions of the panels. Then cut the panels to size.

Assembling the Box

1. Dry-assemble all the pieces of the box and make any necessary adjustments.

2. Sand the panels and inside carcase surfaces to 180 grit.

3. Tape the carcase pieces together, apply glue, and assemble the box just as you would a four-sided box. If you're using white or yellow PVA glue, work quickly because gluing up this box will take longer than a typical four-sided box. If you want more time to work, use a slower-setting glue, such as hide glue. Test the assembly for "square" by measuring diagonals; they should be equal.

4. Cut slots for the keys. To hold the box at the proper angle to the sawblade, make a 60° carriage jig, as shown in the bottom drawing at right. I used a thin-kerf sawblade that cuts ³/₃₂-in.-wide slots.

5. Cut the keys and glue them into the slots. Then trim the keys, sand the box sides flush, and ease the corners with 180-grit sandpaper.

6. Cut the box apart to separate the lid and the tiers. Use the index piece to locate the cuts

precisely. Butt the box's bottom against the rip fence and saw the lid off first. Then adjust the fence, using the index piece as a guide, and saw off the upper tier.

7. After separating the box pieces, both the lid and the upper tier should have inside rabbets exposed in their undersides. The next step is to cut mating outside rabbets in the top edges of the top and bottom tiers. Cut the outside rabbets to complement the inside rabbets (for more on cutting mating rabbets, see the sidebar on p. 50).

8. Fine-sand and finish the box (for more on finishing, see pp. 17-21).

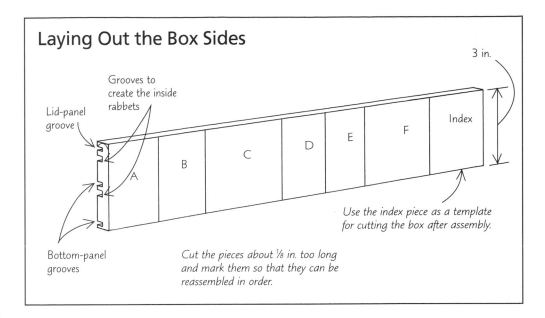

Laying Out the Box Sides

3 in.

Grooves to create the inside rabbets

Lid-panel groove

A B C D E F Index

Use the index piece as a template for cutting the box after assembly.

Bottom-panel grooves

Cut the pieces about ⅛ in. too long and mark them so that they can be reassembled in order.

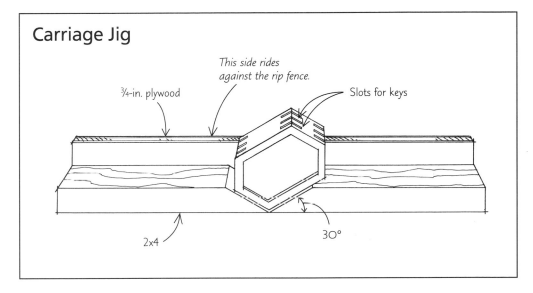

Carriage Jig

This side rides against the rip fence.

¾-in. plywood

Slots for keys

2x4

30°

4 BOXES WITH SLOT HINGES

Techniques

I enjoy making boxes without hinges because they're uncomplicated. When the box is small, you can lift off the lid with one hand and take something out of the box with the other hand. But a lid on a box larger than 4 in. or 5 in. wide is difficult to remove with one hand. That's why I attach lids for large boxes with hinges and incorporate a finger relief to make opening the box easier.

Slot Hinges

For a box maker stepping into the world of hinged boxes for the first time, I'd recommend slot hinges (also called barbed hinges or production hinges) because the installation is forgiving and the hinges are inexpensive. A slot hinge has a barrel in the center, on which the two leaves pivot. The leaves are inserted in slots cut in the carcase and lid frame. Barbs die-cut into both leaves lock the hinge in the slot (see the left photo on the facing page). This provides an almost invisible hinge where only the barrel shows (see the photos below).

Slot hinges are commonly available in two different sizes (measured with the leaves open): a small hinge is $\frac{7}{8}$ in. long and $\frac{9}{16}$ in. wide, and a large hinge is $1\frac{1}{8}$ in. long and $\frac{7}{8}$ in. wide. If a box is made of $\frac{1}{2}$-in. stock, I recommend using the larger hinge; if it's made of $\frac{3}{8}$-in. stock, use the smaller hinge.

You can buy slot hinges through many woodworking stores and catalogs (they cost about $1.75 each). Since I've never received instructions with any slot hinges I've purchased, I've had to learn to install them by trial and error. The pages that follow describe the tools you'll need to install slot hinges and the procedure I've fine-tuned over the years.

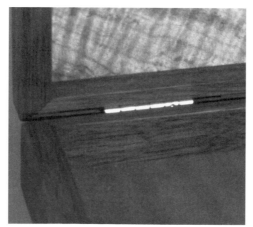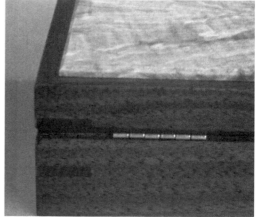

The barrel is the only part of the slot hinge visible from both inside and outside the box.

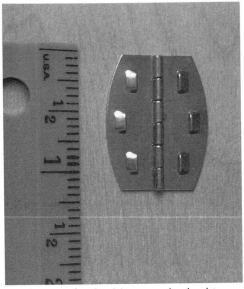

The leaves of a slot hinge are barbed to prevent them from sliding out after installation. A large hinge is shown here.

A slot cutter is essentially a miniature circular saw blade mounted on an arbor.

TOOLS YOU'LL NEED

To install slot hinges, you'll need a slot cutter, which is essentially a miniature circular saw blade on an arbor that mounts in a drill press (see the right photo above). The cutter, which is intended to run at 3,000 rpm, typically costs around $14, plus another $15 for the arbor. Slot cutters are available in two sizes: a large size for 1⅛-in.-long slot hinges, and a smaller version for ⅞-in.-long hinges. (You can use the same arbor for both cutters.)

Some woodworkers use the slot cutter in a router because setting the depth of cut on the router table is easy. However, the high speeds of a router can cause the cutter to burn the wood and leave a black residue on the cutter. (One solution is to use a variable-speed router or a router speed control, but even then you should be certain your slot cutter is rated for the higher rpm.) On production runs where you're making a lot of boxes, a fast-spinning cutter will generate so much heat that it could present a fire hazard. And if the router is connected to a dust collector, it could draw the heat into your sawdust bin and cause an explosion. For all the above reasons, I prefer to mount the slot cutter and arbor in the drill press and select a slow speed.

SETTING UP

Before you can cut the slots you'll need to lay out their location and build a simple jig to support the workpiece.

1. Start by marking the locations of the slots on the mating edges of the carcase and the lid frame. Make corresponding marks on the outside edge and on the rim, where the hinges will be installed.

The slot for a large hinge should be centered about 1½ in. from the end of the carcase. A slot for a small hinge should be centered about 1 in. from the end.

The larger slot hinge needs at least ³⁄₁₆ in. of wood supporting it, but the smaller hinge can get by with ⅛ in. (If your box is made of softwood, add ¹⁄₁₆ in. to those measurements.) With the locations laid out, it's time to set up the slot cutter in the drill press.

2. Chuck the cutter in your drill press and set the speed to 3,000 rpm. Clamp an auxiliary table to the drill-press table.

3. To ensure accuracy, build a simple right-angle carriage jig to help slide the workpiece upright along the auxiliary table into the cutter, as shown in the drawing on p. 62. Without the support of the carriage jig, the workpiece will tend to wobble as you move it into the cutter, causing a sloppy slot cut or bending the thin cutter. Worse yet, your hand could be drawn into the blade.

Cutting Slots on the Drill Press

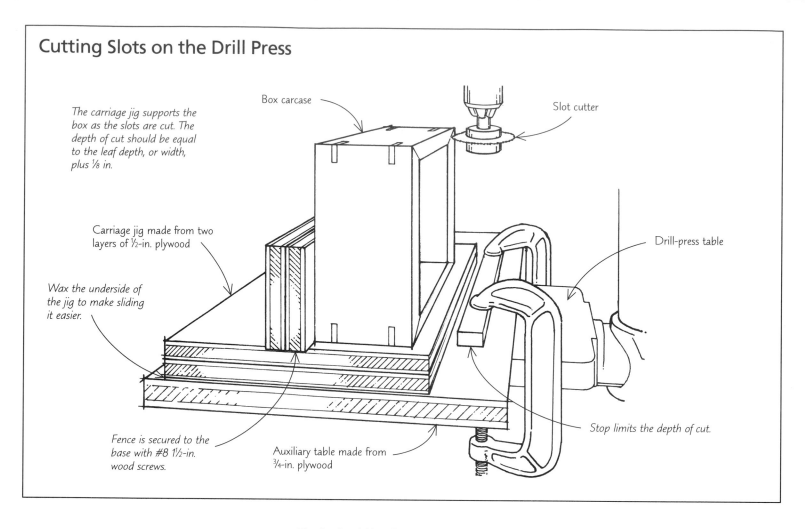

The carriage jig supports the box as the slots are cut. The depth of cut should be equal to the leaf depth, or width, plus 1/8 in.

Box carcase

Slot cutter

Carriage jig made from two layers of 1/2-in. plywood

Drill-press table

Wax the underside of the jig to make sliding it easier.

Stop limits the depth of cut.

Fence is secured to the base with #8 1½-in. wood screws.

Auxiliary table made from 3/4-in. plywood

The jig should be about the same length as the box. Wax the bottom of the jig so that it will slide smoothly on the auxiliary table.

4. To prepare the setup, set the carcase on the carriage jig, with the box's bottom against the fence of the jig. With the power off, slide the jig toward the cutter until the carcase's rim almost touches the cutter's teeth. Adjust the table and/or the chuck up or down to align the cutter with the layout marks on the rim of the carcase. Then lock the chuck and the table.

5. Set a stop to limit the depth of cut. Measure the width of one hinge leaf (at its widest point) and add 1/8 in. to give you some flexibility in case the mated slots aren't precisely positioned.

With the carcase's rim still almost touching the cutter, measure 3/8 in. from the leading edge of the carriage jig and make a pencil mark on the auxiliary table at that point. Then clamp a stop to the auxiliary table touching your mark, parallel to the carriage jig's leading edge and fence. This setup will ensure that your cutter will make a slot exactly 3/8 in. deep.

CUTTING THE SLOTS

1. With the setup complete, it's time to cut the slots in the box carcase. Hold the carcase tightly to the carriage jig and slowly slide the jig forward, toward the stop. Aim the left-hand mark on the carcase back toward the cutter first. You don't have to be precisely on the mark because you're making your cut a little deeper (and therefore wider) than required. As soon as the cutter enters the box edge, be ready to feel the jig hit the stop. When it does, back the jig away from the cutter. Repeat the procedure for the right-hand mark.

2. With a narrow slip of paper, measure the depth of the slot to make sure it's deep enough for the hinge. When the paper hits the bottom of the slot, mark it and compare it to the hinge leaf. Another option is to check the fit with a test hinge. Remember to flatten the barbs on the hinge, or they will tear the wood fibers as you attempt to remove it.

3. After the carcase slots are cut, repeat the process for the lid. (You'll need to reset the stop block.)

PROVIDING CLEARANCE

There are two more things to do before you can install the hinges. First, to provide clearance so the lid can open fully, the outside back edges of the lid and carcase need to be chamfered (see the drawing at right). Second, to allow the lid to sit flat on the carcase, you need to cut small rabbets on the inside back edge of the lid and carcase to provide clearance for the hinge barrel.

Cut the chamfers in the lid and the carcase using a 45° chamfer bit. The chamfer should end about 3/64 in. from the slot to accommodate the rabbet for the hinge barrel. If the chamfers are cut accurately, they will meet when the box is open at just over 90° and hold the lid open in that position.

I use a 1/4-in. straight bit in the router to cut the rabbets, setting the router-table fence so that the rabbet cuts just into the slot.

By the way, I know a professional box maker, Alexander Thomas of California, who hired a machine shop to fabricate a router bit that cuts both the chamfer and the rabbet in one pass. His custom-made bit cost him $90 several years ago. But because Alexander sells thousands of boxes a year, the cost was well worth it. Some router-bit suppliers can make custom bits if you send them specifications.

INSERTING THE HINGES

Once the chamfers and rabbets are cut, sand and finish the box. After the finish cures, insert the hinges in the slots.

1. Slide one hinge's leaf into a slot in the carcase, with the barrel facing the back. You can shift the hinge laterally to adjust it but don't try to pull it back out, unless you really need to (use pliers and pull slowly). Slide the second hinge's leaf into the other slot in the carcase.

2. Slip the free leaves into the slots in the lid, keeping the sides of the lid flush with the sides of the carcase. Close the box and press the lid and carcase together at the hinge locations. Adjust the lid so that the sides are flush.

Routing a Finger Relief

If a box is wider than 4 in. or 5 in., you may not be able to open the lid easily with one hand. To make opening a larger box easier, I like to rout a finger relief in the front of the carcase, where a finger can gain purchase (see the photo at right).

The simplest way to cut a finger relief is on the router table, with a cove bit (you can also use a corebox bit). You can rout a cove on the

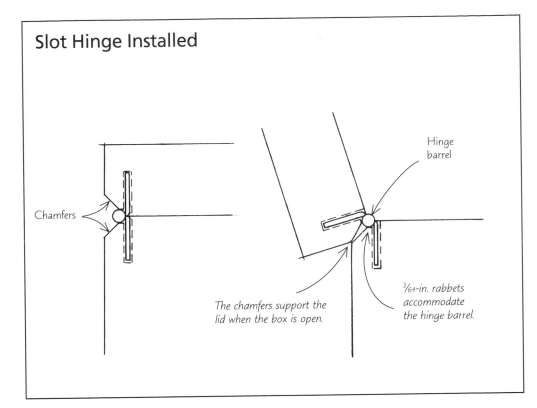

Slot Hinge Installed

Chamfers

Hinge barrel

The chamfers support the lid when the box is open.

3/64-in. rabbets accommodate the hinge barrel.

A finger relief makes it easy to open a box with one finger.

Router Setup for Finger Relief

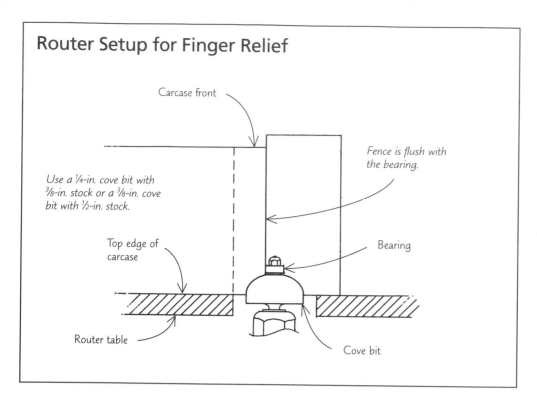

Carcase front

Fence is flush with the bearing.

Use a ¼-in. cove bit with ⅜-in. stock or a ⅜-in. cove bit with ½-in. stock.

Top edge of carcase

Bearing

Router table

Cove bit

front of the carcase before or after you assemble the box. I prefer to do it after, because it's easier to maneuver the assembly rather than one piece of wood. The size of the router bit depends on the thickness of your stock. I use a ⅜-in. cove bit with ½-in. stock and a ¼-in. cove bit with ⅜ in. stock. Here's how to rout the finger relief:

1. Mount the cove bit in the router and set the table fence flush with the bit's bearing (see the drawing above).

2. The final height of the cut will be equal to the bit's cutting radius. But to minimize

burning and tearout at the end of the cut, I always rout the cove in two or more passes. So, for starters, set the bit height to about one-third or one-half of the final depth of cut.

3. Locate the finger relief on the carcase front. First, mark the center of the carcase on the top edge of the carcase front.

The finger relief should be at least 1 in. long, but not more than a couple of inches (the actual size is a matter of personal taste). From the centerline, measure and mark the ends of the finger relief: Each side should be half the length of the entire relief.

4. Set two stops on the router-table fence— one to the left and one to the right of the bit—to limit the length of the finger relief.

To locate the stops, draw a vertical line on the fence centered over the router bit (it may not necessarily be the middle of the fence). To determine the distance (D) from the fence's centerline to each stop, use this formula:

$$D = L/2 + F/2 - R,$$

where L is the length of the box, F is the length of the finger relief, and R is the cutting radius of the cove bit. For instance, if the box length is 6 in., the finger relief is 1 in., and the cove bit is ¼ in., the distance from the centerline on the fence to each stop would be 3¼ in.

5. Turn the carcase upside down and rout a cove in the front. Place one edge of the carcase against the right-hand stop and slowly turn it into the bit. Then move the carcase from right to left between the stops (against the bit's rotation) until it hits the left-hand stop. After the first pass, turn off the router, raise the bit height, and repeat until you've reached the final finger-relief depth.

Projects

HIS-AND-HER RING BOXES

This pair of boxes makes a great wedding or anniversary gift. The boxes rest on a cherry base with two raised platforms to hold them in place. To distinguish between his box and her box, I made the lid panels of contrasting wood: In this case one is walnut, and the other is maple (see the photos above and at right). The lid panels are decorated with contrasting veneer strips sandwiched between sections of the panel, plus laminated dowel plugs. The boxes shown here have cherry carcases.

For these ring boxes, use the dimensions given in the drawings on pp. 66 and 67 and in the instructions, or feel free to adapt the dimensions and materials to fit your own tastes. A cutlist is included with the drawings.

Both boxes are identical in dimension and should be made at the same time from the same stock.

Keys coordinate with the lid panels (they can be solid wood or laminated): The box on the left has a walnut panel, with keys of walnut veneer and cherry; the box on the right has a maple panel, with keys of maple veneer and cherry.

Ring Box and Base

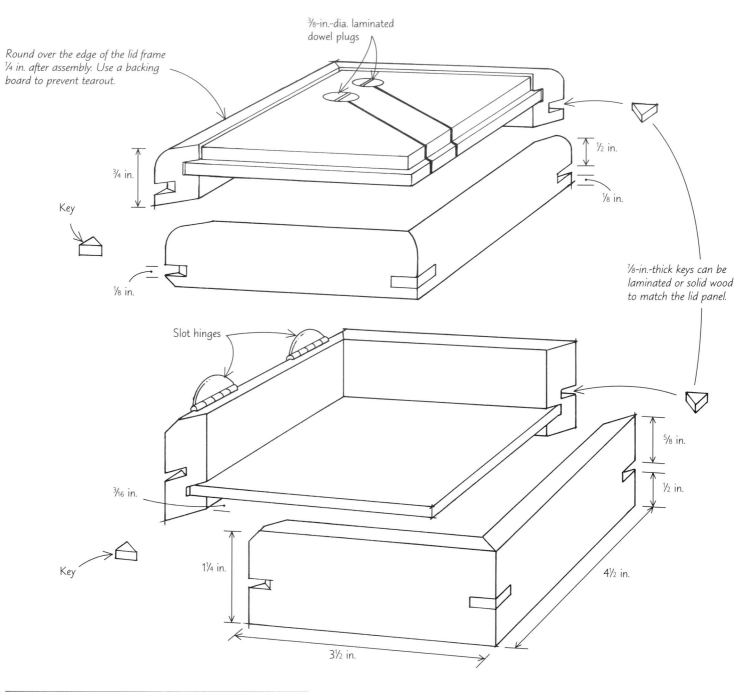

⅜-in.-dia. laminated dowel plugs

Round over the edge of the lid frame ¼ in. after assembly. Use a backing board to prevent tearout.

¾ in.

½ in.

⅛ in.

Key

⅛ in.

⅛-in.-thick keys can be laminated or solid wood to match the lid panel.

Slot hinges

³⁄₁₆ in.

⅝ in.

½ in.

Key

1¼ in.

4½ in.

3½ in.

Ring box

CUTLIST

Description	Quantity	Dimensions
Front/back*	4	⅜ x 2⅛ x 4½
Sides*	4	⅜ x 2⅛ x 3½
Bottom panel	2	⅛ x 3⅛ x 4⅛
Lid panel	2	⅜ x 3⅛ x 4⅛
Base	1	¾ x 4½ x 10¼

*Make oversized to allow for saw kerf.

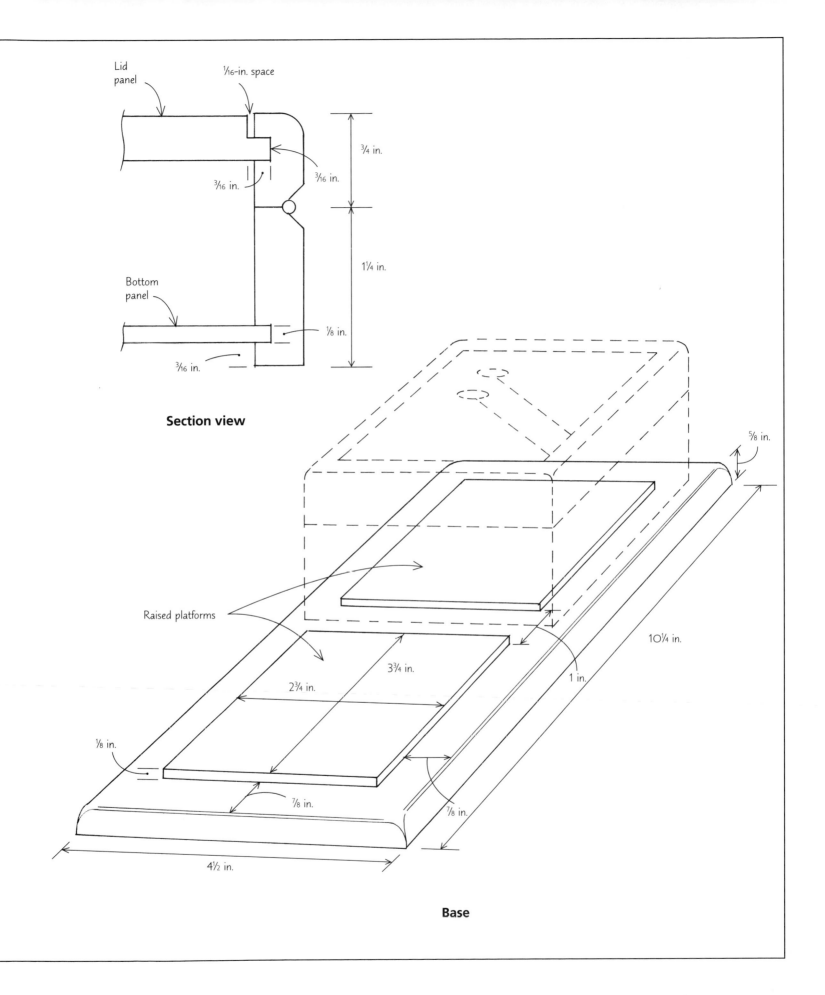

Lid panel

¹⁄₁₆-in. space

³⁄₄ in.

³⁄₁₆ in.

³⁄₁₆ in.

1¹⁄₄ in.

Bottom panel

¹⁄₈ in.

³⁄₁₆ in.

Section view

⁵⁄₈ in.

Raised platforms

10¹⁄₄ in.

3³⁄₄ in.

1 in.

2³⁄₄ in.

¹⁄₈ in.

⁷⁄₈ in.

⁷⁄₈ in.

4¹⁄₂ in.

Base

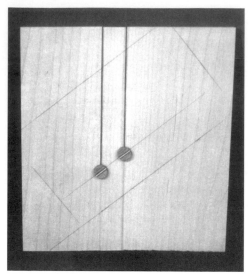

Lay out the lid pattern, including the location of the dowel plugs.

Making the Lid Panel and Carcase

1. Make two oversized blanks for the lid panels (in this case one walnut and one maple), each around 6 in. by 6 in. Use blanks with straight grain so that the decorative laminations won't have to compete against a wild grain pattern. If you can't find boards that are 6 in. wide with straight grain, glue up two or more boards to make each blank. (If possible, use stock that's $\frac{1}{16}$ in. too thick because you'll be planing and/or sanding the faces after you've glued the laminations together.)

2. Lay out the lid pattern on graph paper and then transfer it to the panel.

3. Rip each blank along the pattern lines and cut the veneer strips to size. The strips should be slightly wider than the thickness of the boards (see the drawing at left).

4. Reassemble each lid blank, with the veneer strips in place, and glue up each assembly. Be sure to orient the grain of both veneer strips in the same direction as the lid because they will be planed or scraped flush after the glue dries. Use rubber bands to clamp the pieces together.

5. After the glue dries, plane or sand the front and back faces of the lid-panel blanks to make them flat and of uniform thickness.

6. Drill $\frac{3}{8}$-in. holes for the laminated dowel plugs at the points where the contrasting veneers meet. To learn how to make the laminated plugs, see the sidebar on the facing page. If you prefer, you can use solid hardwood dowel plugs instead of laminating them. Dowel stock is commonly available in walnut, cherry, birch, and oak.

7. Glue the plugs into the holes. After the glue dries, trim the dowels flush.

8. Sand both faces of each panel until they're smooth. The final thickness should be around $\frac{3}{8}$ in. It doesn't have to be exact, but it does have to be uniform (the same thickness all the way around).

9. Draw pencil or chalk lines to indicate the final shape of the lid panels. Then cut each panel to its final dimensions.

10. Rip a board for the sides of both boxes to width. Cut a $\frac{3}{16}$-in. groove for the lid panel and a $\frac{1}{8}$-in. groove for the bottom panel (the bottom grooves will be about $\frac{3}{16}$ in. above the carcase bottom so that the box can rest on the raised platforms of the base). Then miter-cut the carcase pieces to length.

Assembling the Lid Panel

2⅞ in.

6 in.

⅝ in.

2 in.

3⅝-in.-long strip

4³⁄₁₆-in.-long strip

Veneer strips match the lid-panel stock.

Veneer strips contrast with the lid-panel stock.

Draw cutlines to indicate the final shape of the panel.

Contrasting plugs (can be laminated or solid)

Making Laminated Dowel Plugs

I think laminated dowel plugs are a nice design touch. For the boxes on p. 65, I used ⅜-in.-diameter plugs, but you can use plugs of any diameter, as long as you have the appropriate-size drill bits and plug cutters. You'll need a ⅜-in. brad-point or Forstner drill bit and a ⅜-in. plug cutter.

Assemble the plug blanks as shown in the left drawing below. (In the drawing I've indicated particular veneers and stock used to create the plugs for the boxes shown here, but feel free to use different stock and veneers to make a pattern that pleases you.) The solid pieces should be ¾ in. thick and about 1 in. wide. Sandwich the veneer strips between the solid

pieces, glue up the blank, and sand the faces smooth. Make sure the edges of the blank are parallel to the veneer strips and that they're straight, so you can make the repetitive cuts on the drill press. To help with the cuts, make an auxiliary table with a fence.

For accurate centering, temporarily chuck a ⅛-in. brad-point drill bit (or the smallest brad-point bit you have) in the drill press. Butt the edge of the plug blank against the fence and lower the bit until it almost touches the blank. Adjust the table, keeping the blank butted against the fence, until the bit is positioned directly above the middle veneer strip (assuming you use an odd

number of strips) in the blank. Clamp the table in position.

Remove the ⅛-in. brad-point bit and chuck in the plug cutter (see the right drawing below). Cut the plugs to a depth of ⅜ in. to ½ in. While you're at it, it's a good idea to cut extra plugs for future projects.

To separate the plugs from the blank, turn the blank on its edge and run it through a bandsaw or a table saw. If you put a strip of masking tape across the tops of the plugs before separating them, they won't pop out and roll away.

Gluing Up the Dowel-Plug Blank

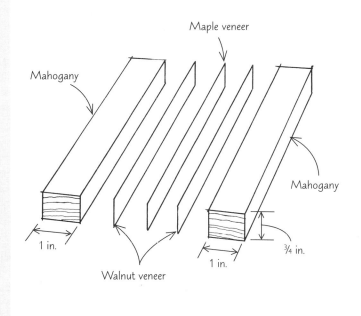

Maple veneer

Mahogany

Mahogany

1 in.

Walnut veneer

1 in.

¾ in.

Drilling the Plugs

Line up the plug cutter over the middle veneer strip.

⅜-in. plug cutter

Glued-up dowel-plug blank

Use the fence to guide the blank.

Plywood auxiliary table with fence

Drill-press table

A recess in the bottom of each box fits over the raised platform in the base to hold the boxes in place.

11. Raise a field in each lid panel. Rabbet the edges to form a ³⁄₁₆-in.-thick tongue all the way around the panel, which will fit into the grooves cut in the carcase (for more on raising a field and assembling a lid panel, see pp. 40-50).

12. Final-sand the panels. Ease the sharp edges and corners around the fields only slightly.

13. Prefinish the panels, but don't apply finish where you intend to spot-glue the panels into their grooves. In this case, the glue spots will be opposite corners so that the panel can expand across the grain (see p. 47).

14. Assemble the two boxes and reinforce them with keys (see pp. 22-30).

15. Separate the lid from each carcase, and then cut the slots, chamfers, and rabbets for a pair of small slot hinges (for more on installing slot hinges, see pp. 60-64).

16. Finish the boxes. The boxes shown here were finished with two coats of Danish oil (for more on finishing, see pp. 17-21).

17. Install the hinges and then turn your attention to the base.

Shaping the Raised Platforms

1. Glue up a ³⁄₄-in.-thick base (or you can use solid stock), and cut it to its final dimensions. If your box dimensions are different from those given in the drawing, your base dimensions will be different as well. In that case, to calculate the length of the base, measure the length of one box and double it (assuming the boxes are identical). Then add 1¼ in. To calculate the width of the base, measure the width of one box and then add 1 in.

2. Turn one of the boxes upside down and measure the inside distances between the front and back, then between the sides. This will give you the dimensions of the two raised platforms: Each should be 2³⁄₄ in. by 3³⁄₄ in., if you're using the dimensions shown in the drawings on pp. 66 and 67.

3. Mark the locations of the dado in the center of the base and the two rabbets on the ends. With the base upside down on the table saw or router table, cut the dado and rabbets to a depth of ¹⁄₈ in. Avoid making these cuts too wide—you want almost a friction fit of the box bottom to the raised platform.

4. Next, lay out and cut the rabbets on the front and back of the base to the same depth (¹⁄₈ in.).

5. Fit the boxes onto the platforms. The recessed box bottoms should capture the platforms with very little play. If the fit is too tight, widen the rabbets a bit to shrink the length or width (or both) of the platforms.

6. When the boxes fit on the platforms just right, round over the edges of the base. I use a ³⁄₈-in. roundover bit in my router. To avoid tearout, rout the ends first and then the front and back. The ³⁄₈-in. roundover bit is fairly large, so make multiple passes rather than trying to make the cut in one pass.

7. Scrape the rabbets and the roundovers smooth with a cabinet scraper and then sand the base, finishing with 180-grit paper.

8. Finish the base with two coats of Danish oil (or whatever finish you used for the boxes). For the finishing touch, apply self-stick felt disks to the bottom of the base.

The carcase for this stationery box is made of Honduras mahogany, and the lid panel is mahogany veneer. The keys are $5/32$-in.-thick solid mahogany.

Even in this world of cellular communications and e-mail, many people still prefer stationery, envelopes, and pens. In fact, these traditional tools for communicating deep sentiments may seem ever more precious compared with electronic devices. A stationery box gives paper and ink a place of honor.

This box is made to accommodate standard stationery ($5 5/8$ in. by $7 3/4$ in.) and envelopes (4 in. by $5 7/8$ in.) available at most stationery and greeting-card shops. You can scale the box up or down for other stationery sizes. For example, make the box larger to fit full-size letterhead ($8 1/2$ in. by 11 in.). If you're making this box as a gift, consider bestowing it fully stocked with stationery, envelopes, and a pen or two.

A box of this size calls for $1/2$-in.-thick stock, along with large slot hinges ($1 1/8$ in. long). I made the carcase for the box shown above and at right out of Honduras mahogany, and the lid panel is mahogany veneer laminated to a hardboard substrate. The keys are $5/32$-in.-thick mahogany, and the finish is Danish oil.

By sawing and routing the carcase to create "feet," I lightened its appearance yet at the same time added strength and visual interest. Another interesting feature of the box, and

The lid for this stationery box is held on with slot hinges. The pen-and-pencil tray is mahogany, and the feet are sawn and routed into the carcase.

Stationery Box with Tray

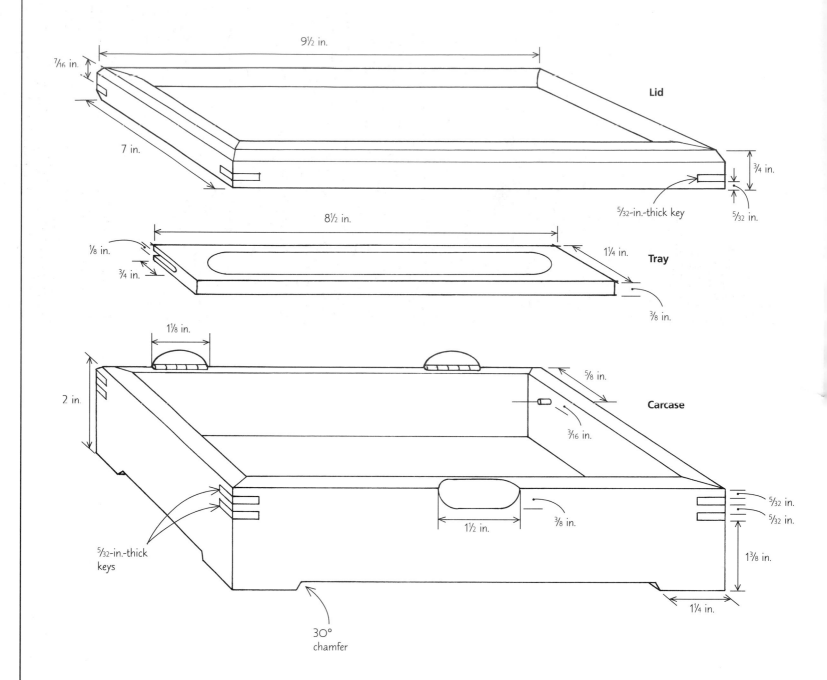

Lid

9½ in.

7/16 in.

7 in.

¾ in.

5/32-in.-thick key

5/32 in.

Tray

8½ in.

1¼ in.

⅛ in.

¾ in.

⅜ in.

Carcase

1⅛ in.

⅝ in.

2 in.

3/16 in.

1½ in.

⅜ in.

5/32 in.

5/32 in.

1⅜ in.

1¼ in.

5/32-in.-thick
keys

30°
chamfer

CUTLIST		
Description	**Quantity**	**Dimensions**
Front/back*	2	½ x 2⅞ x 9½
Sides*	2	½ x 2⅞ x 7
Bottom panel	1	⅛ x 6½ x 9
Lid panel	1	⅛ x 6½ x 9
Tray	1	⅜ x 1¼ x 8½

Cut width oversize to allow for saw kerf.

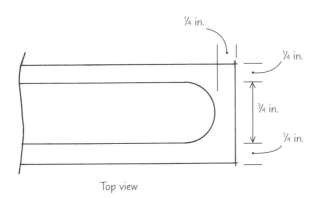

¼ in.

¼ in.

¾ in.

¼ in.

Top view

Detail of tray

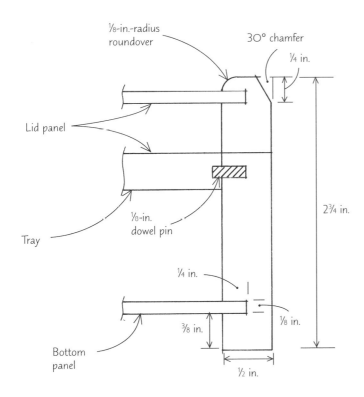

⅛-in.-radius roundover

30° chamfer

¼ in.

Lid panel

Tray

⅛-in. dowel pin

2¾ in.

¼ in.

Bottom panel

⅜ in.

⅛ in.

½ in.

Section view

one that adds to its complexity, is the interior pen-and-pencil tray, which is held in the box with "blind" dowel pins.

For this box, use the dimensions given in the drawings at left and in the instructions, or adapt the dimensions and materials to fit your own tastes. A cutlist is included with the drawings.

The basic techniques for assembling the carcase and the lid are covered in the previous chapters. In the following pages I'll show you how to rout the feet in the carcase and how to make and install the pen-and-pencil tray.

Making the Feet

1. Rip the ½-in.-thick carcase stock to a rough width of 2⅞ in. (this width allows ⅛ in. extra for the saw kerf when the lid is separated from the carcase). Rout the grooves for the lid panel and the bottom panel, and round over the inside top edge. Then miter-cut the front, back, and sides to final length.

I waited until after assembly to cut 30° chamfers on the outside top edges of the carcase. This chamfer angle matches the angle cut on the feet.

2. Set up to cut two 30° kerfs in each carcase piece, where the feet will begin. I found this easiest to do accurately on the table saw, although you could use a bandsaw or cut them by hand.

On the table saw, tilt the sawblade to 30° and set the blade height to ¼ in.

3. Attach an auxiliary fence to the table saw's miter gauge. The fence should be at least 2 in. by 14 in. and should extend several inches past the sawblade. After you attach the fence, run it through the blade to establish a 30° kerf for reference.

4. Clamp a stop to the auxiliary fence, 1¼ in. from where the blade will enter each carcase piece. The stop must be thicker than ½ in. to ensure that the point of the miter hits the stop. Test the setup with a scrap piece. Place the scrap on its edge and butt one end against the stop. Then turn on the saw and cut the kerf.

Make any necessary adjustment, and take another test cut. When you've got the settings just right, cut two 30° kerfs in each carcase piece. Make the first kerf in one piece, then flip the piece end for end and make the second cut. Repeat for all four pieces.

5. Connect the highest points of the kerfs with a pencil or marking knife (see the drawing on p. 74). Then rough out the waste area using a bandsaw or a coping saw. Make the cuts on the waste side of the line.

Making the Feet

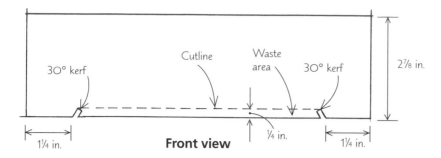

Front view

30° kerf · Cutline · Waste area · 30° kerf · 2⅞ in. · 1¼ in. · ¼ in. · 1¼ in.

1. Cut the kerfs, then remove the waste area on the bandsaw.

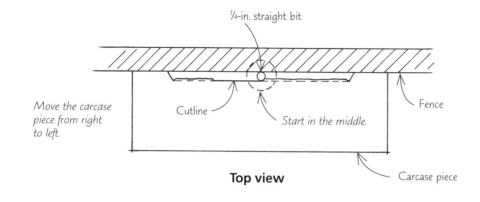

Top view

¼-in. straight bit · Move the carcase piece from right to left. · Cutline · Start in the middle. · Fence · Carcase piece

2. Smooth the rough edge on a router table with a ¼-in. straight bit.

6. Next, install a ¼-in. straight bit in the router and mount it under the router table. Set the fence ¼ in. behind the front of the bit. Place each carcase piece flat on the router table and ease its roughed-out edge into the spinning bit, so that the bit enters around the middle of the rough-cut edge (see the drawing above). Then move the carcase piece from right to left until the bit almost touches the kerf. Flip the piece over and repeat the operation, ending the cut just short of the opposite kerf. This should leave a straight, smooth edge most of the way along the line between the kerfs. Clean out the remaining waste near the kerfs with a chisel.

7. Drill ⅛-in. dowel-pin holes in each of the carcase sides to accept the dowels that will support the tray. Drill the holes about ¼ in. deep, and then assemble the carcase. Now you're ready to begin work on the tray.

Making the Tray

1. After separating the lid from the carcase, measure the box's interior length. Then cut a 1¼-in.-wide piece of ⅜-in.-thick mahogany to that length for the tray.
2. Rout a ¾-in. by 8-in. flat-bottomed recess in the tray for the pen or pencil. It should be ¼ in. deep. I used a ¾ in.-diameter "bowl-and-tray bit" to rout the recess in one pass. If you don't have a bowl-and-tray bit, you can use a straight bit and/or a corebox bit and complete the operation in several passes.
3. Ease the front edge of the tray. Fine-sand the flat top surface, the dished-out recess, and the bottom. Do not ease the back or side edges.

INSTALLATION
The tray for this box is glued to the back of the carcase and is supported by two blind, or concealed, dowel pins on the ends.
1. Insert ⅛-in. dowel pins into the holes you drilled earlier. The dowels should be about ⅛ in. proud of the holes. Round over the protruding end of each dowel slightly. Do not glue the dowel pins into the carcase just yet.
2. Rout ⅛-in. by ⅛-in. stopped grooves into the ends of the tray; use a zero-clearance auxiliary table on your router table to keep the workpiece from falling into the throat surrounding the bit.
3. Test-fit the tray by sliding it into place. When you've got the fit you want, glue the dowel pins into the holes in the carcase, apply glue to the tray's back, slide the tray in place again, and clamp it to the back of the box (I used three large spring clamps).
4. When the glue cures, cut the slots, chamfers, and grooves for the large slot hinges. Also rout the finger relief in front with a ⅜-in. cove bit (see pp. 63-64). Then fine-sand and finish the entire box, and install the slot hinges.

5 BOXES WITH PIN HINGES

Techniques

In this chapter, you'll learn how to install pin hinges to make a box with a lid that opens traditionally or a box with a lid that swivels open. You'll see some alternative joinery methods, which will allow you to make boxes that are stronger and more visually appealing. You'll also learn how to create dazzling box interiors using fabric, dividers, and trays.

Pin Hinges

Pin hinges—the most rudimentary of all hinge mechanisms—are simply rods (made of wood or brass) inserted into the carcase and lid, which allow the lid to be opened. Pin hinges (also called pivot pins) are used mostly in contemporary boxes. They are often used in boxes in which traditional hinges will not work or in boxes where a traditional hinge method would detract from the box design.

Because pin hinges are made from brass rod or wood dowels, they are by far the

cheapest hinge mechanism available. For instance, a 1-ft.-long, 1/8-in.-diameter brass rod can yield several pairs of hinge pins but costs less than $1 at most hobby shops. Hardwood dowels are even more inexpensive.

Although pin hinges will work on many box designs, I don't recommend using them on boxes made of softwood unless the hole is reinforced. The repeated pivoting action of the pin will wear down softwood, resulting in a sloppy mechanism. One reinforcement option is to line the pin hole with a brass tube.

PIN SIZE AND MATERIAL

What size pin you use and whether you use wood or brass pins will depend on the size of the box you are making.

For small boxes with lightweight lids, use at least a 3/32-in.-diameter brass rod or 1/8-in.-diameter hardwood dowel. For medium-sized boxes, use 1/8-in.-diameter brass rod or 3/16-in.-

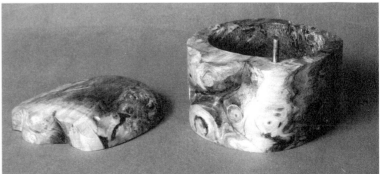

This buckeye burl box, made by Doug Muscanell and Karen Harbaugh of Colorado, has a lid that swivels open on a pin hinge.

diameter wood dowel, at minimum. For large boxes or medium-sized boxes with heavy lids, use ³⁄₁₆-in.-diameter brass rod (I don't recommend using wood dowels here).

Brass and hardwood are easy to cut, sand, and polish. Regardless of whether you're using brass or wood pin stock, round over the ends to make the pins slide into their holes easily.

CONFIGURATIONS

Pin hinges are typically used in two configurations: vertical and horizontal. Using a vertical pin is an easy way to make a swivel-lid box (see the photos on p. 75). Installing pins horizontally allows you to open a lid by lifting its front, as you would with traditional hinges (see the drawing below). Depending on the box design (and on your tastes), you can leave the pins visible, or you can conceal them.

The biggest advantage to leaving the pin ends visible is that installing the pins is easy. Simply drill holes through a carcase side and

into the lid simultaneously, with the lid taped or wedged in position.

Glue the pin to the carcase, so that the pivoting action takes place in the lid. (To glue brass to wood, use epoxy or cyanoacrylate glue.) Then trim and sand the pin flush with the carcase (see the top drawing on the facing page).

When you don't want the pin hinges to be prominent (or if you simply want to avoid trimming and sanding the brass flush), there are two ways to conceal them. The main difference between the two methods is when you drill the holes for the pins (see the bottom drawing on the facing page).

The first method is to use blind pins. To install blind pin hinges, you must drill holes partway through the carcase before assembly, and then drill mating holes in the lid. No glue is needed for this method because the pin "floats" in the holes after the box is assembled. The second method of concealing pin hinges is to use a wood plug. After assembling the

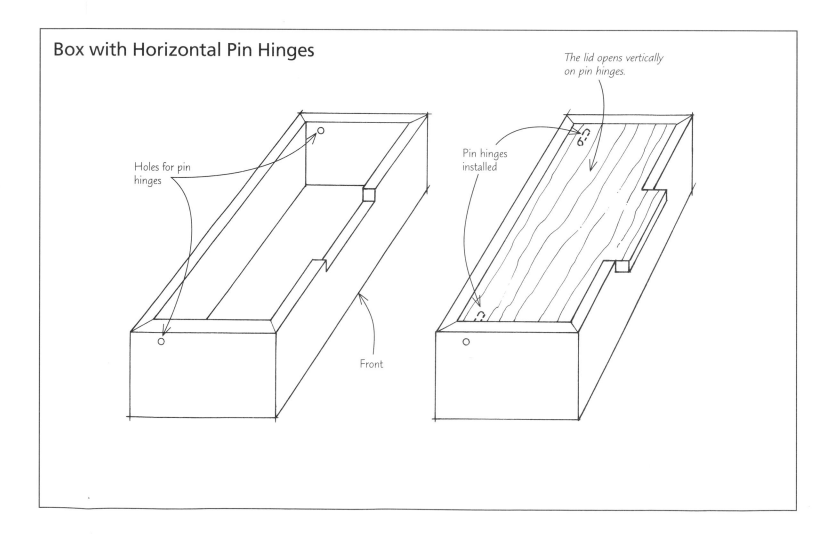

Box with Horizontal Pin Hinges

Holes for pin hinges

Front

The lid opens vertically on pin hinges.

Pin hinges installed

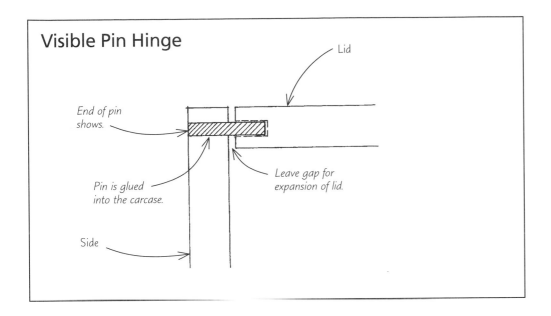

Visible Pin Hinge

Lid

End of pin shows.

Pin is glued into the carcase.

Leave gap for expansion of lid.

Side

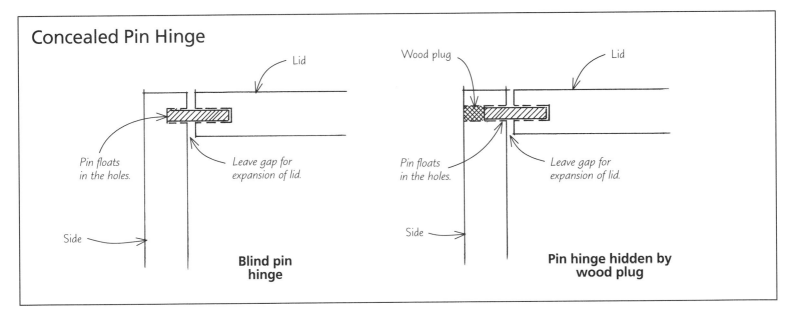

Concealed Pin Hinge

Lid

Pin floats in the holes.

Leave gap for expansion of lid.

Side

Blind pin hinge

Wood plug

Lid

Pin floats in the holes.

Leave gap for expansion of lid.

Side

Pin hinge hidden by wood plug

box, drill through the box sides and into the lid. Again, no glue is needed because the pin will float in the hole. After inserting the pin, glue a dowel in the hole, then trim and sand it flush to the carcase.

INSTALLATION TIPS
The techniques for installing pin hinges vary, depending on the design of the box. Overall, it's a fairly simple process, but there are a few general guidelines that you should keep in mind.
• The pin holes must be exactly 90° to the surfaces in which they're drilled. You need either a drill press or a 90° drill guide for this operation.

• In a rectangular box where the pins are installed horizontally, the carcase must be glued up square so that the two pins line up.
• In a box with horizontal pin hinges, the back of the lid has to be rounded to allow the lid to open. This is the case whether the lid is inset (see the drawing on the facing page) or whether it rests on the back (see the drawing on p. 78). If the lid is rounded just enough and no more, it'll provide its own stop. I don't have any formula for this: You have to round a little and test the fit until the lid stops where you want it to.

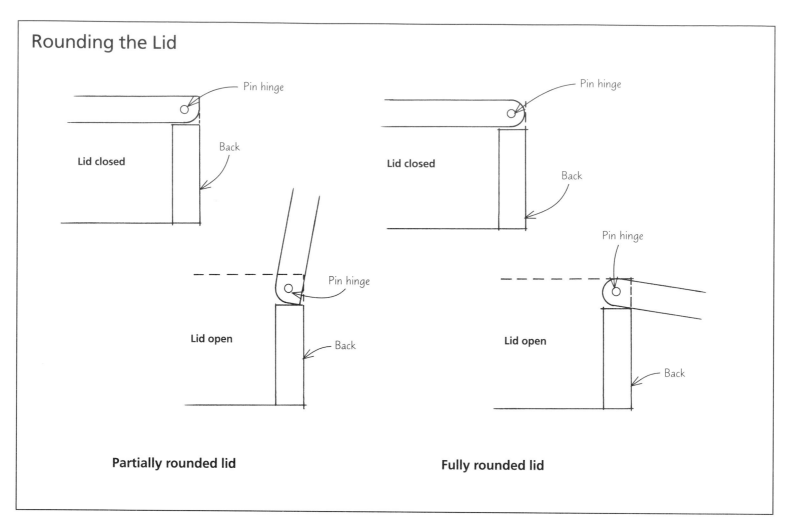

Rounding the Lid

Pin hinge

Lid closed

Back

Lid open

Back

Pin hinge

Partially rounded lid

Pin hinge

Lid closed

Back

Pin hinge

Lid open

Back

Fully rounded lid

Alternate Joinery Methods

Up to this point, all the projects in this book have used miter joints to hold the carcases together. Although miters are attractive and easy to make, there are times when you'll want to use other types of joinery.

For example, use of miter joinery in a pin-hinged box in which the lid lies between two tall sides would be inappropriate because the mitered edges on the taller sides would be exposed. Or, if you're making a box that needs to stand up under stress—a lap desk, for instance—miter joints may not be strong enough. If you're making a large box, or a box with a heavy lid, miter joinery similarly may not be strong enough. In these instances it's better to use stronger joinery (such as dovetail or finger joints).

You may also choose alternate joinery for purely aesthetic reasons. Many woodworkers prefer one joinery method over others because of the final appearance.

Although this book is not intended as a comprehensive text on joinery, I'll discuss a few alternatives. These include butt, rabbet, finger, and dovetail joints.

BUTT JOINTS

A butt joint is the simplest method of joinery because all cuts are 90°, and you clamp in just one direction during assembly (see the top drawing on the facing page).

However, a butt joint isn't very elegant because it leaves large expanses of end grain exposed. Another problem is that butt joints are weak because half the joint is end grain. That's why some sort of reinforcing method should be used. I recommend using biscuits or splines to reinforce the joints. Don't use screws—not only are they visually distracting, but the shrinking and swelling of the wood fibers around the screws over the years will loosen their grip.

When gluing up butt joints, I've found that it helps to "prime" the end grain before final assembly. That is, apply a very thin film of glue on the end grain and let it dry for a few minutes to seal the pores in the grain. Then apply a second layer of glue and assemble the box.

RABBET JOINTS

Rabbet joints, like butt joints, are simple to cut and assemble. However, they offer a slightly larger glue surface than butt joints, so they're a bit stronger. Also, there's less end grain showing than with butt joints, and the shoulders of the rabbet serve as an alignment aid during glue-up and assembly.

As with butt joints, I've found it best to prime the end grain before glue-up to seal the pores in the grain. Apply a second layer of glue and assemble the box. You have to clamp in two directions during assembly (see the bottom drawing on the facing page).

Butt Joint

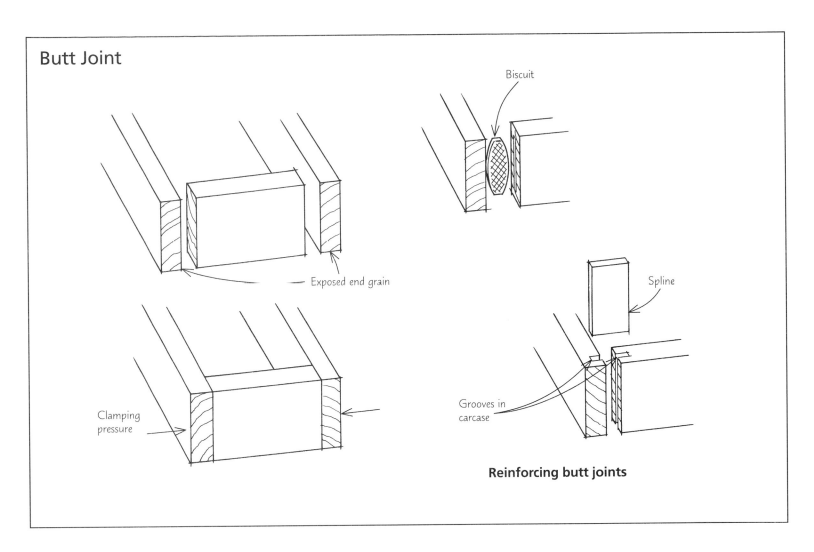

Biscuit

Exposed end grain

Clamping pressure

Spline

Grooves in carcase

Reinforcing butt joints

Rabbet Joint

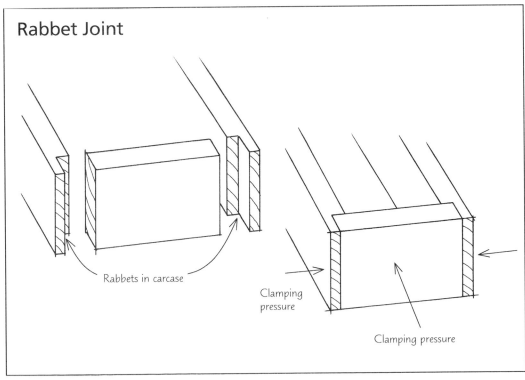

Rabbets in carcase

Clamping pressure

Clamping pressure

Finger Joint

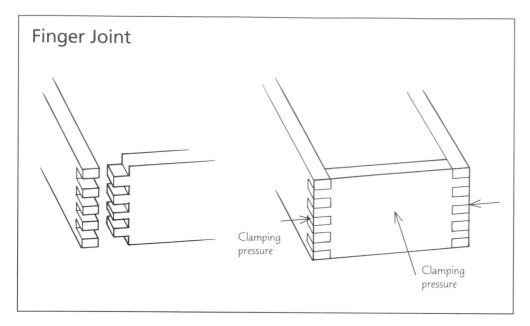

Clamping pressure

Clamping pressure

Dovetail Joint

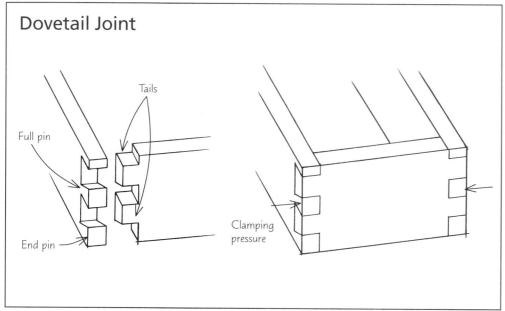

Tails

Full pin

End pin

Clamping pressure

FINGER JOINTS

Finger joints (also referred to as box joints) are much stronger than butt or rabbet joints. Their strength comes from the interlocking fingers that greatly increase the long-grain to long-grain glue surface. The more fingers in the joint, the stronger the joint will be.

You can cut finger joints on the table saw or router table; I use an indexing jig to ensure accuracy. An indexing jig is fairly simple to make (many basic woodworking books show you how), or you can buy one through woodworking mail-order catalogs.

When gluing up a finger-jointed box, you have to spread glue on all the mating surfaces and clamp in two directions (see the top drawing above).

DOVETAIL JOINTS

Dovetails offer the maximum strength in a single direction, which makes them best suited for drawer fronts and cabinet sides. Many people consider dovetails the most elegant of all joints, so they use them for box carcases, even if the extra strength they offer isn't necessary (see the bottom drawing at left).

Dovetails are tricky to cut by hand and require a lot of practice to learn. But if you shop around in woodworking catalogs and specialty shops, you'll be able to find a commercial jig that can be used with the router to cut dovetails. As with finger joints, you'll need to apply glue to all the mating surfaces.

Once you've experimented with different kinds of carcase joinery, you'll be able to design almost any sort of box. Studying the projects in subsequent chapters will help you select the best joinery method for your project.

Frame-and-Panel Lids

In previous chapters you learned how to make a few different types of lid panels, from solid-wood to integral lid panels (in which the lid is assembled as part of the box—called carcase-and-panel construction). Now let's take a look at a frame-and-panel lid that is constructed separately from the box carcase: The framed lid is assembled in one operation, the carcase is built in another, and the pieces are united with hinges.

Making the lid separate from the carcase allows you to make a frame of any width or design you choose and of any species—it doesn't have to be the same wood as the carcase.

PLANNING IS KEY

Making a frame-and-panel lid is a challenging task that requires careful planning and thought. Here are some guidelines for making your frame-and-panel lids more precise, stable, and attractive.

• Use straight-grain, knot-free wood for the frame. Cut all frame members from the same board.

• The frame members should be no thicker than the carcase stock. However, they can be thinner, depending on how large the lid panel is. But remember, a heavy, expansive panel needs more frame support.

- Unless your rails and stiles have perfectly straight grain, try to arrange them so that their overall grain pattern creates an oval effect (see the top drawing at right).
- Save the scrap pieces of the dimensioned frame stock. They can be used for adjusting and testing blade and bit height, for fence settings, and for setting up jigs on your table saw and router table.
- Prepare your panel before cutting the frame joints—you can trim the panel later for a final fit. The panel's tongue should be at least 1/8 in. thick. Wider panels need thicker tongues.
- Ease the panel's edges and corners slightly with a sanding block so that the panel slides into the frame's grooves easily.
- As you're gluing up the lid, remember to spot-glue the panel in two places. This will keep the panel from shifting off center while still allowing expansion and contraction across the grain (see the drawing on p. 47).

With these guidelines in mind, let's look at some different joinery methods for making the frame. (To learn how to make the lid panels, see pp. 40-46.) I commonly use three methods to assemble a frame around a panel: miter joinery, bridle joinery, and stub-tenon-and-groove joinery.

A FRAME WITH MITERS

Using miter joinery to assemble a lid frame (see the bottom drawing at right) offers a number of advantages. Miters give you clean-looking frame edges because there is no end grain showing, and they're easy to cut, especially if you have an accurate miter saw. Use of miters also allows you to cut full-length grooves for the panel, and you can round over or chamfer the inside edges before assembly.

On the downside, a mitered frame is difficult to clamp and to square up, and it is weak, unless you reinforce the joints with biscuits or keys. I prefer to use biscuits because they are hidden, and they help in the assembly process (more about this later). Even though a lid with a mitered frame is not as strong as a lid assembled with other joinery methods, the lid should have sufficient strength for small- or medium-sized boxes. Here's how to make a mitered frame:

1. Miter-cut the frame pieces to length. The 45° miters can be cut on the table saw, but a miter saw will make the job easier.

2. Cut the grooves for the panel on the inside edges of the frame pieces. This can be done on the table saw or with a router with a straight bit.

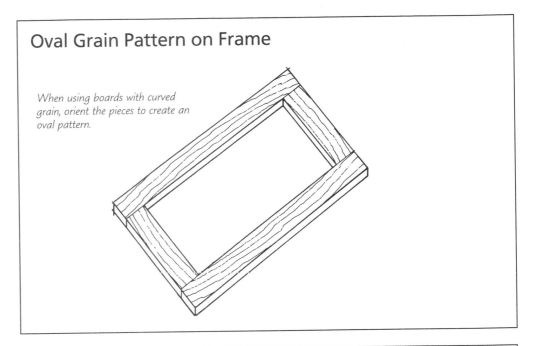

Oval Grain Pattern on Frame

When using boards with curved grain, orient the pieces to create an oval pattern.

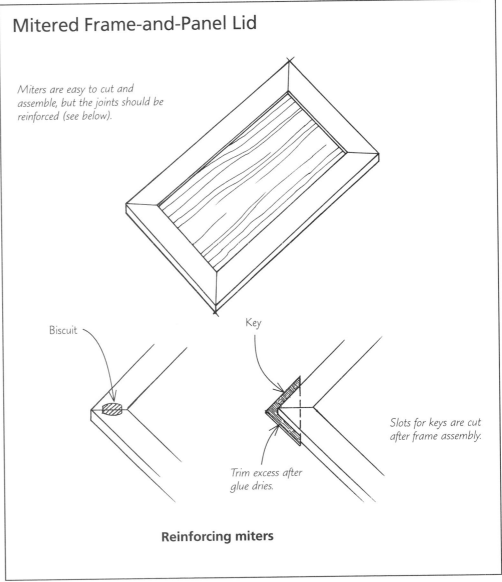

Mitered Frame-and-Panel Lid

Miters are easy to cut and assemble, but the joints should be reinforced (see below).

Biscuit

Key

Slots for keys are cut after frame assembly.

Trim excess after glue dries.

Reinforcing miters

3. If you're reinforcing the frame with biscuits, cut the slots for them before assembling the frame. (If you're using keys, the slots for these will be cut after the lid is assembled.)

4. Glue up the assembly. Put glue on all mitered surfaces, on the biscuits, and in their slots. Also put a dot of glue on opposite edges of the panel. This will allow the panel to sit tight in its grooves and still allow for wood movement.

The most common way to clamp a mitered frame after gluing and assembling it is with band clamps (or with rubber bands for very small frames). The problem with band clamps is that it's often difficult to keep the frame members perfectly aligned and square while you're tightening them. (But biscuits will help keep the pieces in alignment.)

Commercial tenoning jigs slide in the table-saw's miter-gauge slot. The distance from the jig's face to the sawblade is adjustable. Check with a square to make sure the jig's face and backstop are set *exactly* 90° to the saw table. (Photo courtesy of Delta International Machinery.)

A FRAME WITH BRIDLE JOINTS

Bridle joints (also called slip joints or through mortise and tenons) are very strong because they offer the most long-grain-to-long-grain glue surface. They are relatively easy to clamp and are practically self-squaring. They are also attractive because they show sufficient end grain to contrast with edge grain and create what some consider a classic look.

The drawback is that bridle joints are more difficult to cut than miter joints. I find that a tenoning jig helps. You can buy a commercial jig (see the photo at left), or you can make one yourself from scrap wood (see the top drawing on the facing page). Another challenge of using bridle joints in a frame-and-panel assembly is that you'll have to rout stopped grooves in the rails for the panel and unstopped grooves in the stiles (see the bottom drawing on the facing page). Here's how to cut bridle joints:

1. Cut the frame members to final thickness and width. Then crosscut them about 1/16 in. longer than final length. (After assembly, you can plane or belt-sand the frame to its final dimensions.)

2. Mount a flat-tooth rip blade in your table saw, and set the blade height 1/32 in. higher than the width of your frame stock.

3. Mark the edge of one stile to show the width of each through mortise. This width should be slightly more than one-third of the total thickness. Position this stile upright in the tenoning jig, as shown in the top drawing on the facing page. Adjust the jig (or the rip fence) so that the table-saw blade will slice through the approximate center of the stile's end.

Cut a kerf in one end, then rotate the stile 180° and cut it again. This way you'll end up with a centered mortise. If the mortise you've cut is the correct width, flip the stile end for end and repeat this procedure on the opposite end. Do the same with the other stile. If the mortise is not wide enough, readjust the jig (or rip fence) and make another cut, rotating the stile between cuts. Continue like this until the mortise is the correct width. Now you're ready to cut the tenons on the ends of the rails.

4. Keeping the blade height the same as for the through mortises, position a scrap piece (the same thickness as the frame members) in the jig. Set the jig or fence so that the sawblade cuts on the outside face of the scrap. Make the cut, rotate the scrap 180°, and make another cut on the opposite face, so that you now have a tenon that's too thick to fit in the

Shopmade Tenoning Jig

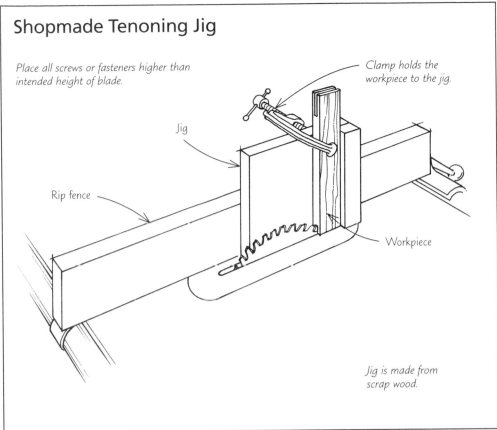

Place all screws or fasteners higher than intended height of blade.

Clamp holds the workpiece to the jig.

Jig

Rip fence

Workpiece

Jig is made from scrap wood.

through mortises. Move the jig or fence a little closer to the blade and cut the tenon again. Test-fit with the stiles. Readjust the jig or fence in very small increments and make fine cuts in the scrap piece, shaving away at the tenon until it fits nicely into the stile mortise.

5. Now you can make your final cuts in both rails. If you accidentally cut the tenons too thin for their mortises, all is not lost. You can glue thin pieces of veneer to the tenon faces to build them back up, and then use your tenoning jig again to shave them down to the right thickness.

6. Dry-assemble the frame and clamp it to check the fit. The ends of the frame members should protrude from the joints very slightly. If you want to ease or round over the inside edges with a sanding block, now is the time to do it, while the frame is dry-clamped without the panel.

7. Cut grooves in the inside edges of the frame members for the panel. Because the grooves in the stiles are hidden in the joint, they can be full length. But the grooves in the rails must be stopped because you don't want to groove the tenons. I've found that it's easiest to cut the grooves in the rails on the router table, using a straight bit or spiral bit that matches the panel's thickness.

Frame-and-Panel Lid with Bridle Joints

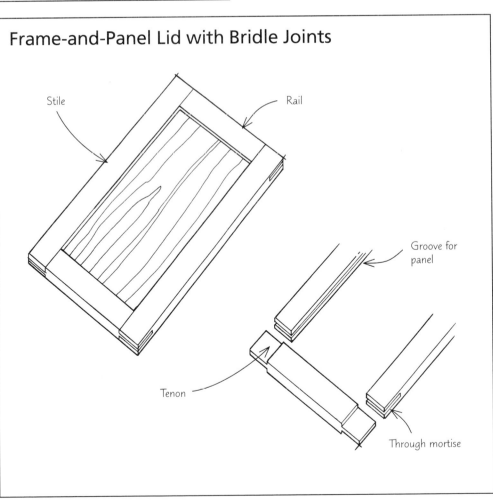

Stile

Rail

Groove for panel

Tenon

Through mortise

Routing Stopped Grooves

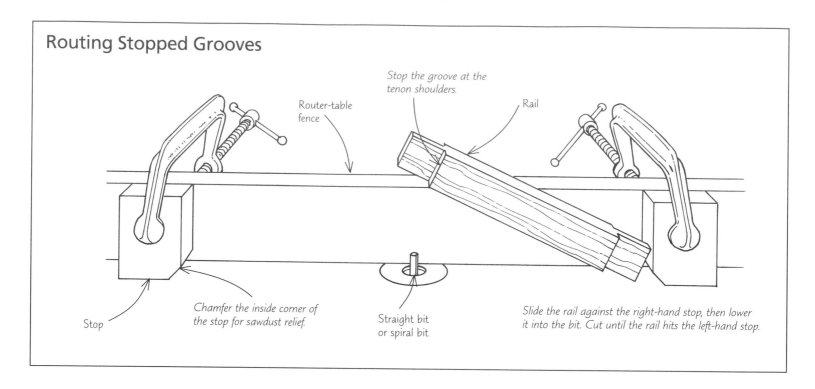

Stop the groove at the tenon shoulders.

Router-table fence

Rail

Stop

Chamfer the inside corner of the stop for sawdust relief.

Straight bit or spiral bit

Slide the rail against the right-hand stop, then lower it into the bit. Cut until the rail hits the left-hand stop.

Set the bit height to cut the groove about ¼ in. to ⅜ in. deep. The groove width is the same as your panel's thickness if it's a veneered plywood panel or the same as the thickness of the panel's tongue if it's a raised, solid-wood panel.

You don't absolutely have to center the groove, but you can do so by routing close to the center in one pass, flipping the piece end for end, and making a second cut. Then adjust the fence away from the blade or bit and repeat the cuts, test-fitting the panel after each pair of cuts until the groove is the right width for the panel.

To make the stopped grooves in the rails, clamp stops to your router-table fence at either end to limit the cut (see the drawing above). Place the rail on the table, slide one end against the right-hand stop, then slowly lower the rail onto the bit. Cut until you reach the other stop and then lift off the rail. If you want to center the groove, flip the rails end for end after each cut and repeat.

8. Practice assembling and clamping the frame and panel before glue-up. To clamp the frame together, place bar clamps or band clamps just inside the joints. Avoid tightening the clamps too much, or the frame members will bow inward—just a little clamping pressure will bring the joined surfaces into full contact.

9. Glue up the assembly. Apply glue to all mating surfaces but be extra careful to avoid excessive squeeze-out around the joints'

shoulders. At the corners, you'll have to clamp down the through mortises (use spring clamps or C-clamps).

10. If you want to shape the outside edges of the frame, do so after assembly. Use a backup board to prevent tearout.

A FRAME WITH STUB TENONS AND GROOVES

Stub-tenon-and-groove joinery is very similar to bridle joinery, but it's not as strong because the glue surfaces are not as large. To compensate for this, you should always use a plywood- or hardboard-veneered panel. Since these panels, unlike solid wood, won't move with changes in humidity, you can glue the panel in the grooves. The result is a very strong lid.

There are a couple of differences between stub-tenon-and-groove joinery and bridle joinery. First, the stub tenons are shorter than the tenons in a bridle joint, and, second, they mate with grooves, not through mortises (see the drawing on the facing page).

One situation that's particularly suitable for stub-tenon-and-groove joinery is when you have more than one panel in the lid (see the photo on the facing page). When there are two panels in a lid, you need an extra rail between the panels. If your frame has miter joints or bridle joints, consider how difficult it would be to cut that middle rail to the exact length. Also, what sort of joint would you use to attach the middle rail to the stiles? If a frame has stub-tenon-and-groove joints, the middle rail can be the same length as the other two rails, and all the stub tenons can be cut in the same operation.

Stub tenons and grooves are cut in a procedure similar to bridle joints, and you can use the same jigs. With stub tenons and grooves, however, the tenons are smaller, so the sawblade will be set lower. As a bonus, all of the grooves for the panel are unstopped.

Dazzling Interiors

Once you start experimenting with joinery to enhance the construction and appearance of your boxes, it's only logical that you experiment with different interior treatments to add pizzazz to your boxes.

You can transform the interior of any box from dull to dazzling by using one or more of the following methods: lining the interior to create a plush resting place for valuables and items of beauty; installing dividers to keep items compartmentalized; or adding trays that rest (and slide) on either the dividers or on rails to provide more storage and to create interesting levels.

LINING A BOX INTERIOR

Lining a box is simple, and it gives you an opportunity to work with materials other than wood and hardware—a refreshing change of pace.

Your choice of lining depends on your tastes and on the type of box you are making. I used to line most of my jewelry boxes with suede leather. Then I learned that the chemicals used to tan leather can tarnish the metals in jewelry. Now I use fake suede, known as suedecloth (100% polyester), or velvet.

The choice of lining also depends on the color of the wood. In cherry and walnut boxes, for example, I like to use dark-brown suedecloth. In mahogany boxes I have used dark green velvet, which turned out to be quite elegant—and popular. You can be creative in your choices, since both materials come in a variety of colors. Browse around a fabric shop to get ideas, and bring some boxes or wood samples with you. Many craft catalogs and shops offer other lining materials, such as velveteen, felt, and flocking.

To cut fabrics and leather cleanly, I like to use a rotary fabric cutter. These tools are inexpensive (around $10) and available at fabric stores, hobby shops, and leather-supply retailers.

Frame-and-Panel Lid with Stub-Tenon-and-Groove Joints

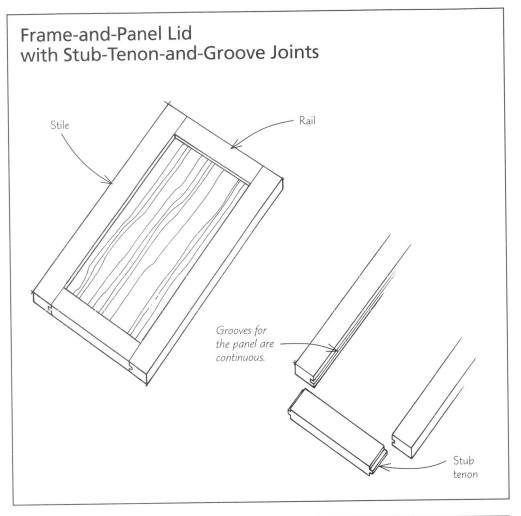

Stile

Rail

Grooves for the panel are continuous.

Stub tenon

The lid for this box was made with two lid panels. Stub tenons and grooves were used to assemble the frame and panels.

Mounting Velvet on Cardboard

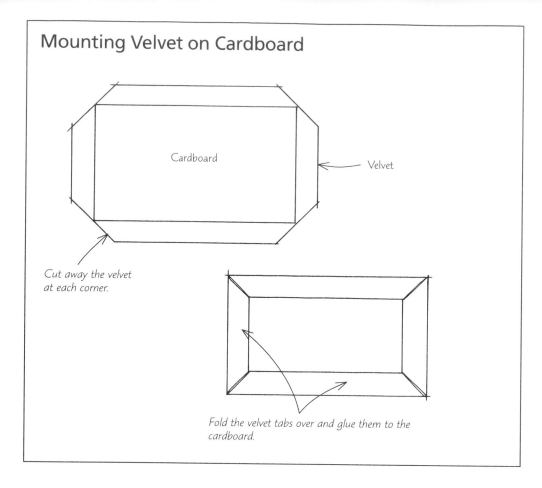

Cardboard

Velvet

*Cut away the velvet
at each corner.*

*Fold the velvet tabs over and glue them to the
cardboard.*

The lining material you choose will dictate how you install it. The methods for installing suedecloth and velvet are different but fairly simple.

Suedecloth Suedecloth is a highly workable material. It's smooth and doesn't get ragged around the edges after being cut. It makes a fine lining material, especially for someone who's adding a liner for the first time. Here's how to line a box with suedecloth:

1. Cut a piece of cardboard to fit snug in the bottom of the box. If it fits tightly enough, you won't have to glue it down. If it's too tight, the cardboard will buckle. The cardboard should be at least $1/32$ in. thick (posterboard or gift boxes work well). For large boxes, and for use with real suede, the cardboard should be $1/16$ in. thick.

2. Cut an oversized section of suedecloth. Measure your cardboard and add 1 in. to each dimension. Brush the smooth side (not the show side) lightly to remove dust. Then lay the cloth smooth-side up on a flat plastic or wood cutting mat. Smooth out the cloth so there are no wrinkles.

3. Coat one side of the cardboard with adhesive. I use spray adhesive, which doesn't soak into the fabric much yet creates a strong bond.

4. Wait 10 seconds or so for the adhesive to reach maximum tackiness, and then lay the tacky side of the cardboard on the suedecloth, keeping the cardboard flat as you lay it down.

5. Trim the extra cloth with the rotary fabric cutter. Place a metal straightedge on the edge of the cardboard to keep the cutter from straying.

6. Flip the finished lining over and press it into the box. Tap it down along the edges and in the corners with the rounded end of a paper clip.

Velvet When velvet is cut, it tends to have ragged edges, so you'll need a different method for lining than you would for suedecloth. Here's the installation procedure to ensure that edges remain neat and luxurious:

1. Cut a piece of cardboard $1/16$ in. smaller in each dimension than the box's interior. The cardboard should be $1/32$ in. to $1/16$ in. thick.

2. Cut a piece of velvet about 1 in. larger in each dimension than the cardboard.

3. Mount the velvet on the cardboard with spray adhesive. Lay the velvet show-side down on a flat plastic or wood cutting mat. Smooth it out. Coat one side of the cardboard with adhesive. Wait for the adhesive to become tacky, then lay the tacky side of the cardboard on the velvet, keeping the cardboard flat as you lay it down.

4. With scissors or a rotary cutter, trim the velvet away from the four corners, as shown in the drawing at left.

5. Fold the remaining velvet tabs over the cardboard and glue these tabs down to the back with rubber cement or hot-melt glue.

6. Press the completed lining into the box.

Lining a box is an easy way to spice up the interior of a box. Another method used to create an interesting, yet functional interior is to use dividers.

MAKING DIVIDERS

Making dividers calls for a high degree of precision. The fit is very important. Where the members intersect, you need snug-fitting joints: If they're loose, the glue joint will be weak; too tight, and the narrow pieces will distort and won't sit flat on the bottom.

Although some box makers permanently install dividers in their boxes by means of dadoes or dowel pins, I prefer to install removable dividers to give the user more flexibility.

I use two different methods of cutting and assembling dividers, depending on whether or not I intend to have a tray sitting on top of them (see the top drawing at right).

If there's no tray (or if the tray slides on separate rails), the divider members don't have to be flush. You can make cross members shorter then the main (longest) member, which allows you to cut just one notch per joint. And you can ease the sharp edges before assembly (which is easier than waiting until afterward).

You can cut all the notches on the table saw, with the help of an auxiliary miter fence that extends beyond the blade. Mark the locations and height of the notches first, then sneak up to the desired width of each notch by making repeated passes through the blade. As you get close to the final width, check the fit after each pass.

If there is a tray, the tops of the divider members must be flush to allow free-sliding movement over them. This requires that you cut mating notches at each joint. It also requires that you ease the sharp edges after the divider assembly is glued up, not before.

Flush-top dividers can be used to support a removable tray, which can add a whole new level (literally) to your box making.

MAKING TRAYS

A removable tray is essentially a small box without a lid, and it can be made using the same box-making techniques described earlier (on a smaller scale). The tray has to fit the interior dimension of the box and needs some form of support.

There are three basic methods of supporting the tray (see the bottom drawing at right): It can rest on dividers if their top edges are flush; it can be supported by rails glued to the sides of the box; or it can sit on rabbets cut into the sides of the carcase itself. The rabbets are cut in the carcase pieces before they're assembled.

Be sure to apply several coats of finish to the tray's bottom edges, as well as to the divider tops or supporting rails, to protect those surfaces from wear. Also line the tray with the same fabric or other material as the box bottom.

Two Types of Dividers

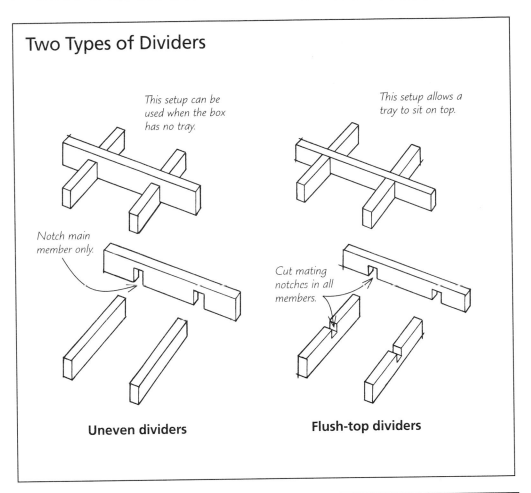

This setup can be used when the box has no tray.

This setup allows a tray to sit on top.

Notch main member only.

Cut mating notches in all members.

Uneven dividers

Flush-top dividers

Supporting a Tray

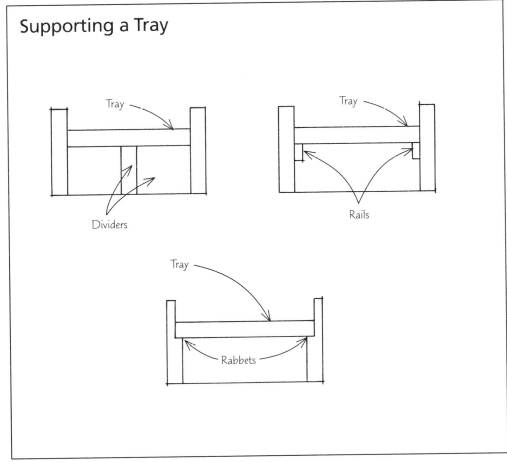

Tray

Dividers

Tray

Rails

Tray

Rabbets

Projects

BOX WITH TWO-PIECE SWIVEL LID

Will Wipperfurth, a box maker in Lake Mills, Wisconsin, makes splendid swivel-lid boxes with one, two, three, and four lid sections. Some of his creations are rectangular, some are elliptical, and some are neither. For this project, I decided to feature one of Will's fairly simple rectangular boxes. This box, shown in the photos below, has a swivel lid with two sections and a lined and divided interior.

The box carcase is made of oak, with walnut keys for reinforcement. The lid is a lamination of oak, walnut, and padauk. The interior is lined with brown suedecloth and has walnut dividers.

For this project, you can use the dimensions given in the drawing on the facing page and in the instructions, or you can adapt the dimensions and materials to fit your own needs. A cutlist is included with the drawing.

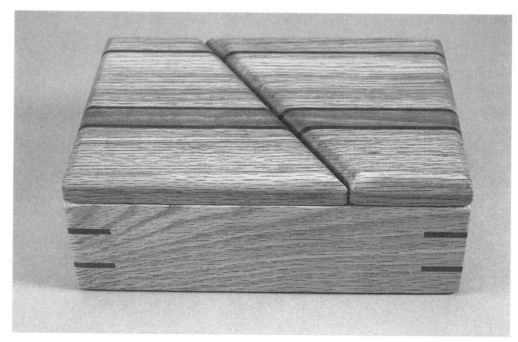

This box, made by Will Wipperfurth, is oak, with laminations of walnut and padauk and walnut keys. The two-piece lid swivels on pin hinges.

The box interior is lined with brown suede-cloth and furnished with walnut dividers. (Photos by Sally Ann Photography.)

Two-Piece Swivel-Lid Box

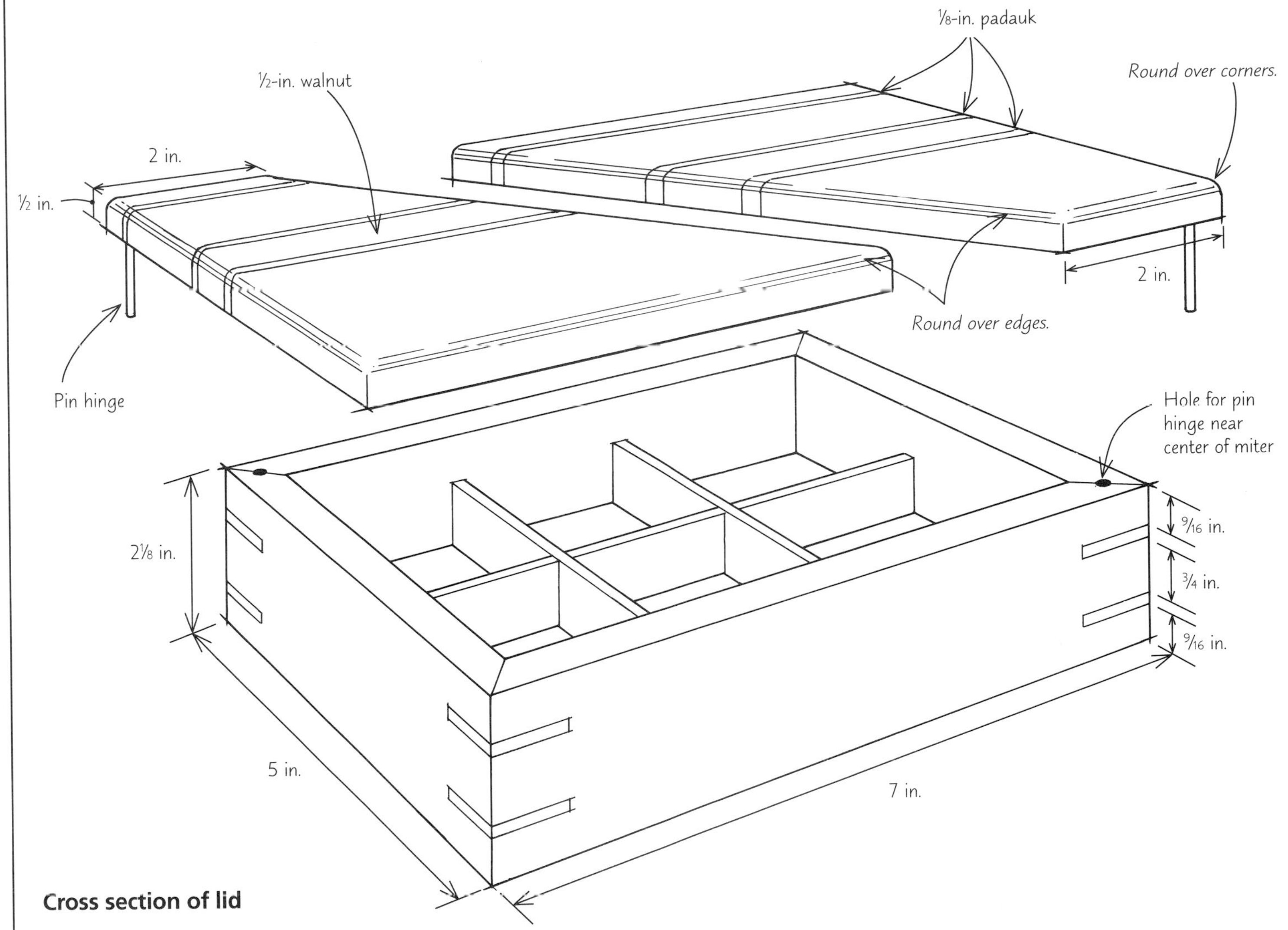

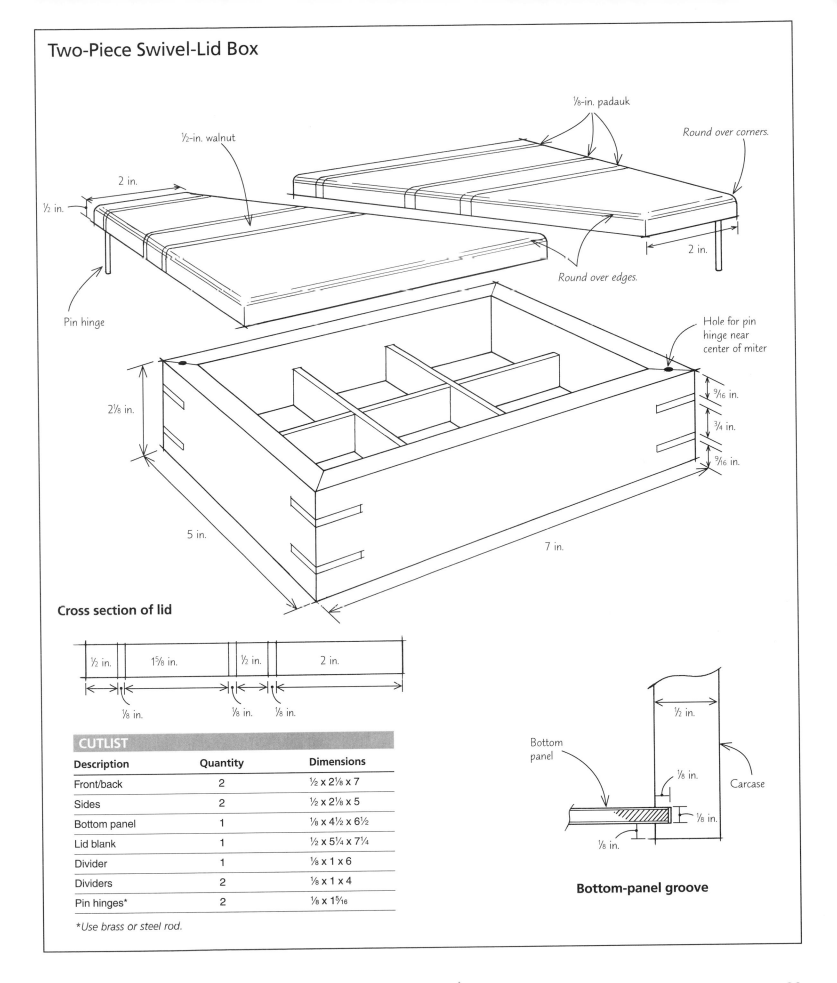

⅛-in. padauk
½-in. walnut
Round over corners.
2 in.
½ in.
Pin hinge
Round over edges.
2 in.
Hole for pin hinge near center of miter
2⅛ in.
9/16 in.
¾ in.
9/16 in.
5 in.
7 in.

Cross section of lid

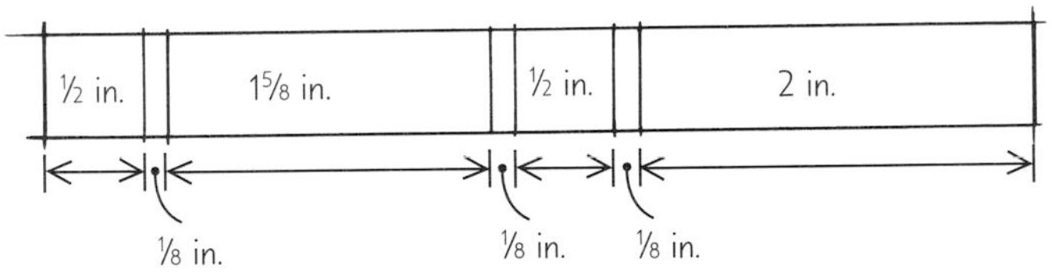

½ in.
1⅝ in.
½ in.
2 in.
⅛ in.
⅛ in.
⅛ in.

CUTLIST

Description	Quantity	Dimensions
Front/back	2	½ x 2⅛ x 7
Sides	2	½ x 2⅛ x 5
Bottom panel	1	⅛ x 4½ x 6½
Lid blank	1	½ x 5¼ x 7¼
Divider	1	⅛ x 1 x 6
Dividers	2	⅛ x 1 x 4
Pin hinges*	2	⅛ x 1 5/16

**Use brass or steel rod.*

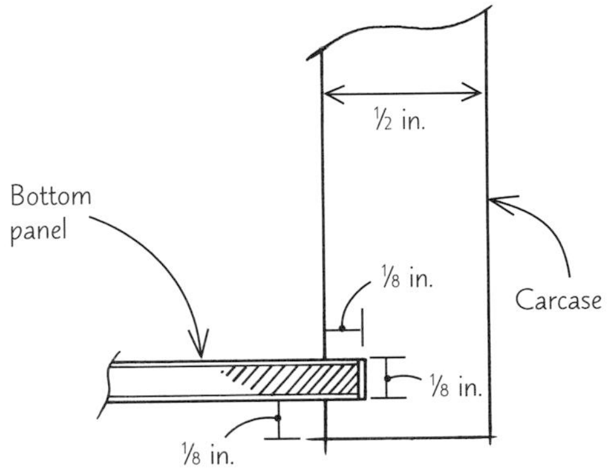

½ in.
Bottom panel
Carcase
⅛ in.
⅛ in.
⅛ in.

Bottom-panel groove

Making the Carcase

1. For the box carcase, cut a 25-in. piece of ½-in. stock to a width of 2⅛ in.
2. Cut a ⅛-in. by ⅛-in. groove for the bottom panel.
3. Miter-cut the sides, front, and back to length.
4. Cut a ⅛-in. plywood bottom panel to fit the carcase. It should measure 4½ in. by 6½ in.
5. Glue up the carcase, with the panel in place.
6. After the glue dries, reinforce the carcase with keys (for more on gluing up a mitered box and reinforcing with keys, see pp. 26-30). Once the carcase is assembled, you can begin work on the lid panel.

Making the Lid Panel

1. Glue up an oversized lid blank (for more on laminating lid panels, see pp. 40-45). The lid for the box shown here is an asymmetric design that uses quartersawn oak with ⅛-in.-wide padauk strips and a ½-in.-wide walnut strip. Clamp the assembly and let the glue dry.
2. Trim the lid blank to size, in this case 5¼ in. by 7¼ in.
3. Cut the blank into two pieces at an angle. When making a two-piece swivel lid, you can't cut the lid into two rectangular sections along a 90° line. Doing so will not allow the lid pieces to swing open. A two-piece swivel lid must be divided along a slanted line. This lid blank is cut at a 60° angle, but you may vary this angle as you wish. (Test your lid configuration with heavy cardboard or scrap wood before you start your project.)

Laying Out the Hinges

1. The next step is to lay out the pin-hinge locations. To do this, start by taping the two lid halves back together. Make sure the grain pattern lines up nicely where they meet. Apply masking tape along the seam, on both the top and bottom, for extra holding power.
2. With a pencil, mark the two pin-hinge locations on the top edge of the carcase, as shown in the drawing on p. 89. They should be located near the center of the miter.
3. To align the hinges with the lid and the carcase, first cut the head off a small brad and chuck it in the drill press. Then use the brad to drill tiny holes about ¼ in. deep at the pin-hinge locations.

4. Clip the heads off two more brads. Then lightly tap the brads into the holes in the carcase edge so that they stick out about ⅛ in. to 3/16 in.
5. Place the lid upside down on your bench. Then turn the carcase upside down and lower it onto the inverted lid, centering the carcase over the lid. Press the carcase down on the lid so the brads imprint their locations on the lid. Push down enough that the lid temporarily attaches to the carcase.
6. With the carcase and lid still attached to each other, flip them over so that they're right-side up. Make sure the lid has not shifted its position on the carcase. Trim the lid almost flush to the carcase on the bandsaw.
7. Sand the lid flush to the carcase. Will Wipperfurth uses an edge sander, which is essentially a long stationary belt sander. (If you prefer, you can use a flush trim bit in the router to trim the lid.)
8. Remove the lid and pull out the brads. Then rout the lid's edges with a ¼-in. roundover bit.

Installing the Hinges

1. Drill ⅛-in.-diameter holes, ⅜ in. deep, in the lid's underside at the points where the brads made their impressions. Do the same in the carcase, but to a depth of 1 in.
2. Now cut two ⅛-in.-diameter pin hinges. Their length will be *almost* the combined depth of the holes you drilled in the lid and carcase—in this case about 1 5/16 in. Will uses steel welding rod for the pins because it's stronger than brass rod. Using steel is fine here because the pins in this project are concealed, unless you remove the lids entirely.
3. Sand a slight chamfer on the ends of the pins. Insert the pins in the carcase, and then test-fit the lid. If the fit is too tight to allow the lid to swivel freely, remove the pins and drill the carcase holes 1/64 in. larger, to 9/64 in. Then test the fit again.

Finishing Touches

1. Separate the lid pieces from the carcase and do your final sanding.
2. Before finishing, glue a pin into each lid section with cyanoacrylate glue or epoxy (for more on pin-hinge installation, see pp. 75-77). Will finished this box with two coats of polyurethane.
3. After finishing, line the interior and furnish it with dividers (for more on lining a box and making dividers, see pp. 85-87).

This box has a spectacular, two-piece bookmatched lid of spalted maple that swings open on blind pin hinges.

The idea for this box came to me after I had resawn a beautiful piece of spalted maple. The two halves formed a spectacular bookmatch, which I thought would be perfect for a box lid. Unfortunately, the edges were decayed and too soft and porous to glue together for a one-piece bookmatched lid. So I decided to make the lid in two pieces and to let them swing open on pin hinges, which allowed me to preserve the wonderful bookmatch and create a stunning box (see the photos this page).

This box has a few subtle yet elegant features that are also functional. When closed, the lid pieces rest on two rail inserts, which are a variation of end inserts (see p. 49). The inserts are attached to the side pieces of the carcase. The box is opened using a finger hole drilled into the lid pieces.

Because the lid is divided in the middle, it seemed logical to me that the box be divided that way as well. So I cut a walnut divider to run the length of the box, but then I found that each compartment seemed small. To make the compartments appear more spacious, I cut a

When closed, the lid pieces rest on two rail inserts glued to the sides of the walnut carcase. Inside, the box has two compartments separated by a removable walnut divider.

Box with Two-Piece Lid

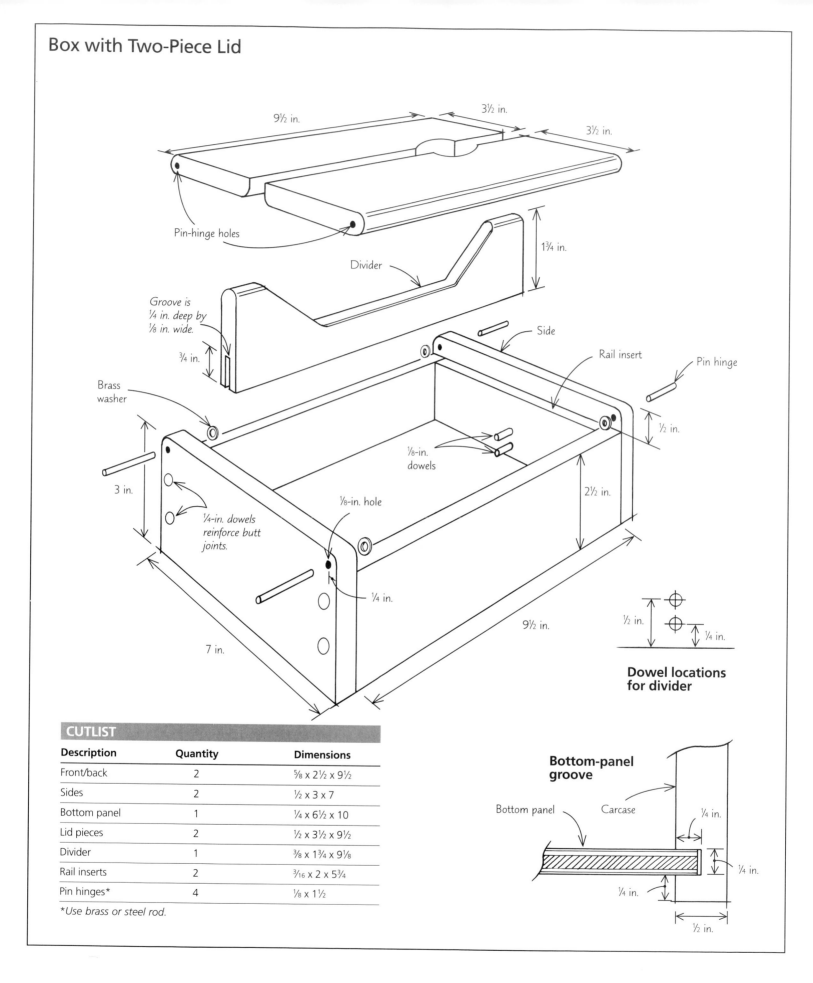

9½ in.

3½ in.

3½ in.

Pin-hinge holes

1¾ in.

Divider

Groove is ¼ in. deep by ⅛ in. wide.

¾ in.

Side

Rail insert

Pin hinge

Brass washer

½ in.

3 in.

⅛-in. dowels

¼-in. dowels reinforce butt joints.

⅛-in. hole

2½ in.

¼ in.

9½ in.

7 in.

½ in.

¼ in.

Dowel locations for divider

CUTLIST

Description	Quantity	Dimensions
Front/back	2	⅝ x 2½ x 9½
Sides	2	½ x 3 x 7
Bottom panel	1	¼ x 6½ x 10
Lid pieces	2	½ x 3½ x 9½
Divider	1	⅜ x 1¾ x 9⅛
Rail inserts	2	3/16 x 2 x 5¾
Pin hinges*	4	⅛ x 1½

Use brass or steel rod.

Bottom-panel groove

Bottom panel

Carcase

¼ in.

¼ in.

¼ in.

½ in.

recess in the top edge of the divider. The divider is removable—it slides up and down on two ⅛-in. dowels in each box side—and the dowels are removable as well, in case the user wants to leave the divider out permanently.

Feel free to adapt the dimensions given in the drawings and the cutlist on the facing page. Although the box shown here has a bookmatched spalted-maple lid, you can use any kind of figured wood and choose the carcase stock to match (or contrast) the lid stock. Begin the construction with the carcase.

Making the Carcase

1. Prepare the bottom panel and the front, back, and side pieces (see the cutlist and the drawing). Because this box employs simple butt joinery, the front and back pieces are planed ⅛ in. thicker than the side pieces to provide extra glue surface on the end grain (for more on butt joinery, see pp. 78-79). The bottom panel is ¼-in. walnut plywood.

2. Cut ¼-in. grooves in the carcase pieces for the bottom panel. The grooves in the sides must be stopped so that they won't show on the exterior (for more on cutting stopped grooves, see p. 84).

3. Bore ⅛-in. holes for the pin hinges ¼ in. down from the top of the side pieces and ¼ in. in from the edge. Setting stops will eliminate tedious measuring and will ensure that all four holes are drilled exactly the same distance from the corner. If you use stops, test the accuracy of the setup on a scrap piece. When you've achieved the setup you want, drill the holes all the way through the stock. To prevent tearout, place a scrap piece under the stock or clamp a wood auxiliary table to the drill-press table.

4. Sand the inside surfaces and assemble the carcase. Take extra care during assembly to square the carcase by measuring the diagonals and adjusting as necessary.

5. Because I used butt joinery, the carcase needed reinforcement. I used walnut dowels, but you can use biscuits or splines if you prefer (see the drawing on p. 79). Wait until the glue dries, and then insert two ¼-in. dowels into each joint; trim the dowels flush.

Making the Rail Inserts

1. Cut the two rail inserts to length. They should fit snug in the ends of the boxes and must be flush with the top edges of the front and back pieces of the carcase.

2. Once you've achieved the fit you want, drill two ⅛-in. holes along the centerline of each insert. One hole is ¼ in. from the bottom of the insert, and the other is ½ in. from the bottom (see the detail drawing on the facing page). These holes accept the dowels that keep the divider in place.

3. Sand the inside faces and top edges of the inserts, then glue them in place. Clamp them with C-clamps or spring clamps.

Cutting the Lid Pieces

1. Cut two ½-in. pieces of stock to size (each should be 3½ in. by 9½ in.). The best design for this type of lid is a bookmatch. To achieve a bookmatch, you may want to resaw a piece of stock for the lid.

2. Drill a finger hole in the lid pieces. Locate the hole anywhere along the dividing line. To create the hole, place a ⅛-in.- to 3/16-in.-wide spacer between the two pieces; the spacer should be as thick as the lid pieces (see the drawing below). Tape the lid pieces and the spacer together.

Drill into the center of the spacer. For best results, clamp the lids to the drill-press table so they can't shift while they're being drilled and

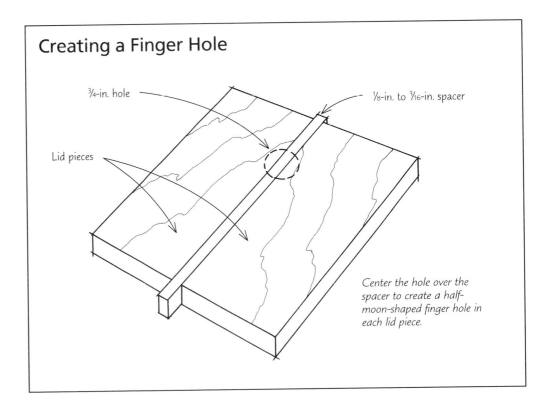

Creating a Finger Hole

¾-in. hole

⅛-in. to 3/16-in. spacer

Lid pieces

Center the hole over the spacer to create a half-moon-shaped finger hole in each lid piece.

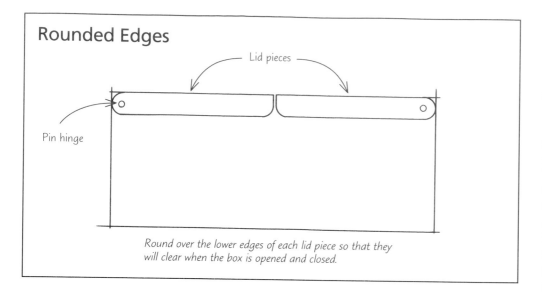

Rounded Edges

Lid pieces

Pin hinge

Round over the lower edges of each lid piece so that they will clear when the box is opened and closed.

use a ¾-in. Forstner bit for a smooth cut. Place a scrap piece or an auxiliary table beneath the workpieces to minimize tearout. If you want a perfectly round finger hole, follow the same procedures but leave out the spacer.

3. Remove the tape and place the lids on the carcase so that they're butted together in the middle. If you've made the cuts correctly, the lid pieces will be resting on the front and back pieces of the carcase and on the rail inserts.

4. Tape the two lid pieces together along the middle, and then tape them to the carcase, making sure their edges are flush with the front and back.

Installing the Hinges

1. Using the holes for the pin hinges as guides, drill ⅛-in. holes about ½ in. deep into each lid piece.

2. Cut four 1½-in. lengths of ⅛-in. brass rod for the pin hinges. Insert these into the pin holes to make sure the holes are clear. If the pins won't go in fairly smoothly, drill out the holes again to remove any debris, and reinsert the pins. When you're satisfied with the fit, remove the pins with a pair of pliers; remove the tape and the lid pieces, too.

3. To avoid wood rubbing against wood when the box is opened and closed, I slide a #4 brass washer over each pin hinge between the lid pieces and the carcase. You may have to trim the ends of the lids a bit until you can fit the washers. (If you've bookmatched the lids, trim them equally to preserve the match.) Put the pieces back on the carcase: The washers shouldn't have any side-to-side play. Once the lids are trimmed, sand the ends lightly, concluding with 180-grit paper.

4. Glue a washer to each carcase side, centered on the pin hole. Use the brass pins to keep the washers in place. A dab of cyanoacrylate glue on each washer should be sufficient—don't let the glue seep into the pin holes or onto the pins. After the glue dries, remove the pins.

5. To prevent the lids from binding due to expansion in humid seasons, plane or rip about ¹⁄₆₄ in. from the inside edge of each lid piece (the edge with the finger hole).

6. Round over the lower inside and outside edges of each lid piece (see the drawing at left). This will allow the lid pieces to swing open easily, without obstruction. You can round the edges on a belt sander or with a ¼-in. roundover bit in the router. Be sure to round over the curved edges of the finger holes, too.

7. Now put the lid pieces in place on the carcase and insert the pins (don't trim them to length yet). If the lids are still restricted from opening fully, find where they're binding, and then round over those edges further. When the lid pieces open freely, remove the pin hinges and take the lid pieces off the carcase.

Cutting the Divider

1. Cut and shape the divider, following the dimensions given in the cutlist on p. 92.

2. Rout stopped grooves into the ends of the divider so that it will slip over the dowels in the rail inserts. Use a ⅛-in. straight bit in the router. The grooves should be ¾ in. high and ¼ in. deep.

Finishing Touches

1. Fine-sand and finish all the parts. I used Danish oil, which brings out the dramatic figure in spalted wood, but you can use whatever finish you like (for more on finishing, see pp. 17-20).

2. After the finish cures, cut the four brass pin hinges to a length of ¾ in. and file the ends smooth. Once you insert the pins now, you'll never get them out. Use a ⅛-in.-diameter or smaller rod or dowel to shove the hinge pins all the way into the lid pieces. Then glue ⅛ in. wood dowels into the pin holes as plugs. I used birch dowels for contrast. (For more on installing pin hinges, see pp. 75-77.)

3. When the glue dries, trim and sand the dowels flush and refinish the areas around the dowels that you just sanded.

4. Open both lid pieces and insert ⅛-in.-diameter dowels, ⅜ in. long, into the holes in the rail inserts. Slide the divider into place over the dowels.

Mike Jagielo of Almond, Wisconsin, designed and made this unusual box. The bottom edges of the carcase pieces are gently curved, and the legs are slightly tapered (see the photo below). This combination of curves and tapers gives the box an Oriental flavor.

This box has a curly maple carcase, with legs and lid made of bubinga. The lid is flush-mounted, and it has a "handle" that fits into a cutout in the front of the carcase. It opens on blind pin hinges. The legs are joined to the carcase pieces with biscuits.

Use the dimensions given in the drawing on pp. 96-97 and in the instructions, or adapt the dimensions and materials given here to fit your own needs. A cutlist is included with the drawings.

Making the Carcase and Lid

1. Cut the carcase pieces to the dimensions shown in the drawing and cutlist. Then cut the curves on the front, back, and side pieces with a bandsaw or scrollsaw. To make the curves exact for each side, make a pattern on paper, attach it to the carcase stock, and follow the pattern as you cut. Then sand the curves smooth (a drum sander works well).

2. Form the cutout in the front carcase piece for the lid's handle. A dado blade in the table saw makes this job easy. Raise the blade to $3/8$ in. and set a stop on the miter gauge $6\frac{1}{4}$ in. from the blade. Make the end cuts first to form the cutout's shoulders, flipping the front end for end between the two cuts. Then remove the waste between the shoulders by making repeated passes through the blade. Smooth the edges of the cutout with a narrow sanding block.

3. Cut $1/4$-in. grooves in all four carcase pieces for the bottom panel. Then cut the bottom panel to size from $1/4$-in. plywood ($5\frac{3}{8}$ in. by $10\frac{3}{8}$ in.). It will be notched for the legs later.

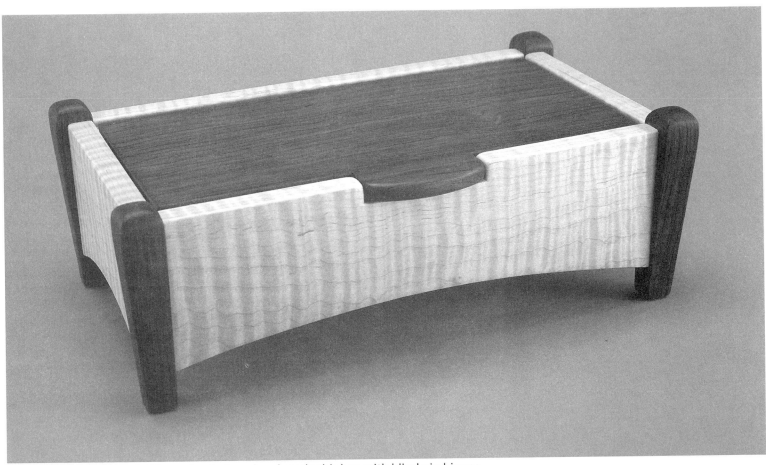

Mike Jagielo of Almond, Wisconsin, designed and made this box with blind pin hinges. The curves in the carcase and the tapered legs give the box an Oriental feel. (Photo by Sally Ann Photography.)

Box with Blind Pin Hinges

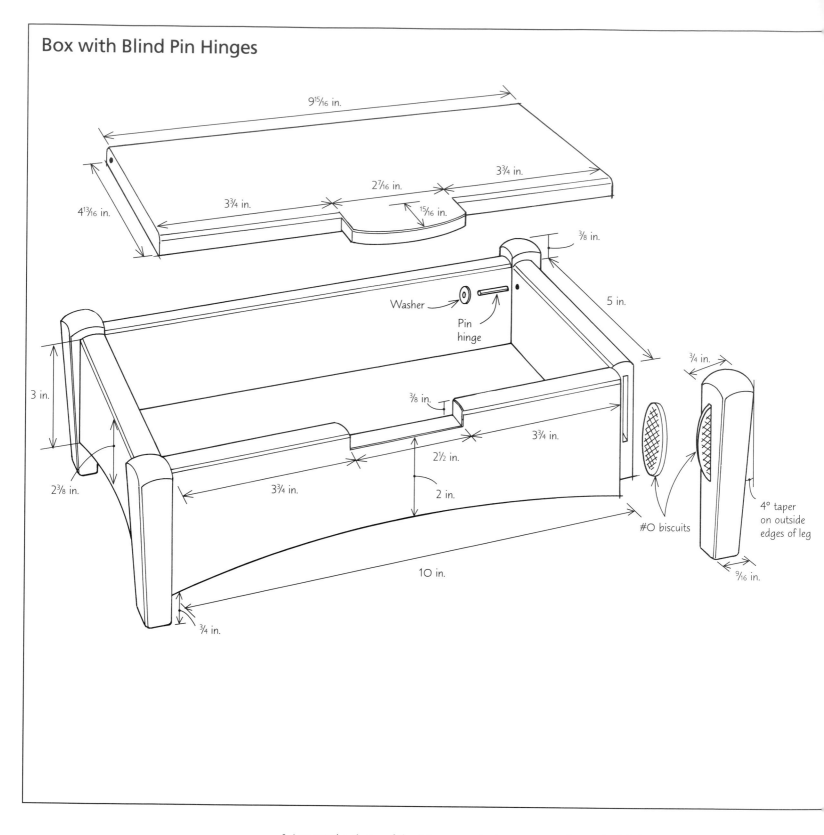

9¹⁵⁄₁₆ in.

4¹³⁄₁₆ in.

3¾ in.

2⁷⁄₁₆ in.

3¾ in.

¹⁵⁄₁₆ in.

⅜ in.

Washer

Pin hinge

5 in.

3 in.

⅜ in.

¾ in.

2⅜ in.

3¾ in.

3¾ in.

2½ in.

2 in.

#0 biscuits

4° taper on outside edges of leg

⁹⁄₁₆ in.

10 in.

¾ in.

4. Lay out the shape of the lid on your stock using a pattern. Again, you can simply attach the pattern to the stock and cut around it. Mike drew the handle's curve by tracing around the rim of a 1-gallon paint can.

Cut the lid to shape on a bandsaw or scrollsaw, and sand the edges smooth. Then round over the lid's back edge slightly to ensure clearance when it opens.

Cutting the Legs

1. Cut the leg stock to rough dimension.
2. To shape the legs, start by tapering them to a 4° angle on the table saw. Taper only two

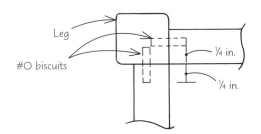

Biscuit layout

CUTLIST		
Description	**Quantity**	**Dimensions**
Front/back	2	1/2 x 3 x 10
Sides	2	1/2 x 3 x 5
Bottom panel	1	1/4 x 5 3/8 x 10 3/8
Lid blank	1	3/8 x 5 3/4 x 9 15/16
Legs	4	3/4 x 3/4 x 4 1/16
Pin hinges*	2	1/8 x 5/8

Use brass or steel rod.

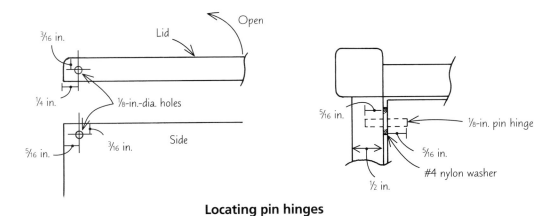

Locating pin hinges

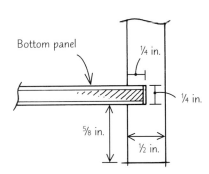

Bottom-panel groove

adjacent edges of each leg, and mark them; leave the other two edges square. The two tapered edges of the legs will face outward. Because the leg blanks were so small, Mike made a tapering jig for this operation (see the drawing on p. 98), which offers better accuracy and safety than the typical commercial taper jig.

3. Round over the tops of the legs on your router table, using a 1/4-in. roundover bit. Be sure to use a backing board to help control the workpiece and to minimize tearout. Use a low clearance auxiliary fence to prevent the leg

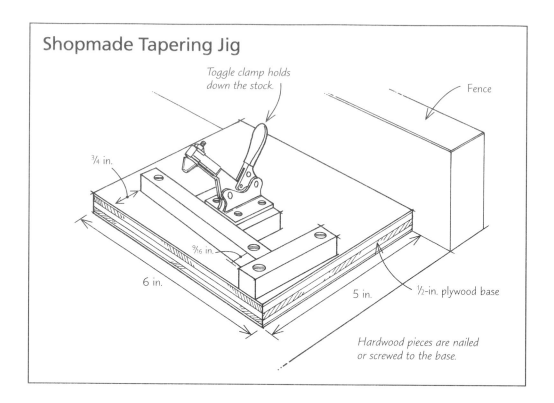

Shopmade Tapering Jig

Toggle clamp holds down the stock.

Fence

3/4 in.

9/16 in.

6 in.

5 in.

1/2-in. plywood base

Hardwood pieces are nailed or screwed to the base.

from dipping into the router bit. Sand the legs smooth, including the roundovers and tops, and ease the sharp corners slightly.

4. Notch the corners of the bottom panel for the legs. These notches must be exactly 1/4 in. by 1/4 in. so that they won't show on the inside of the box.

5. Cut slots for the biscuits that join the legs to the carcase. Mike used #0 biscuits. Be careful to cut the slots on the two inside edges (not the tapered edges) of the legs.

The slots in the carcase pieces must be located toward the outside of the box, not through the center of the pieces, so that the biscuits don't intersect inside the legs (see the detail drawing on p. 96).

Assembling the Box

1. With all the pieces cut, dry-assemble the carcase with biscuits in their slots to make sure everything fits well.

2. Disassemble the pieces and drill 1/8-in.-diameter, 5/16-in.-deep holes in the two sides for the blind pin hinges. Then drill mating pin holes to the same depth in the lid.

3. Cut two pieces of 1/8-in. brass rod to a length of 5/8 in. for the pin hinges. Then dry-assemble the box again with the lid, the pin

hinges, and #4 nylon or brass washers, which prevent wood from rubbing against wood. If the lid doesn't open smoothly, you'll have to trim the lid and/or round over the back edge more.

4. When everything fits nicely, sand all the pieces and apply a coat of finish to the lid. Let the lid dry overnight. Don't apply finish to the carcase yet.

FINAL ASSEMBLY

1. Apply glue to the biscuits and in their slots (but not to the legs or the ends of the carcase pieces). It's also a good idea to spread some glue into the bottom panel's grooves to add strength to the assembly.

2. Clamp the assembly with three or four strong rubber bands. Before the glue sets, open the lid to make sure it moves easily; if not, check the carcase for square and adjust as necessary.

3. Finish the entire box. (Mike applied two coats of Danish oil.)

4. After the finish cures, attach 3/8-in.-diameter felt disks to the bottoms of the legs.

6 BOXES WITH BUTT HINGES

Techniques

The boxes presented in this chapter are finely crafted and slightly more complex to make than those shown in earlier chapters. With a more elegant box design, you'll want to incorporate hardware that is as elegant as the box and that won't detract from the box's appearance. You'll also want the hardware to fit precisely.

In this chapter, you'll learn how to install butt hinges, both mortised and surface-mounted. You'll also learn how to support the box lids using a variety of methods. Let's begin by looking at methods of installing butt hinges.

Installing Butt Hinges

Polished brass butt hinges can add a feeling of richness and reliability to any wood project. That's why they are the most traditional hinges seen on jewelry boxes. Butt hinges are available in many shapes and sizes, and the kind you use and where to mount them is mostly a matter of personal taste.

In general, you want to use the smallest pair of hinges that will support the weight of the lid. Butt hinges can be mounted in two different positions: between the lid and the carcase or on the back of the box (see the photos at right). The position you choose will depend on the look you want to achieve and on how much time you want to spend installing the hinges.

The easiest and quickest way to install butt hinges is to surface-mount them on the back of the box. For a cleaner look, the hinges can be mortised into the lid and the box carcase—either between the lid and carcase or on the outside. Let's begin with hinges surface-mounted on the back of the box.

For a clean look on the exterior of a box, mortise the butt hinges between the lid and carcase.

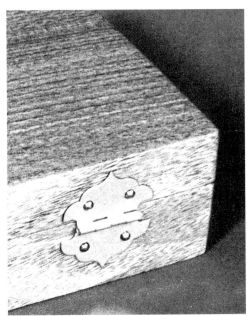

Decorative butt hinges are designed to be surface-mounted on the back of a box.

An Easy Way to Locate Surface-Mounted Hinges

A simple way to locate surface-mounted hinges (especially if their bottom edges aren't straight) is to fold them over the back rim of the carcase, as shown in the drawing at right. Make sure the barrel is facing out and mark the centers of the holes on the carcase. With one leaf resting on the rim, the hinges align themselves. Drill pilot holes and screw the lower leaf onto the carcase. Tape the lid to the carcase, mark the centers of the holes on the lid, drill pilot holes in the lid, and then screw the upper hinge leaves to the lid.

The only drawback of this method is that the barrels of the hinges won't be centered on the seam but above it. (Or, if you fold the hinge over the lid's rim in the first place, the barrels will be centered below the seam.)

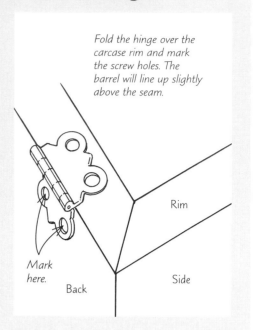

Fold the hinge over the carcase rim and mark the screw holes. The barrel will line up slightly above the seam.

Rim

Mark here.

Back

Side

SURFACE-MOUNTING HINGES

Because hinges mounted on the outside of a box are visible, box makers often use decorative or ornamental hinges for this type of installation. Decorative hinges are available in a wide variety of shapes and styles.

Although I have seen boxes with surface-mounted butt hinges displayed in some prestigious art fairs and galleries, I have not seen many. That's because, in general, surface-mounted hinges signify craft rather than art. So you tend to see them in greater profusion at craft fairs. In my opinion, surface-mounted butt hinges are appropriate for a softwood box, a painted box, a country-style or primitive-style box, or a utility box.

Here's how to install surface-mounted butt hinges:

1. Hold the lid in place with masking tape and/or clamps. Measure an equal distance in from each side and mark the locations of the hinges on both the lid and the carcase.

The distance from the sides and between the hinges is arbitrary, from a mechanical point of view. Aesthetically, though, the hinges should be closer to the sides than to the middle of the box. A good trick is to divide the back into fourths and locate the hinges in the outer fourths, touching the dividing lines.

2. Lay the hinges in place, with the barrels facing out. Center the barrels over the seam between the lid and carcase. If you trust your

hand and your eye, mark the centers of the hinges' screw holes at this point.

If you're installing butt hinges that have straight edges, you can ensure precision by using a straightedge to act as an alignment aid. Hold the straightedge across the back of the box against the bottom edge of the hinges and adjust until the hinge barrels are centered on the seam. Then tape the straightedge to the box. Hold each hinge in place with a finger and mark the centers of the screw holes. This technique won't work, of course, with hinges that have curved or rounded edges. These type of hinges require a different method (see the sidebar above).

3. If your box is hardwood, drill pilot holes in both the lid and the carcase. If it's softwood, you can drill smaller pilot holes, or if the screws are very small, simply punch a starter hole with an awl to make sure the screw doesn't wander when you start to torque it in.

4. Screw the hinges in place. If after installing the hinges you discover that one is a bit askew and the lid doesn't open easily, it's probably because a screw is off-center. Loosen the screws one at a time until you figure out which screw is pulling the hinge out of alignment. Then remove the hinge and plug the screw hole with a toothpick and fast-setting epoxy glue.

The No-Mortise Gap

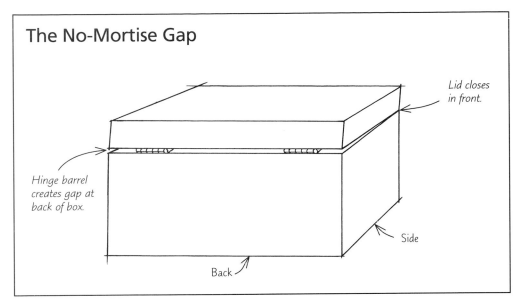

Lid closes in front.

Hinge barrel creates gap at back of box.

Side

Back

Full-Width Hinges

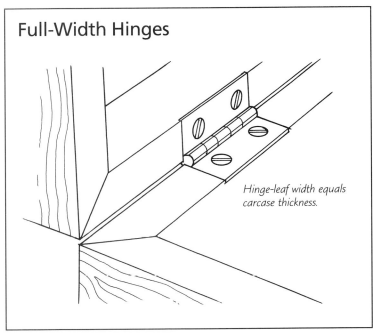

Hinge-leaf width equals carcase thickness.

Part-Width Hinges

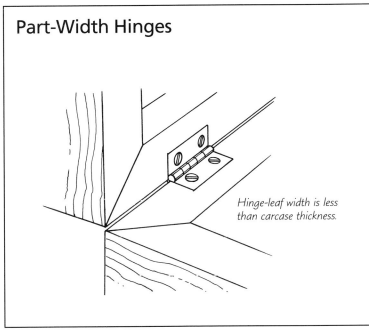

Hinge-leaf width is less than carcase thickness.

After the epoxy sets, trim the toothpick flush with a chisel. Then mark and drill a new pilot hole, and reinstall the hinges.

MOUNTING HINGES
BETWEEN LID AND CARCASE

Although a box with surface-mounted butt hinges can be attractive, having the hinges visible on the outside can be distracting (say, on a box made of exotic hardwood with beautiful figure). In such cases you may want to mount the hinges between the lid and carcase for a box that has the marks of fine craftsmanship. A bit of careful planning will help you achieve a clean, professional look.

To avoid an unsightly gap at the back of the box, you'll need to mortise the hinges in (see the top drawing above). The gap is created by the hinge's barrel, which causes the lid to slope down toward the front of the box. Mortising the hinge lets the lid close without a gap.

The mortise for the hinge should be exactly as long and at least as wide as the hinge's leaf. Box makers often use hinges whose leaves are as wide as the thickness of the carcase, which I call full-width hinges (see the bottom left drawing above). But occasionally you'll see narrower hinges used, mainly for aesthetic reasons—to minimize the expanse of flashy metal inside the box. I call these part-width hinges (see the bottom right drawing above).

There are two common ways to install mortised butt hinges (see the drawing below). You can cut mortises in both the carcase and the lid, with each mortise as deep as the barrel's radius. I call these radius-depth mortises. Alternatively, you can cut mortises in the back rim of the carcase only (not in the lid), in which case the mortise is as deep as the barrel's diameter. I call these diameter-depth mortises. In this type of installation, the hinge's top leaf will be surface-mounted to the underside of the lid. Let's look at the radius-depth mortises first.

Cutting radius-depth mortises

1. Sand the edges of the lid and carcase smooth.

2. Clamp the back of the lid to the back of the carcase, as shown in the drawing on the facing page. I like to use spring clamps, but you can use whatever works for you. The thing to remember here is that the sides and the top edges must be flush.

3. Measure in from each side to locate the outside edge of each hinge. Using a square, score a layout line across the grain with a sharp knife.

4. Lay the hinge in position and mark the location of its inside edge. Use the square to score a second layout line. (For part-width hinges, mark and score the front and back edges of the hinge, too.)

5. Using a straight bit or a mortising bit, rout the mortises freehand almost to the layout lines. Finish them off with a chisel.

The depth setting of the router bit must be precise. Test this setting on two pieces of scrap before you start routing the box. Then place the scrap mortises face-to-face and check the clearance with the hinge barrel—the barrel should fit snugly between the mortises.

It may be necessary to replace your router base with a larger auxiliary base if the box is so large that it doesn't support the router during these cuts. The router base must span the

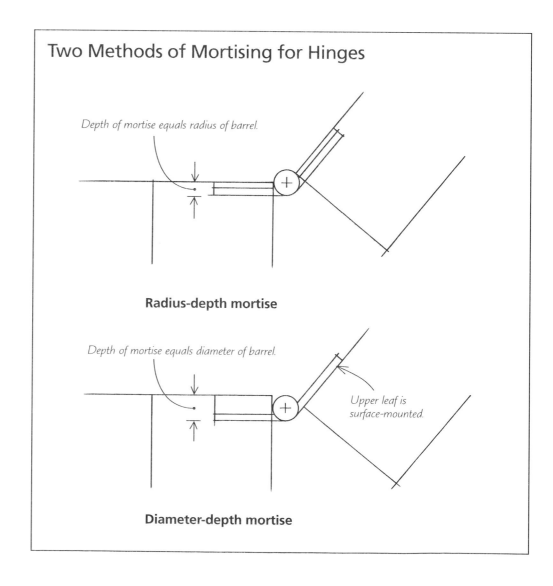

Two Methods of Mortising for Hinges

Depth of mortise equals radius of barrel.

Radius-depth mortise

Depth of mortise equals diameter of barrel.

Upper leaf is surface-mounted.

Diameter-depth mortise

box's back and front to keep the router level while in operation.

On small boxes, I use a laminate trimmer, which is essentially a small-scale router, to avoid knocking into the clamps.

On very small boxes, routing mortises is practically impossible, because the clamps would get in the way of even the smallest router. So you have to cut the mortises with hand tools. That's one reason why very small boxes typically have slot hinges or no hinges at all.

6. After routing and chiseling out the mortises, clamp the lid and the carcase back together, set the hinges in their mortises, and mark the centers of the screw holes. Then drill pilot holes and install the hinges. Make any necessary adjustments and remove the hinges for finishing.

Cutting diameter-depth mortises

There are two ways to cut diameter-depth mortises: with a router after the carcase is assembled; or on the table saw before the carcase is assembled.

To rout the mortises after the carcase is assembled, simply follow the instructions for routing radius-depth mortises. The only difference is that you'll be mortising just the carcase, not the lid. Set the depth of cut to equal the diameter of the hinge barrel. A hinge-mortising jig makes this job easier, especially if you'll be making the same box design in the future or are making a lot of boxes at once (see the sidebar on p. 104).

I've found that the easiest way to cut diameter-depth mortises, however, is to cut them in the back before assembling the carcase. This operation can be done on a table saw, using a single blade or dado head. Here's how:

1. Score layout lines on the top edge of the back carcase piece and extend the lines to one face.

2. Set the height of the blade or dado head to the hinge barrel's diameter. Test this setting on scrap.

3. Place the back upside down against the miter gauge with a long auxiliary fence attached. You should be able to see the layout-line extensions on the face. Make repeated passes until you've removed the waste between the layout lines. As the blade nears the layout lines, test the mortise length and depth by laying the hinge in place.

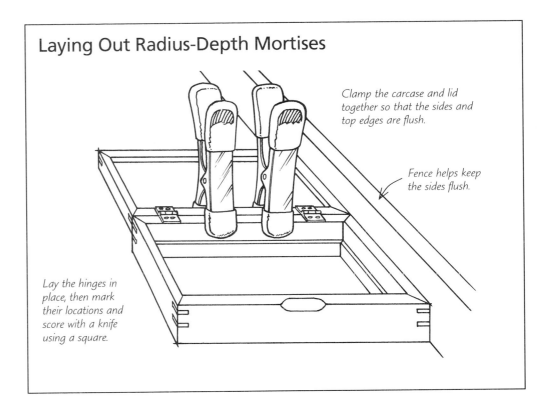

Laying Out Radius-Depth Mortises

Clamp the carcase and lid together so that the sides and top edges are flush.

Fence helps keep the sides flush.

Lay the hinges in place, then mark their locations and score with a knife using a square.

4. On the bottom of the mortise you'll see cross-grain hatch marks made by the sawblade. These can be sanded out quickly with 150-grit sandpaper and a small, flat sanding block.

Surface-mounting hinges under the lid

When mounting hinges into diameter-depth mortises, the lid does not have to be mortised. Instead, the upper hinge leaf is surface-mounted. It's just a matter of drilling pilot holes and screwing the upper leaf to the lid. But it's not quite as simple as it sounds, especially if the lid overhangs the carcase. Here's a foolproof way to locate the pilot holes:

1. Grind four wood screws into "pilot pins." I started with four #6 x ¾-in. flat-head wood screws. (The hinges I use have ³⁄₁₆-in.-diameter holes.) Cut off the threaded section of the screw with a hacksaw. Then grind the shanks into points (see the photo at left on p. 105), holding the screw heads with pliers. If you don't have a grinder, you can file the shank to a point.

2. Place the four pilot pins, pointed end up, on top of the hinges that you already installed in the carcase—center them over the screws. Then flop the upper hinge leaves down over the pins, so the pins are captured and can't move.

3. Put the lid into position—take your time and get it aligned perfectly. Press down over the two hinges. The pilot pins will leave dimples in the lid, indicating where you should drill pilot holes.

Making and Using a Hinge-Mortising Jig

A hinge-mortising jig is simple to make, and it's perfect for production runs. The jig lets you rout all the way up to the hinge layout lines, so that you have to use a chisel only to square up the corners. It's essentially three pieces of scrap nailed together: the top, which has two cutouts that guide the router, and two cleats, which align the jig on the box. The top must be big enough to clamp onto the carcase with at least two clamps, to stabilize the jig while you're routing. Here's how to make it:

1. Cut a piece of ½-in. plywood a little longer than the carcase and at least 4 in. wide. This will be the top of the jig. Lay it on the carcase and transfer the hinge-location marks from the carcase to the edge of the plywood.

2. Using a square, extend the layout lines to the top face of the jig top. Since this jig is used with a guide bushing on the router, the cutouts must be bigger than the hinges.

3. Calculate the dimensions of the cutouts (this is the tricky part), as shown in the drawing below. The width (W) of the cutout (the distance between the cutout's guide edges) should equal the hinge's length (L) plus the difference between the router bit's diameter (r) and the guide bushing's outside diameter (g). To formulate it neatly, $W = L + (g - r)$.

If your mortises are full-width (one hinge leaf is as wide as the carcase's thickness), the depth (D) of the cutout is arbitrary, as long as it's greater than the thickness of the front cleat plus the thickness of the carcase, plus the distance between the bushing and the bit, which is $(g - r) \div 2$.

However, if your mortises are part-width (the hinge leaves are narrower than the carcase's thickness), the depth of the cutout is critical. The depth (D) must exactly equal the thickness of the front cleat plus the width of the hinge leaf plus $(g - r) \div 2$. And the back of the cutout must be straight and perpendicular to the sides.

Don't let the math scare you—it's easy once you get the concept. If you make the jig's cutouts too wide or too deep on your first try, throw away the scrap and start over. Always make a test mortise to check for accuracy.

4. Glue and nail the jig top to the hardwood cleats. The face of the front cleat must be flush to the front edge of the jig top. Sink the nail heads so they don't interfere with the router base. Now you're ready to use the jig.

USING THE JIG

1. Score layout lines for the hinges on the carcase with a sharp knife, to prevent tearout.

2. Clamp the jig to the back of the carcase, with the cleats outside the carcase, so that you can see your layout lines centered between the cutouts' guide edges.

3. Install a straight bit (at least ¼ in. diameter) and guide bushing in the router. The bit and bushing must be the same ones you measured when you performed the calculations for making the jig. Set the depth of the bit to the thickness of the jig's top plus the hinge barrel's diameter.

4. Rout between the edges of the jig until the mortises are clean. The first time you use the jig you'll be routing into the jig's front cleat, as well as into the carcase. Before removing the jig, test-fit a hinge into the mortises.

Jig Dimensions

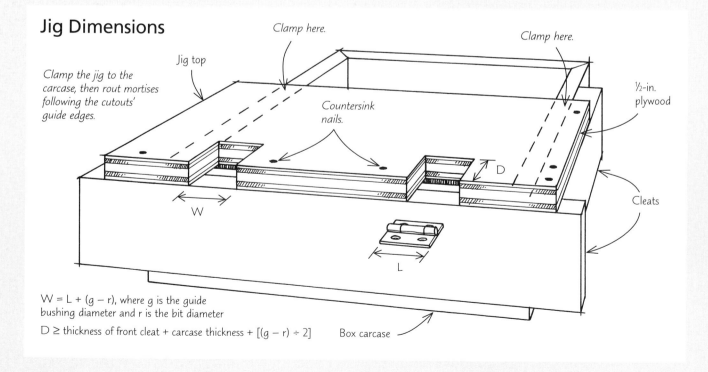

Clamp here.

Clamp here.

Jig top

Clamp the jig to the carcase, then rout mortises following the cutouts' guide edges.

Countersink nails.

½-in. plywood

Cleats

Box carcase

W

D

L

$W = L + (g - r)$, where g is the guide bushing diameter and r is the bit diameter

$D \geq$ thickness of front cleat + carcase thickness + $[(g - r) \div 2]$

To make a pilot pin, cut off the threaded portion of a wood screw and grind or file it to a point.

A precision butt hinge was mortised into the back of this box made by Claire Wright so that the hinges would not detract from the elegant interior.

4. Before you drill the pilot holes, measure the length of the screws to make sure they won't bore all the way through the lid. If the screws that came with the hinges are too long, grind them down or buy shorter screws.

5. Drill pilot holes in the lid and install the hinges. When you close the lid, see if it's properly aligned all around the box. If not, you'll either have to sand the sides and lid flush or reposition the lid by filling one or more screw holes and drilling new pilot holes.

MORTISING HINGES INTO THE BACK

There will be times when you make a box whose interior is so beautiful that you don't want to detract from it by showing the hinges inside. An option is to mount the hinges in the back, so only the barrel will show inside. But to preserve the box's "fine" status, you can use precision hinges and mortise their thick leaves into the back (see the photo at right above). Here's how:

1. Tape and/or clamp the lid to the carcase. Lay the hinges in position and score around their edges with a knife.

2. Mount a straight bit in your router and set the bit's depth to the thickness of the hinge leaf (which equals half the barrel's diameter).

3. If the box is short, you'll need to clamp it between some ¾-in.-thick boards to give the router a larger bearing surface. Make sure the boards' edges are flush with the back of the box.

4. Mount the workpiece in a vise and rout out the mortises freehand, stopping short of the scored lines.

Common and Precision Hinges

There are two different kinds of butt hinges that can be installed between the lid and carcase: common hinges and "precision" hinges (see the photo below).

Common butt hinges have thin leaves. Specifically, the combined thickness of the two leaves is less than the diameter of the barrel. They're fairly inexpensive and are available in brass, stainless steel, zinc-plated steel (not as rust-resistant as stainless), and "antique" finishes. You can buy common butt hinges at hardware stores, from hobby and craft suppliers, and through woodworking catalogs.

Precision hinges have thicker leaves, typically ³⁄₃₂ in. to ³⁄₁₆ in. thick. Their combined thickness equals the barrel's diameter exactly. They're several times more expensive than common hinges, but they are also very durable and elegant. Precision butt hinges are available in solid brass through many woodworking catalogs and specialty woodworking stores.

One advantage of precision hinges is that their thick leaves completely hide the shoulders of the mortises, so that the leaves are flush with the box's top edges. With common hinges, a small part of the mortise shoulders shows because of the thin leaves.

Common butt hinges (left) have thin leaves, while "precision" butt hinges (right) have thick leaves

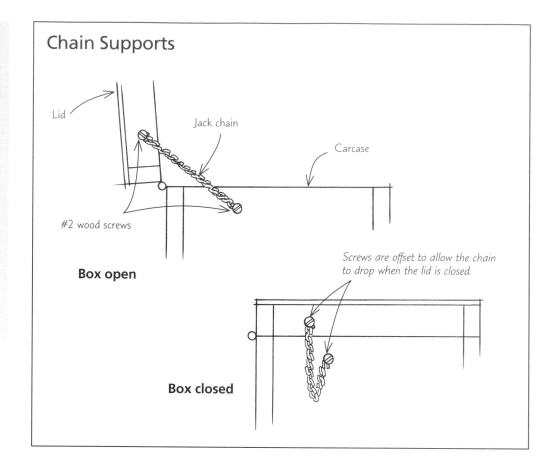

Chain Supports

Lid

Jack chain

Carcase

#2 wood screws

Box open

Screws are offset to allow the chain to drop when the lid is closed.

Box closed

5. Square up the mortises with a chisel.

6. Before you unclamp the lid from the carcase, mark the screw locations and drill pilot holes. Install the hinges and test the fit. You may need to tweak the mortises a bit with a chisel to achieve a good fit.

7. Remove the hinges, finish the box, and replace the hinges.

Supporting the Lid

In this book I've shown you a few different methods of hinging a lid. The problem with hinged lids is that some of them need help supporting the lid while it's open—this is especially true with large boxes. In the next few pages, I'll show you some different ways to support a lid.

Certain kinds of hinges allow the lid to open just past a vertical position, typically 100° to 105°, and no farther. Slot hinges and some (expensive) butt hinges support lids in that nearly vertical position. Many kinds of hinges, however, don't stop the lid from falling all the way open (past 180°), including pin hinges and most cheap butt hinges. Normally you don't want the lid to fall all the way open because it may damage the lid.

When you install hinges that do not support the lid in a near-vertical position, you're expecting the user to hold the lid open with one hand—unless you also install some mechanism that supports the lid. Generally, there are three kinds of manufactured lid-support mechanisms that work independently of the hinges: chain supports, surface-mounted pivoting supports, and mortised lid supports.

CHAIN SUPPORTS

One of the simplest ways to support a lid is with chain (see the drawing above). You can buy brass-plated chain at some hardware stores for less than $1 per foot—look for #16, #18, or #19 "jack chain," which you can mount with small (#3 or smaller) wood screws. (If you need help finding polished brass jack chain, see the sidebar above.) Installing chain supports is easy. Here's how:

1. Lay out the locations of the screws and drill pilot holes into the carcase and lid. You can do this before or after assembly. There's no magic formula for locating the screws, but remember that the farther away from the back of the box you put them, the longer the chain will need to be. Make sure the two holes are not in a vertical line when the lid is closed—offset them

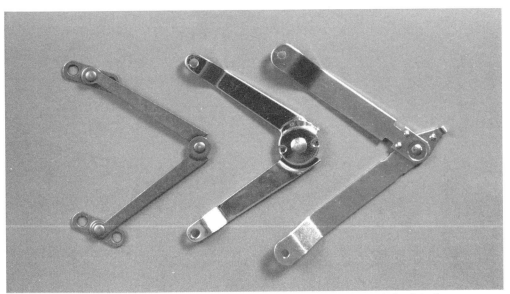

These supports mount on the vertical surfaces of the carcase side and the lid of a carcase-and-panel box.

so that there will be space for the chain to drop down between the screws into the box when the lid is closed.

2. Cut the chain a little long to begin with.

3. Screw one end of the chain into the lid. Leave the screw just loose enough so that the link can swivel.

4. Hold the lid open just past the vertical position, pull the chain taut so that it intersects the layout mark in the carcase, and note which link is closest to the mark. Then screw that link to the carcase.

5. Trim off the excess chain.

SURFACE-MOUNTED PIVOTING SUPPORTS

Surface-mounted pivoting supports offer a more elegant alternative to the simple chain support. Though I don't use them much, I know many box makers who do. Surface-mounted pivoting hinges can be divided into two categories—vertical mounting and horizontal mounting. The type you choose will depend on how your box and lid are constructed.

With the vertical-mounting support, the lower arm mounts on the carcase, and the upper arm mounts on the lid—both are vertical surfaces. This type of support is made for carcase-and-panel boxes (see the top photo above).

The horizontal-mounting support is for solid one-piece lids or frame-and-panel lids, where the lid is constructed separate from the carcase. The upper support arm is mounted on the horizontal lid surface, and the lower

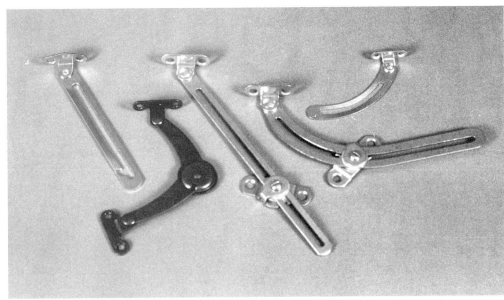

The upper arm of these supports mounts on a horizontal lid surface, while the lower arm mounts on a vertical side.

support arm is mounted on the vertical side surface (see the bottom photo above).

You can find a variety of surface-mounted pivoting supports in woodworking catalogs. Prices vary considerably, ranging from around 70 cents for light-duty supports to more than $15 for heavy-duty ones. Some supports control the lid's rate of descent so that it doesn't slam shut.

Surface-mounted pivoting supports will be fine for most boxes. However, you may want the lid supports to be finely crafted as well. Mortised lid supports are elegant, but

This lid is held open by a mortised lid support.

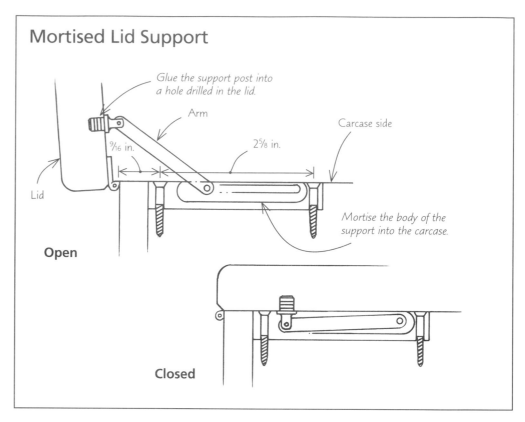

Mortised Lid Support

Glue the support post into a hole drilled in the lid.

Arm

⁹⁄₁₆ in.

2⁵⁄₈ in.

Carcase side

Lid

Open

Mortise the body of the support into the carcase.

Closed

their installation is a lot trickier than surface-mounted supports.

MORTISED LID SUPPORTS

If you're making elegant, high-end boxes, consider using mortised lid supports (see the photo above). These types of supports take up no interior space and thus are perfect for boxes with trays.

The body of the lid support fits into a mortise cut in the side of the box and is screwed in place (see the drawing above). The arm, or "hanger," reaches up to the lid, and it has a post at the end, which is glued into a hole drilled in the underside of the lid. As you close the lid, the arm slides down into a slot in the body.

These deluxe brass supports are available in two sizes—small and large—but the small support should be more than sufficient to hold a lid for any of the boxes in this chapter. The small support is ¼ in. wide, 2⅞ in. long, and ½ in. deep. To use this type of support, the box carcase must be at least ½ in. thick, and the lid should be at least ⁷⁄₁₆ in. thick where the post is glued.

As far as I know, there's only one manufacturer of mortised lid supports: Brusso of Waterford, Michigan, which is known for its precision jewelry-box and cabinet hardware. You can purchase these supports for around $10 in woodworking mail-order catalogs.

In my opinion, the installation instructions that come with these lid supports are inadequate. Here's a more detailed explanation of how to install them:

1. Pick which side of the box you want the support installed in. Mark the locations of two ¼-in. holes in the carcase—one at each end of the mortise. Connect the two end points with a pencil line.

2. Drill a ¼-in.-diameter hole at each end point. Start the holes with a sharp awl to keep your drill bit on target and use a brad-point bit to minimize wandering.

3. Switch to a ³⁄₁₆-in. drill bit and rough out the area between the two end holes. Do not drill more than ½ in. deep.

4. Clean out the mortise on the router table with a ¼-in. straight or spiral router bit. Set the fence so that the bit is centered in the forward ¼-in. hole in the carcase, which you drilled earlier. (With the router unplugged, rotate the bit by hand to make sure it's centered.) Then clamp a stop to the fence where the back of the box hits the fence. Lift the carcase off the table and set it back down with the router bit inside the rear ¼-in. hole. Set the opposite stop.

5. Rout the mortise, taking a series of shallow passes (each no more than ³⁄₁₆ in. deep). Before the final pass, test-fit the lid-support body in the mortise to make sure you don't cut the final pass too deep. The body should end up flush with the box edge.

6. When the support fits perfectly in the mortise, drill pilot holes in the carcase for the two screws that secure the support to the carcase. Use a ⁵⁄₆₄-in.-diameter bit and drill 1 in. deep (½ in. deeper than the mortise). Simply aim your drill bit into the ¼-in. holes at each end of the mortise, and the indent left by the brad-point bit in step 2 will guide the bit.

7. Apply a finish to the carcase and the lid, and then install the hinges and insert the lid-support body into its mortise (no need to screw it in place yet), keeping the lid open.

8. Mark the location of the post hole in the lid's underside. If your lid is perfectly flush with the carcase on all four sides, this is easy. Simply measure from the center of the post to the back and sides of the carcase. Transfer these measurements to the lid (see the top drawing at right).

However, if the lid overhangs the carcase on the sides and front, you'll need to use a different method to find the post hole's location. With the lid open, place a piece of masking tape on the carcase near the hanger's post, and mark on the tape the location of the post's center (see the bottom drawing at right).

Remove the lid-support body from the mortise and place a piece of masking tape on the lid's edge near the location of the post hole. Close the lid and transfer the mark to the lid. Then open the lid and use a square to extend the mark in from the edge of the lid. Reinsert the support body in its mortise (this time you can screw it in place), lean the post against the lid, and mark the location of the post hole.

9. With the post hole marked, unscrew the lid from the hinges. Drill a ¼-in. hole ¼ in. deep in the lid for the post. Use a Forstner bit to make a flat bottom.

10. Screw the lid back on the hinges and dry-fit the post into its hole. Close the lid slowly and check to see if the arm slides smoothly into the slot in the body. If it does, you can glue the post into its hole with cyanoacrylate glue or epoxy.

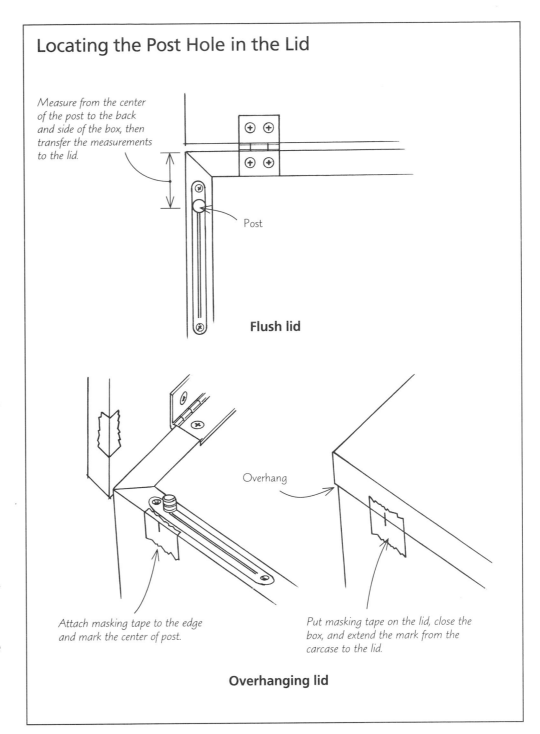

Locating the Post Hole in the Lid

Measure from the center of the post to the back and side of the box, then transfer the measurements to the lid.

Post

Flush lid

Overhang

Attach masking tape to the edge and mark the center of post.

Put masking tape on the lid, close the box, and extend the mark from the carcase to the lid.

Overhanging lid

If the arm doesn't slide down smoothly, you can fix the problem in one of two ways. If the fit is very close, simply file a larger slot or recess in the support body. Use a very fine file made for soft metals. If your post hole is way off, plug it with a ¼-in. dowel (of the same species as your lid frame), measure its location again, and drill a new hole. After you glue in the post, dab some finish on the exposed plug.

Projects

SUNBURST JEWELRY BOX

The most prominent part of the box shown here is its sunburst lid panel, made of 10 individual "rays." The rays are trapezoid-shaped pieces of maple edge-glued together into a fan shape and then trimmed to size. The lid opens on full-width butt hinges mortised into the lid and carcase.

The inside of the box features an integral tray support, in which rabbets cut into the carcase sides act as a ledge. The maple dividers on the bottom are removable (see the photos on the facing page).

Preparing the Parts

You can choose a wood that contrasts with the carcase or the lid frame to highlight the sunburst panel as I did, or you can select complementary woods (e.g., cherry or mahogany on walnut) for subtlety. I used keys

of walnut rather than a contrasting wood so that they wouldn't compete for attention with the maple sunburst panel.

For this project, you can use the dimensions given in the drawings on pp. 112-113 and in the instructions, or you can adapt the dimensions and materials to suit your needs. A cutlist is included with the drawing.

The box carcase is mitered with an integral lid and reinforced with keys. The techniques for making such a box are explained on pp. 28-30 and 46-48 (trays and their supports, as well as dividers, are covered on pp. 86-87).

The trapezoidal rays of this maple sunburst lid (on a walnut carcase) were chamfered to emphasize the diverging lines.

The tray is supported on a ³⁄₁₆-in.-wide ledge cut into the carcase sides before assembly. Notice that the butt hinges are mortised into the lid and carcase.

The interior is lined with suedecloth, and the dividers are removable.

Sunburst Jewelry Box

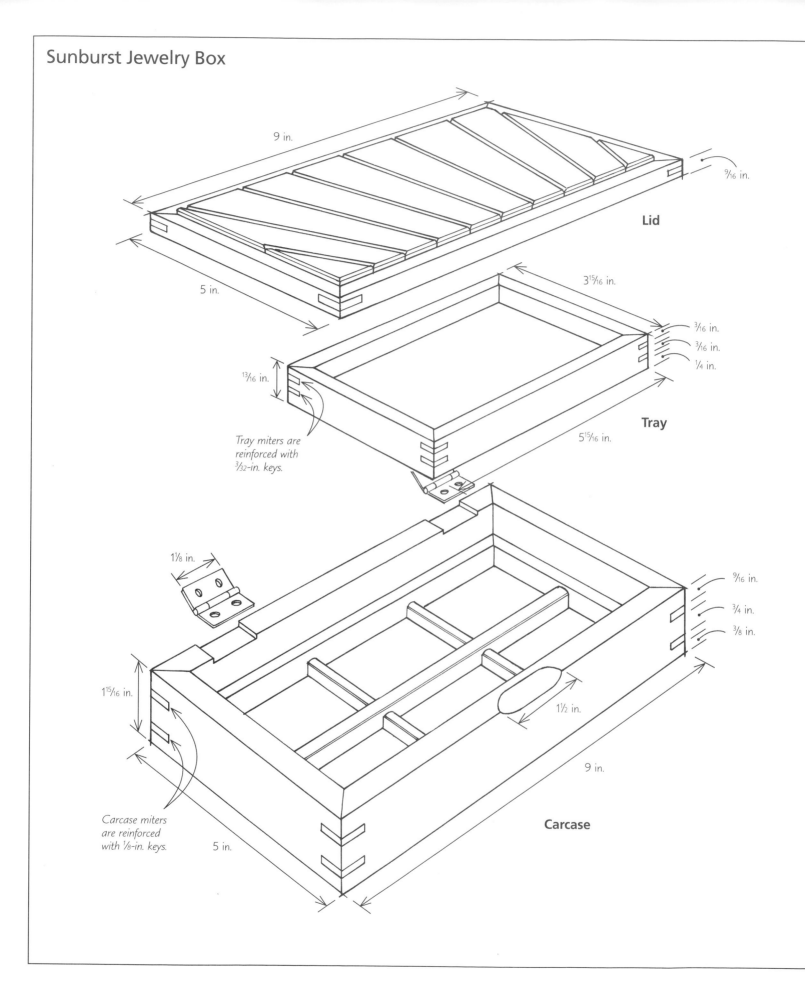

9 in.

5 in.

9⁄16 in.

Lid

3¹⁵⁄₁₆ in.

³⁄₁₆ in.

³⁄₁₆ in.

¼ in.

¹³⁄₁₆ in.

Tray miters are reinforced with ³⁄₃₂-in. keys.

5¹⁵⁄₁₆ in.

Tray

1⅛ in.

9⁄16 in.

¾ in.

⅜ in.

1¹⁵⁄₁₆ in.

1½ in.

Carcase miters are reinforced with ⅛-in. keys.

5 in.

9 in.

Carcase

CUTLIST

Description	Quantity	Dimensions
Front/back	2	⅝ x 2⅝ x 9
Sides	2	⅝ x 2⅝ x 5
Bottom panel	1	⅛ x 4¼ x 8¼
Sunburst rays	10	½ x 1⅞ x 6½
Short dividers	2	⅛ x ⅜ x 3¹¹⁄₁₆
Long divider	1	¼ x ½ x 7¹¹⁄₁₆
Tray		
Front/back	2	⅜ x ¹³⁄₁₆ x 5¹⁵⁄₁₆
Sides	2	⅜ x ¹³⁄₁₆ x 3¹⁵⁄₁₆
Bottom panel	1	⅛ x 3½ x 5½

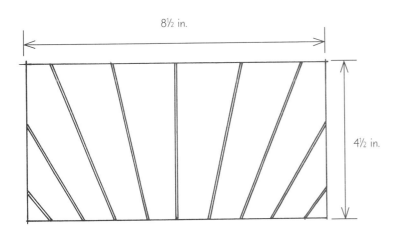

Lid panel

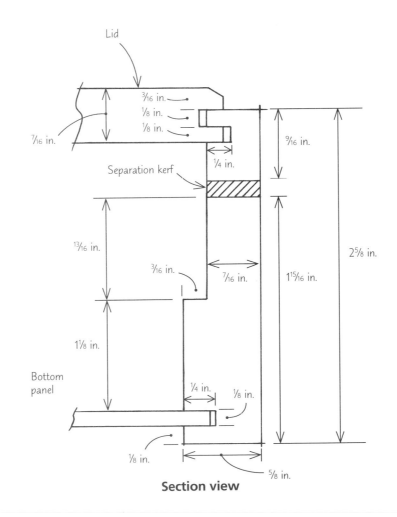

Section view

Sunburst Tapering Jig

The sliding carriage jig shown in the drawing below lets me cut the sunburst blanks for the lid panel quickly and accurately. It is built like a miniature sliding crosscut table, except that the runner (which fits in the table-saw's miter slot) is attached at an angle to the centerline of the jig. For this project, the angle should be 6°.

The base is ¾-in. plywood—it must be perfectly flat for the jig to work—with a pair of front and back support rails attached with wood screws (two on each side of the kerf). Each support rail is ⅞-in.-thick hardwood, although you could use ¾-in.-thick stock. The runner underneath is screwed to the base with four flat-head screws. The kerf for the sawblade should be parallel to the runner, not parallel to the edge of the base.

What makes the jig unique and versatile is the adjustable fence, which is to the right of the kerf, parallel to the

edge of the base. The fence is made of ¾-in. plywood and has two ⅜-in.-wide slots in it. The slots align with two threaded inserts installed in the base. A pair of ⁵⁄₁₆-in. machine screws and washers keep the fence in place and can be loosened to allow the fence to be adjusted left and right. The advantage of having an adjustable fence is that you can vary the width of the tapered rays while keeping the taper angle the same, so you can make rays of different widths but of the same angle.

At the lower end of the fence is an adjustable stop that registers the workpiece for the second taper cut. I made the stop from a piece of hardwood scrap. It has a ¼-in.-wide slot routed into it lengthwise, which corresponds to a threaded insert installed in the fence. The stop can be adjusted left and right by means of a ¼-in. machine screw and washer. The left corner of the stop has a 2-in. length of ³⁄₁₆-in. brass rod, which serves as a fence. When it's not in use, I store the brass rod in a hole in the front support rail.

Using the jig is simple. Here's how:
1. Draw each tapered piece to scale on paper, and then measure the dimensions.
2. Adjust the fence for the width of the wider end of the workpiece (the end that meets the sawblade first).
3. Make the first taper cut, holding the workpiece in place with a push stick to keep your hands clear of the blade.
4. Flip the workpiece over for the second cut. Place the brass rod in the stop and adjust the stop to the left, so that the distance from the rod to the kerf is equal to the trapezoid's narrower end. Do not readjust the fence!
5. Place the workpiece against the fence at the wide end and against the rod at the narrow end, and cut the second taper.

Adjustable Tapering Jig

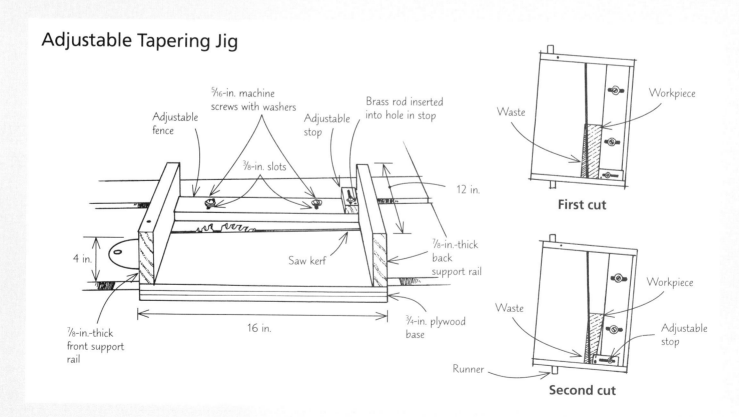

First cut

Second cut

SUNBURST LID PANEL

1. Cut 10 ray blanks. Each blank should be ½ in. thick and at least 1⅞ in. wide and 6½ in. long. Cut a double taper on these blanks to create trapezoids. You can use a commercial tapering jig or, if you're making several of these sunburst lid panels, consider making the custom jig shown in the sidebar on the facing page.

2. On the table saw, cut the first taper at 6° on all 10 blanks.

3. Adjust the taper jig for a 12° taper to make the second cut on the blanks. One end of each blank will be 1¾ in. wide, and the other end will be ⁷⁄₁₆ in. wide (see the drawing at right).

4. Rout a small chamfer (about ³⁄₃₂ in. wide) on the top tapered edges of each blank. (Or for a subtler look, round over the ray edges.) Now you're ready for glue-up.

5. Start by gluing two rays together. When you glue the rays edge to edge, you won't be able to clamp them together. So use masking tape and rubber bands.

First apply glue to each edge, taking care not to get glue on the chamfered surfaces. Let the glue sit for a minute before you put the pieces together, so the glue will get tacky and prevent the pieces from slipping too much. If you get some glue squeeze-out in the chamfered areas, wait until it's rubbery before removing it.

Place waxed paper on a flat surface (such as your table-saw top) and lay the two pieces on the paper. Stretch several pieces of masking tape across the joint line, as shown in the glue up drawing at right. Then flip the pair over, tape the other side, and wrap the pair with rubber bands. Glue up five pairs of rays.

6. After a few hours, remove the rubber bands and the tape, and glue up all the pairs into one assembly (see the bottom drawing at right). You won't be able to use rubber bands for this, but the stretched masking tape should hold the joints well enough.

7. After the glue has dried, cut the fan-shaped sunburst lid panel into an oversized rectangle. The easiest way to square up the sunburst panel is to make a simple squaring-up jig out of a piece of ½-in. plywood (see the drawing on p. 116). Place the panel on the jig so that the sunburst's centerline is perpendicular to the jig's longer edges. Tack or screw two cleats to the jig so that they touch the sunburst panel's two straight edges. Add a third cleat ¼ in. from the top of the sunburst panel's large-

Cutting and Assembling the Sunburst Rays

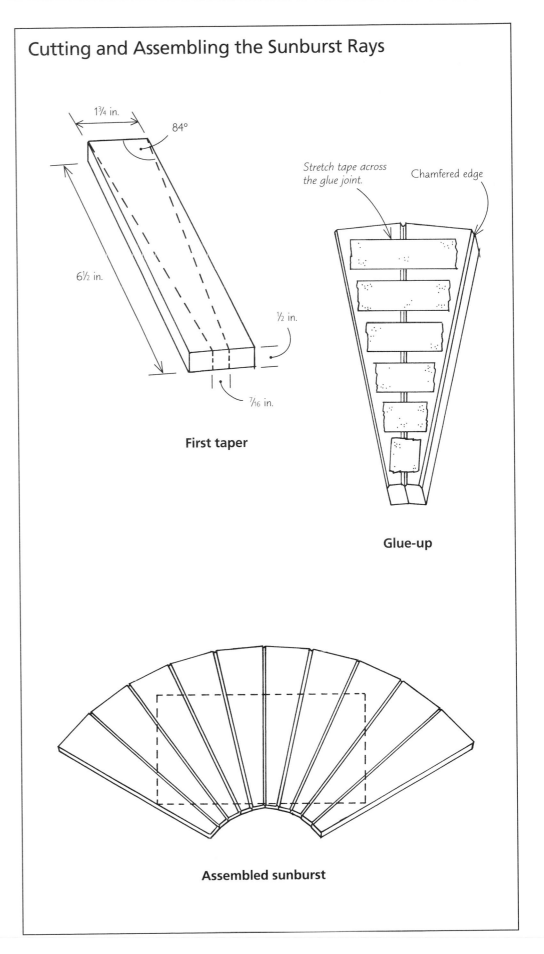

1¾ in.

84°

6½ in.

½ in.

⁷⁄₁₆ in.

First taper

Stretch tape across the glue joint.

Chamfered edge

Glue-up

Assembled sunburst

Jig for Squaring Up Sunburst Blank

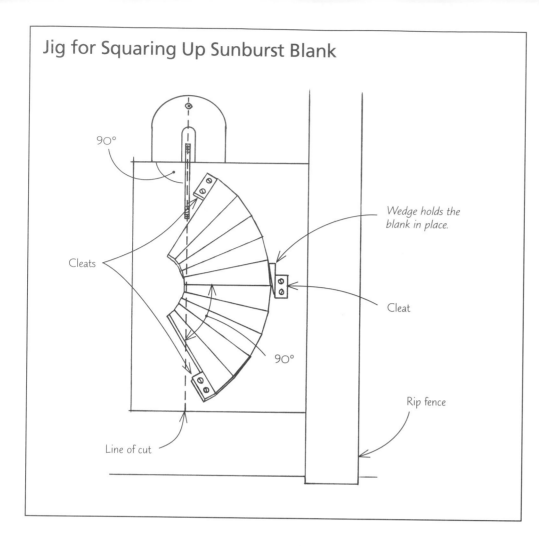

90°

Cleats

Wedge holds the blank in place.

Cleat

90°

Rip fence

Line of cut

CARCASE

1. Rip ⅝-in.-thick stock to a width of 2⅝ in. for the carcase, but don't crosscut it to length yet.

2. Cut a groove for the bottom panel (see pp. 24-25).

3. Cut the rabbet to form the tray ledge (see p. 87).

4. Cut the mating grooves in the lid panel and the carcase stock (see pp. 42-43).

5. Miter-cut the carcase front, back, and sides to length.

6. Prepare and sand the bottom panel, finishing with 180-grit paper.

7. Final-sand the sunburst lid panel by hand with 180-grit paper. Sand the chamfers first, then the edges, and finally the faces. Use a narrow sanding block and sand with the grain, shifting your direction as the grain fans out.

8. Sand the insides and top edges of the four carcase pieces, finishing with 180-grit paper.

9. Apply a coat of finish to the lid panel (except where you'll spot-glue the panel into the carcase) and to the top edges of the carcase pieces. Avoid getting finish on the miter-joint surfaces.

Assembling the Box

1. Now you can assemble the box, as explained on pp. 46-48. Let the glue dry overnight.

2. Cut key slots and install keys (for more on installing keys, see pp. 28-30).

3. When the glue is dry, trim the keys, then sand them flush with 180-grit paper; ease the corners, too.

4. Separate the lid from the carcase (see p. 48) and sand the newly exposed edges with 180-grit paper.

5. Rout the finger relief (see pp. 63-64), using a ⅜-in. cove bit. Set stops on your router-table fence 4¹³⁄₁₆ in. from the fence's centerline to locate the finger relief precisely.

6. Cut the hinge mortises and install the hinges. Check to see if the lid and the carcase close tightly and flush on four sides. If not, adjust the hinges and/or belt-sand the sides flush. Then remove the hinges.

7. Make the dividers and the tray (see p. 87). Measure the inside of the box to get your final dimensions or check the cutlist on p. 113.

8. Finish the box. I applied two coats of Danish oil. When the finish cured, I added a coat of beeswax polish on the outside of the box, and reinstalled the hinges.

9. Line the box and the tray with suedecloth (see pp. 85-86).

radius edge. Lightly tap a wedge between the top cleat and the panel to keep it from moving. Butt the jig's edge against the rip fence for the first cut.

After the first cut, remove the sunburst lid panel from the jig and square up the other edges using the table-saw rip fence and miter gauge. Leave the panel oversized for now.

8. While the panel is still oversized, sand both faces to 180 grit. Use a wide belt sander or a thickness sander, if you have access to one, because it's important to keep the panel flat and uniform in thickness. (I've taken lid panels to a cabinet shop to have them run through a wide belt sander for a modest charge.)

After all of this surfacing, you'll probably lose about ¹⁄₁₆ in. of thickness, so you'll wind up with a panel that's ⁷⁄₁₆ in. thick.

9. Trim the panel to final length and width, and rout a ⅛-in. chamfer around the top edge. Set the sunburst lid panel aside while you prepare the carcase stock.

The profiling on the carcase sets this box apart from other, simpler integral-lid boxes. The box also features banded inlay and ball feet. (Photo by Sally Ann Photography.)

This unusual box was designed and built by Mike Jagielo of Almond, Wisconsin (who also designed the box on p. 126). What makes this integral-lid box unique—aside from the prominent ball feet—are the details, such as the banded inlay in the carcase and the slight profiling around the carcase edges (see the photo above). The box also features part-width hinges mortised between the lid and carcase, and the lid is supported by polished brass chain (see the photo at right).

Preparing the Parts

The box shown here has a curly maple carcase with a bubinga lid panel, but feel free to use whatever woods you think will work together. The box carcase is mitered with an integral lid. (The techniques for assembling such a box are covered on pp. 46-48.) Mike did not reinforce the box with keys; instead, he strengthened the joinery by gluing a plywood bottom panel into grooves in the carcase.

For this project, you can use the dimensions given in the drawings on pp. 118-119 and in the instructions, or you can adapt the dimensions and materials to suit your needs. A cutlist is included with the drawings.

CARCASE

1. Cut ½-in.-thick stock for the carcase 3 in. wide and about 30 in. long. Do not cut the carcase pieces to length yet.

2. Rout a groove on the outside face of the carcase stock for the wood inlay banding. Banding is available through woodworking catalogs and specialty stores in a variety of patterns and widths.

The banding shown here is ½ in. wide and about ⅟₁₆ in. thick, so the groove for it will need to be the same width and slightly less than ⅟₁₆ in. deep. The banding should be located just below where the lid will be separated from the carcase (the top edge of the banding is exposed when the lid is open). It's a good idea to rout the groove on a scrap piece first to make sure the banding fits.

3. After you rout the groove, glue the banding in place. Place a 30-in.-long, ½-in.-thick strip of scrap over the banding, then clamp it in place. The strip will protect the banding and spread the clamping pressure evenly. When the glue dries, sand the banding flush with the carcase stock.

The lid opens on part-width hinges mortised into the back and is supported by polished brass chain. (Photo by Sally Ann Photography.)

Box with Ball Feet

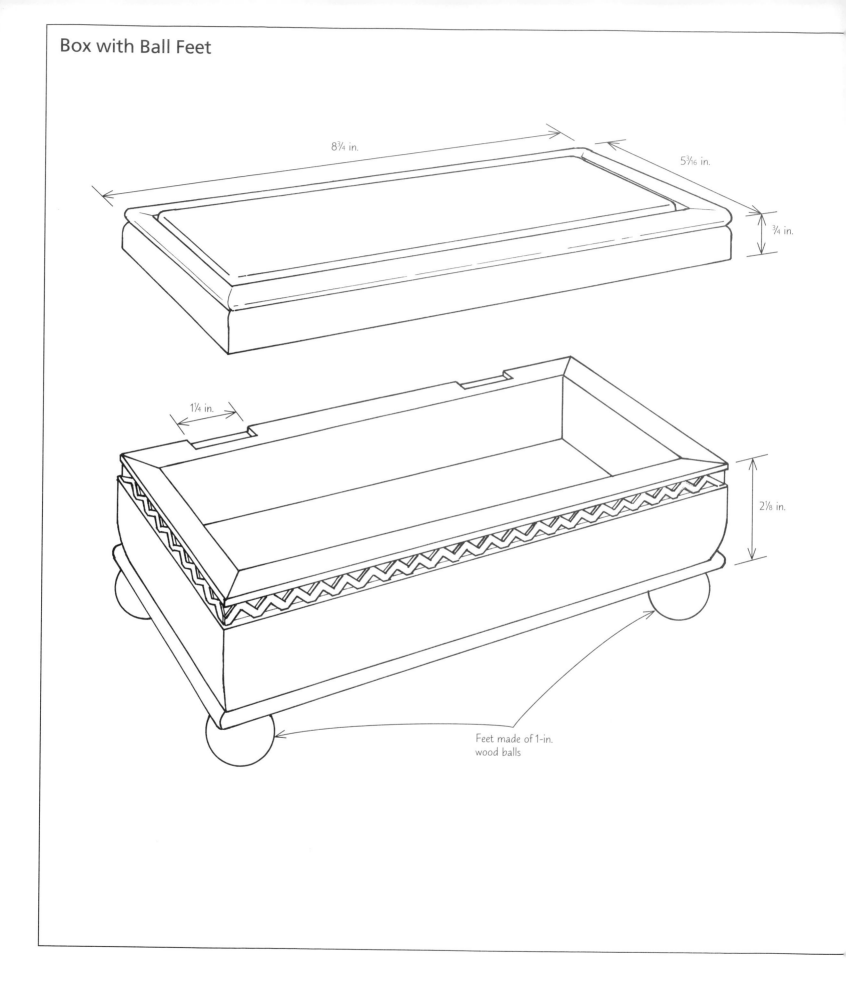

8¾ in.

5³⁄₁₆ in.

¾ in.

1¼ in.

2⅛ in.

Feet made of 1-in. wood balls

Ease edges and corners before assembly.

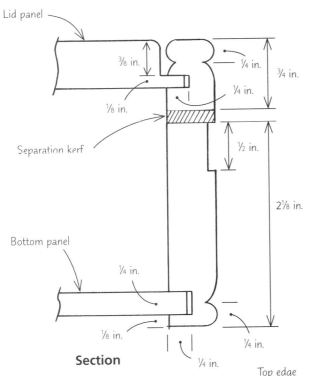

Lid panel

3/8 in.

1/4 in.

3/4 in.

1/4 in.

1/8 in.

Separation kerf

1/2 in.

2 1/8 in.

Bottom panel

1/4 in.

1/8 in.

1/4 in.

1/4 in.

Section

CUTLIST

Description	Quantity	Dimensions
Front/back	2	1/2 x 3 x 8 3/4
Sides	2	1/2 x 3 x 5 3/16
Bottom panel	1	1/4 x 4 9/16 x 8 1/8
Lid panel	1	1/2 x 4 9/16 x 8 1/8
Inlay banding	1	1/16 x 1/2 x 36
Feet	4	1 in. round

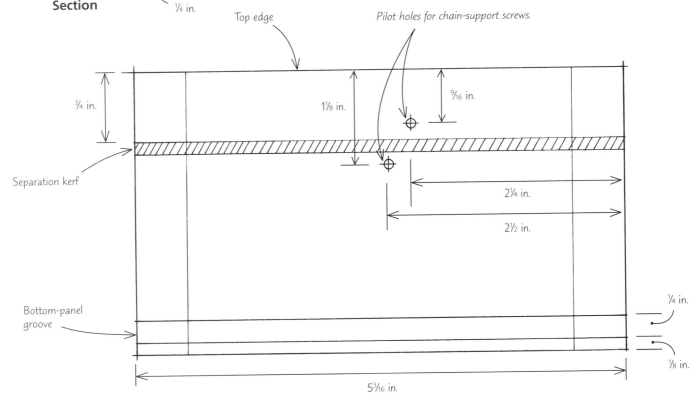

Top edge

Pilot holes for chain-support screws.

3/4 in.

1 1/8 in.

9/16 in.

Separation kerf

2 1/4 in.

2 1/2 in.

Bottom-panel groove

1/4 in.

1/8 in.

5 3/16 in.

Inside face of box side

Routing the Profile

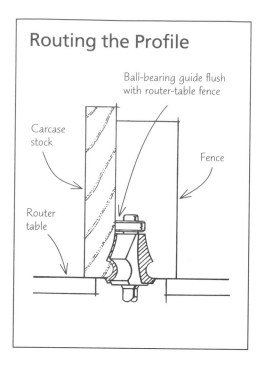

Ball-bearing guide flush with router-table fence

Carcase stock

Fence

Router table

4. Rout the profiles on the carcase stock. To do this, Mike used a special carbide-tipped router bit, with two flutes, and a ball-bearing guide. The bit is commonly used for moldings and picture frames and is available from MLCS, Ltd., P.O. Box 4053, Rydal, PA 19046; 800-533-9298. Order item #526 (¼-in. shank) or #826 (½-in. shank).

Set the fence of your router table flush with the ball-bearing guide on the bit, as shown in the drawing at left. Rout profiles on the upper and lower parts of the outside face and on the upper part of the inside face.

5. Cut grooves for the lid panel and the bottom panel. The groove for the lid panel should be ⅛ in. wide and ¼ in. deep. The groove for the bottom panel should be ¼ in. wide and up to ¼ in. deep.

6. Miter-cut the carcase pieces to length.

7. Drill pilot holes in one side piece for the screws that will anchor the brass jack chain to support the lid. The pilot-hole locations are shown in the bottom drawing on p. 119. For a #6, ⅝-in. flat-head, brass wood screw, drill the pilot holes ⁷⁄₁₆ in. deep. After drilling the pilot holes, put the carcase pieces aside and make the lid panel and the bottom panel.

LID AND BOTTOM PANELS

1. Cut the ½-in. thick lid panel to size (4⁹⁄₁₆ in. by 8⅛ in.). The lid panel of the box shown is made of one solid piece of bubinga, but if you prefer, you can glue up a lid panel (for more on making lid panels, see pp. 40-46).

2. Rabbet the edges of the lid panel to form a ⅛-in.-thick tongue. Check the fit of the tongue in the grooves cut in the carcase. The raised field in the middle of the panel should measure about 4 in. by 7⁹⁄₁₆ in.

3. Cut the ¼-in.-thick bottom panel to size (4⁹⁄₁₆ in. by 8⅛ in.).

4. Sand the lid panel, the bottom panel, and the inside faces of the carcase pieces, finishing with 180-grit paper. Then apply a preliminary finish to the lid panel. Don't finish the areas where you will be gluing the panel into its frame; the finish will prevent the glue from adhering well.

5. Assemble the box, following the instructions on pp. 46-48. The lid panel is spot-glued into the frame. The bottom panel, however, is glued all the way around, which reinforces the miter joints.

6. Allow the glue to dry, then separate the lid from the carcase on the bandsaw (for more on this procedure, see p. 48). For this box, the cut will be made just above the top edge of the banding. Leave a bit extra so that you can sand the carcase edge to remove the saw marks. After sanding, the banding edge should be exposed.

HINGES

1. After separating the lid from the carcase and sanding the edges smooth, cut the hinge mortises. This box uses part-width hinges, whose leaves are narrower than the thickness of the carcase. That means the mortises will be cut partway into the carcase, not all the way across (for more on installing part-width hinges, see pp. 101-102).

2. After cutting the mortises, test-fit the hinges. When you're satisfied with the fit, remove the hinges.

3. Sand all surfaces with 220-grit paper.

BALL FEET

The ball feet for this box are made from 1-in. maple balls, which you can buy at any craft or hobby shop. Here's how to make them into feet:

1. Sand a ½-in.-diameter flat surface on each ball. The easiest way to do this is to touch each ball to a stationary belt sander, checking the diameter frequently.

2. Turn the box upside down and glue the flat surfaces of the balls to the underside of the bottom panel in the four corners. Each ball should touch two edges of the carcase near a miter joint. Mike just twists the balls to spread the glue—he doesn't use clamps.

After the glue dries, if the box rocks on a flat surface, lightly sand the bottoms of the balls with a fine-grit sandpaper until the box no longer rocks. The bottoms of the balls will be covered later with felt disks.

FINISHING TOUCHES

1. Now you can finish the box. Mike applied three coats of Danish oil to the box shown on p. 117, plus a coat of paste wax.

2. After the finish dries, install the hinges permanently.

3. Now install the chain to support the lid (for more on installing chain supports, see pp. 106-107). For this box, Mike used 14-gauge polished brass jack chain.

4. Finally, apply ¼-in.-diameter felt disks to the feet.

I got the idea for the box shown here from a popular woodworking magazine. The first time I built the box, I followed the plan closely. Since then I've gradually modified the design by changing its overall proportions and the way it's constructed. Now the design has evolved so much from the original that I consider it my own.

Preparing the Parts

I call this box "classic" because of its understated combination of wood, the lid joinery, the footed base, and the finely crafted interior (see the photo below). The lid has a cherry panel with a walnut frame and is assembled with bridle joints. The base is made of walnut, and the interior has both cherry and walnut dividers. The cherry carcase and the tray are assembled with miter joints and reinforced with laminated keys.

You can use the same materials and dimensions given here (see the drawings on pp. 122-123), or you can adapt them, as I had done originally. A cutlist is included with the drawing.

CARCASE

1. Dimension the front, back, and side pieces to width and final thickness. Then miter-cut them to final length (see the cutlist on p. 123).

2. Cut mortises in the back piece for the hinges. This can be done on the table saw with a combination blade or a dado blade. The hinges used here are 1¼ in. long, with ½-in.-wide leaves.

3. Rout the 1½-in.-long finger relief in the front piece using a ⅜-in. cove bit (for more on routing a finger relief, see p. 63-64).

4. Now you can glue up the carcase. Since you don't have a bottom panel in the carcase to help align the assembly (the bottom panel is part of the base), you'll need to be careful to ensure that the box remains square. Use rubber bands to clamp the carcase.

5. After the glue dries, cut slots in the carcase and install ⅛-in.-thick keys. I laminated keys from walnut strips and maple veneer. The keys for this box are stepped: The top one is larger than the bottom one. (For more on installing keys, see pp. 28-30.)

6. Sand the carcase, finishing with 180-grit paper.

7. Next, place the carcase on a piece of ¹⁄₁₆-in.-thick cardboard (such as poster board) and

This classic jewelry box features complementary woods, laminated keys, and a footed base.

The interior has a removable tray supported by cherry dividers. (Photos by Skot Weidemann.)

Classic Jewelry Box

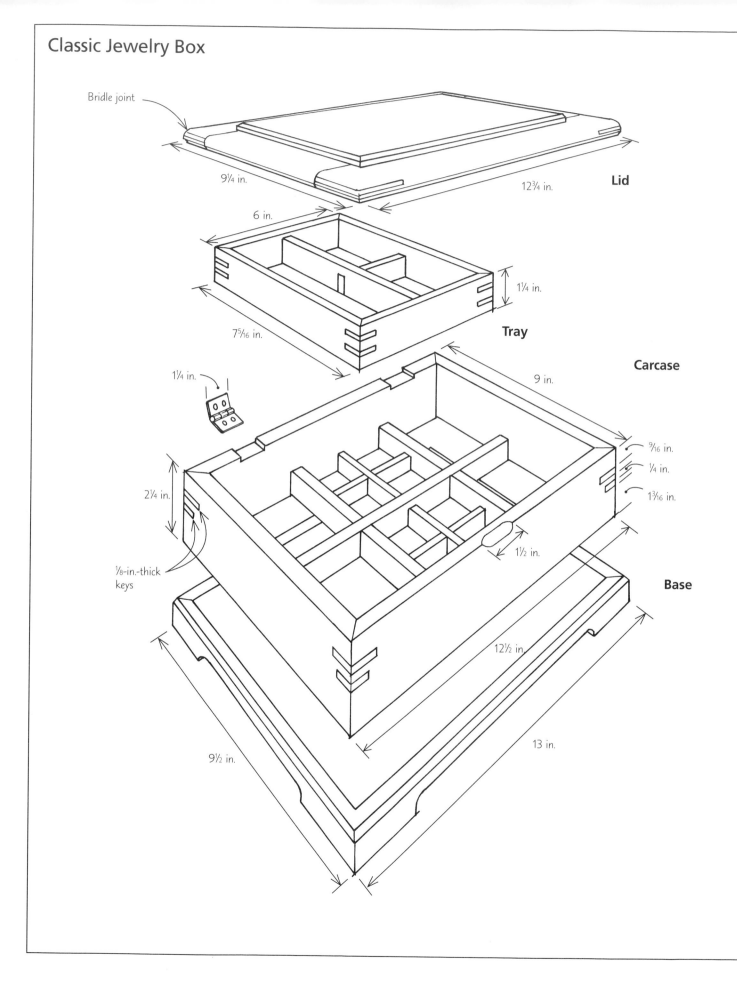

Bridle joint

9¼ in.

12¾ in.

Lid

6 in.

1¼ in.

7⁵⁄₁₆ in.

Tray

Carcase

9 in.

1¼ in.

⁹⁄₁₆ in.

¼ in.

1³⁄₁₆ in.

2¼ in.

1½ in.

⅛-in.-thick keys

Base

12½ in.

9½ in.

13 in.

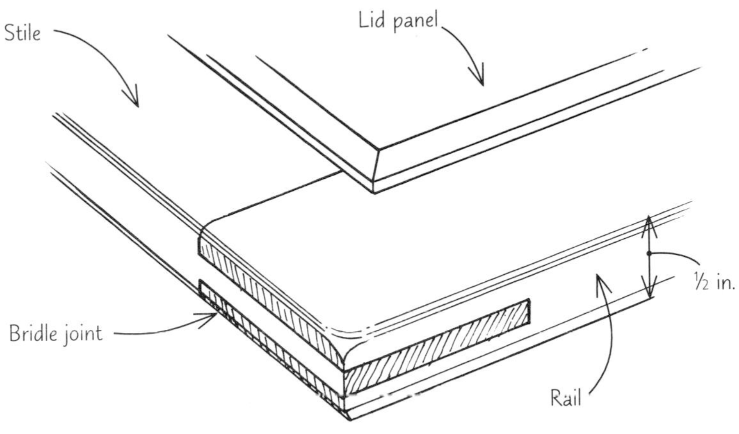
Stile
Lid panel
1/2 in.
Bridle joint
Rail

Bridle-joint detail

CUTLIST

Description	Quantity	Dimensions
Carcase		
Front/back	2	1/2 x 2 1/4 x 12 1/2
Sides	2	1/2 x 2 1/4 x 9
Divider	1	3/8 x 1 x 11 1/2
Divider	2	3/8 x 1 x 8
Divider	1	1/4 x 3/4 x 8
Divider	2	1/4 x 3/4 x 2 3/8
Base		
Front/back	2	3/4 x 1 x 13
Sides	2	3/4 x 1 x 9 1/2
Panel	1	1/4 x 8 3/8 x 11 7/8
Lid		
Rails	2	1/2 x 1 1/4 x 12 13/16
Stiles	2	1/2 x 1 1/4 x 9 5/16
Panel	1	1/2 x 7 1/4 x 10 3/4
Tray		
Front/back	2	3/8 x 1 1/4 x 7 15/16
Sides	2	3/8 x 1 1/4 x 6
Panel	1	1/8 x 5 5/8 x 8 7/8
Divider	1	3/8 x 7/8 x 7 3/16
Divider	1	1/4 x 3/4 x 2 13/16

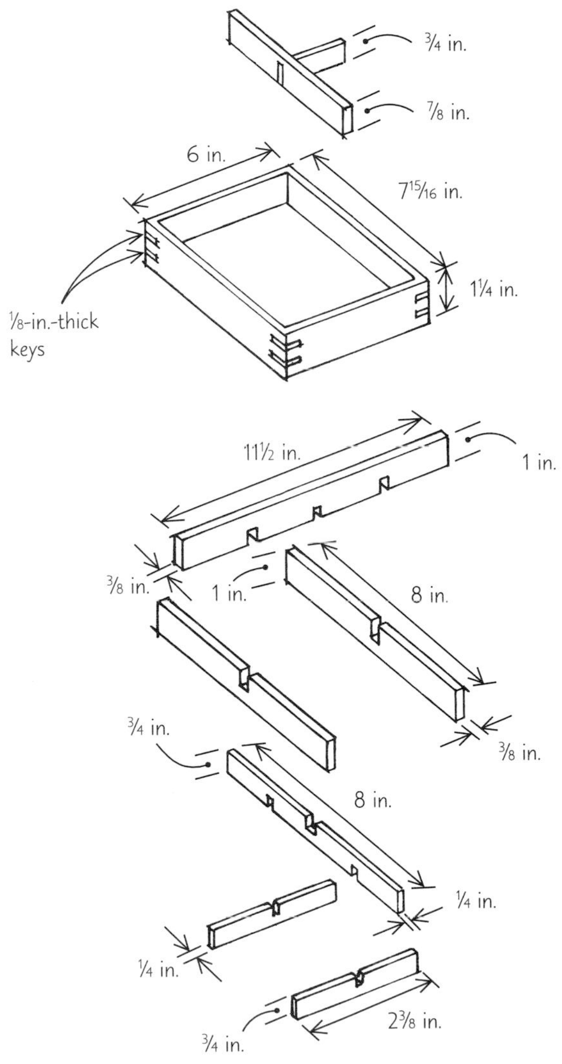
3/4 in.
7/8 in.
6 in.
7 15/16 in.
1 1/4 in.
1/8-in.-thick keys
11 1/2 in.
1 in.
3/8 in.
1 in.
8 in.
3/8 in.
3/4 in.
8 in.
1/4 in.
1/4 in.
3/4 in.
2 3/8 in.

Tray/divider detail

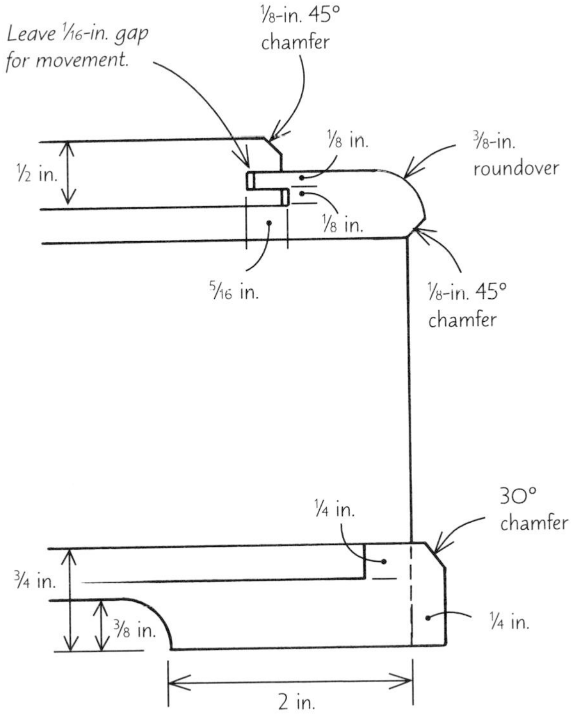
Leave 1/16-in. gap for movement.
1/8-in. 45° chamfer
1/2 in.
1/8 in.
3/8-in. roundover
1/8 in.
5/16 in.
1/8-in. 45° chamfer
1/4 in.
30° chamfer
3/4 in.
3/8 in.
1/4 in.
2 in.

Box profile

Shaping the Feet

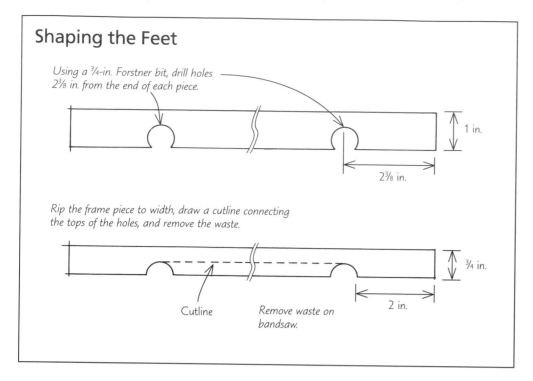

Using a ¾-in. Forstner bit, drill holes 2⅜ in. from the end of each piece.

1 in.

2⅜ in.

Rip the frame piece to width, draw a cutline connecting the tops of the holes, and remove the waste.

¾ in.

Cutline

Remove waste on bandsaw.

2 in.

trace its inside dimensions onto the cardboard. Cut along the line and set the cardboard aside for now. You'll be gluing the lining to this cardboard substrate later.

BASE

The frame of the base is assembled with miter joints, and the bottom panel sits flush in a rabbet cut into the top of the frame. The frame has "feet" cut into all four pieces. It is made of solid walnut, which provides a subtle contrast to the cherry carcase, and the panel is ¼-in. walnut plywood. Here's how to make the base:

1. Begin by cutting the frame stock to a width of 1 in.

2. Cut a ³⁄₁₆-in.-wide rabbet in the top of the frame stock for the bottom panel. The depth of the rabbet should equal the thickness of the bottom panel.

3. To create a subtle transition between the carcase and the base, cut 30° chamfers on the side of the stock opposite the rabbet.

4. Miter-cut the frame pieces to length. The front and back should be 13 in., and the sides should be 9½ in.

5. Now you can create the feet on each piece. The feet of this box are 2 in. long, with subtle curves on their inside edges to match the roundovers on the lid. To make each curve uniform, I drilled ¾-in. holes in the frame pieces and then cut out the waste between the holes, as shown in the drawing above. (If you prefer a straight, sharp transition to

the feet, you can make them using the method on pp. 73-74.) Once the frame pieces are ripped to their final ¾-in. width and the waste is cleared out between the holes, you're left with matching ⅜-in. curves on the feet.

The first step is to set up the drill press. Since all the feet are the same size, this setup will work for each frame piece. Chuck a ¾-in. Forstner bit in the drill press and set the drill-press fence exactly ¾-in. from the center of the bit. To prevent tearout, I clamp a backup board to the drill-press table.

6. Clamp a stop block to the fence 2⅜ in. from the center of the bit and drill the first hole.

7. Flip the piece end for end—keeping the top edge of the piece against the fence—and drill the second hole. Repeat the process for all frame pieces.

8. With the holes drilled, rip each frame member to a final width of ¾ in.

9. On each piece, draw a cutline connecting the tops of the two holes. Then cut out the waste between the holes, using a bandsaw, sabersaw, or coping saw. Keep the blade inside the waste area. Then trim to the cutline using a straight bit in your router. Set the frame pieces aside for now.

10. Cut a ¼-in. plywood bottom to fit the frame (mine measured 8⅜ in. by 11⅞ in.).

11. Dry-assemble the base to check the fit of all the parts.

12. Sand the base and the bottom panel, finishing with 180-grit paper.

13. Next, assemble the base. Glue the bottom panel into the rabbets and hold the assembly together with rubber bands. The panel will help keep the assembly square.

14. After the glue dries on the base, glue the carcase to it. Apply glue to the bottom edge of the carcase only. Clamp the carcase to the base, using clamping blocks to protect the edges of the base. I also placed a ¾-in. piece of plywood on top during the clamping process to prevent the carcase from racking.

LID

The lid of the box overhangs the carcase by ⅛ in. and is a frame-and-panel design assembled with bridle joints. Start by cutting the frame.

1. Cut each ½-in.-thick frame piece to length and width. If I were using miter joints, I would cut one long piece of stock and then cut the grooves in one pass. But with bridle joints, I need to cut stopped grooves in the rails of the frame, so all the pieces must be cut to length before the grooves can be cut.

To determine the lengths of the frame pieces, take the dimensions of the carcase pieces and add ¼ in. to them to allow for the overhang. Add another 1/16 in. to the length (that's an extra 1/32 in. at each end), which will allow you to trim the bridle joints flush after assembly. If your base is exactly 9½ in. by 13 in., the stiles should be 1¼ in. wide and 9⁵⁄₁₆ in. long. The rails should be 1¼ in. wide and 12¹³⁄₁₆ in. long.

2. Cut the bridle joints, as explained on pp. 82-84.

3. Dry-assemble the frame to test the fit and adjust, if necessary.

4. Now make the panel. Because I've chosen to use an overlay-panel design, I could not use plywood, as I did in the base. So I glued up ½-in. stock.

5. Cut the lid panel to its final dimensions: 7¼ in. by 10¾ in.

6. Rout a ⅛-in. 45° chamfer around the top edge of the panel.

7. Sand the panel and the frame pieces, finishing with 150-grit paper.

8. Now rout the interlocking double-groove joints (⁵⁄₁₆ in. deep and ⅛ in. wide) in both the frame and the panel. Because this lid is assembled with bridle joints, the rails require stopped grooves (otherwise, the grooves would show), which are best handled by the router.

Use a ⅛-in. straight bit in the router. Set the bit height at ⁵⁄₁₆ in., and set the fence exactly ⅛ in. from the bit. Make test cuts on a scrap piece and adjust the fence until the double-groove joints fit snug. When you're satisfied with the fit, rout the grooves on the stiles and the panel. Then rout the stopped grooves on the rails (for more on routing stopped grooves, see pp. 83-84).

9. After cutting the interlocking joints, test-fit the frame-and-panel assembly. You should be able to center the panel in the frame. If the fit is too tight, wrap some 100-grit or 120-grit sandpaper around a metal ruler and sand the mating grooves lightly.

10. Sand the entire panel and the top faces of the frame pieces, finishing with 180-grit paper. Then apply a light coat of finish, making sure not to put finish on the bridle joints or in the two areas where the panel will be spot-glued.

11. After the preliminary finish dries, assemble the lid. For this lid I used liquid hide glue to spot-glue the panel in place (yellow glue is used everywhere else). Hide glue affords me more time to center the lid after clamping and squaring up the assembly.

The interior is lined with suede. The dividers are cherry and walnut.

12. After the glue dries, trim the ends of the stiles and rails so the outside edges of the frame are flush. Round over the top outside edges of the frame with a ⅜-in. roundover bit in the router, then cut a ⅛-in. chamfer at the bottom outside edges of the frame.

FINISHING TOUCHES

1. Lay out and install the hinges (for more on installing hinges, see pp. 99-106). Then remove them.

2. Sand the box, finishing with 180-grit paper.

3. Apply the finish. I used three coats of Danish oil, followed by an application of paste wax on the outside.

4. Line the box, attaching the liner to the cardboard you cut earlier. Use whatever lining material you like—I chose suede. (For more on lining a box, see pp. 85-86.)

5. Cut and install the removable interior dividers (for more on making and installing dividers, see pp. 86-87). Then build (and line) the tray, which is a simple mitered carcase reinforced with ⅛-in.-thick laminated keys. The tray dividers are held in place with blind dowel pins in the tray sides (for more on making a tray, see p. 87).

6. Now reinstall the hinges and apply ½-in. felt disks to the bottom of the feet.

Stepped legs, inlaid zigzag fretwork, pine painted with translucent pastel colors, and dyed leather hinges and latch all combine to give this box a distinctive Southwestern flair (see the photo below). This is another box designed by Mike Jagielo.

The leather hinges operate essentially as surface-mounted butt hinges. The only trick is nailing the leather very close to the edges of the carcase and the lid, so that the lid doesn't flop away from the carcase when it's opened. An interesting construction feature is the way Mike created a seamless transition from carcase to lid: He beveled the lid panel and glued it onto corresponding bevels in the carcase.

All the wood in this project—except the fretwork—is ½-in.-thick pine. (The box was designed to survive in the dry Southwest. If you live in an area where wood movement is more pronounced, you might want to substitute pine-veneered MDF or pine plywood for the lid.) The box was finished with pastel gel stains: pink on most surfaces, with green in the fretwork grooves and on the bottom edges of the box.

You can use the same dimensions, materials, and finishes discussed here (see also the drawings on pp. 128-129), or you can adapt them to suit your needs and tastes. A cutlist is included with the drawing.

Preparing the Parts

1. Cut a ½-in.-thick, clear-pine board 5¾ in. wide by 31 in. long for the carcase pieces.

2. Cut the ½-in.-wide groove on the inside face for the bottom panel. Then cut two ½-in.-wide grooves on the outside face for the fretwork inlays. Next, cut a 45° bevel on the inside face of the top edge.

3. Make a slightly oversize ½-in.-thick lid of clear pine—approximately 6¼ in. wide by 9¼ in. long.

This box gains its Southwestern flair from its stairstep legs, inlaid fretwork, pastel colors, and the dyed leather hinges and latch. (Photo by Sally Ann Photography.)

4. Miter-cut the front and back carcase pieces to length on the table saw, and bevel-cut the lid to the same length. Then miter-cut the carcase sides, and bevel-cut the lid's width to match.

5. Cut the stepped legs in the four carcase pieces. Mike did this on the table saw using a ¾-in.-wide dado blade. Clamp the pieces together on the miter gauge, with a backing board to prevent tearout.

Set the blade height to 1½ in. Starting 2¼ in. in from each end, hollow out the front and back pieces to create a 4½-in.-wide cutout. With the same blade height, repeat for the side pieces, but make the cutout 1½ in. wide. Next, set the blade height to 1 in. and cut a ¾-in. cutout 1½ in. from each end (this cut is the same for both front and back pieces and the side pieces). Then set the blade height to ½ in. and make the final pass ¾ in. from each end (see the detail drawing on p. 129). The result will be stepped legs in each carcase piece.

6. Cut the ½-in.-thick bottom panel to its final dimensions (5³⁄₁₆ in. wide and 8¼ in. long).

7. Sand the two panels and the inside faces of the carcase pieces, finishing with 180-grit paper.

Assembling and Finishing the Box

1. Assemble the box, applying glue to all mitered and beveled surfaces. You can use masking tape to hold the joints together. Tape can also be used to hold the lid panel to the carcase, but to add clamping pressure place a small weight (1 lb. to 2 lb.) on the lid. Don't glue the bottom panel in place—it should float in its grooves to allow for seasonal movement.

2. After the glue dries, separate the lid from the carcase. Make the cut 1¼ in. from the top (see the section-view drawing on p. 129). Sand the new edges smooth. Then cut a ¹⁄₁₆-in.-deep, 1-in.-wide mortise in the lid's front edge for the leather latch.

3. Make the zigzag fretwork (but don't install it yet). The sidebar at right explains how to make the fretwork on the table saw.

4. Sand the box and the fretwork, finishing with 220-grit paper.

5. Apply one coat of gel stain to the fretwork and the box (including the stepped edges), using a thick rag or brush. Because pine does not take penetrating finishes well, it's better finished with a nonpenetrating finish, such as gel stain, varnish, lacquer, or paint.

On the fretwork, stain only the show side and the edges; leave the glue side unfinished —otherwise, the glue will adhere poorly.

Cutting the Zigzag Fretwork

Mike Jagielo worked out a way of cutting the zigzag fretwork in this box using a table saw. His method creates a zigzag pattern that is straight, uniform, and equally spaced. Here's how he did it:

1. Start with two strips of ⅛-in.-thick stock: one is ½ in. wide and 36 in. long; the other is ½ in. wide and around 24 in. long. The long strip is the actual stock for the fretwork; the shorter strip will be used to test the miter-fence setup.

2. Screw an auxiliary fence to the miter gauge. To allow for slight adjustments to the right or left, slot the holes for the screws.

3. Set a ⅜-in.-wide dado blade to 45° and to a height of ¹¹⁄₃₂ in. Saw a triangular cutout near one end of the test strip.

4. Then cut a triangle out of ⅛-in. hardwood that fits into the cutout precisely, and set it aside. The triangle will be used to index the angled dado cuts and will guarantee that the triangular cutouts in the fretwork are equally spaced.

5. Glue the indexing triangle to the fence, as shown in the drawing below. The triangle should be located so as to create the next cutout ⁵⁄₁₆ in. from the previous one.

6. Place the test strip against the fence, with the cutout positioned over the indexing triangle. Then make several more cutouts, indexing the previous cutout over the indexing triangle each time.

7. Flip the test strip over and saw a triangular cutout equidistant between the first two cutouts on the opposite side (Mike judges this by eye). If your new cutout isn't quite in the middle between two opposite cutouts, cut off the end of the strip and try again. When you get a perfectly located cutout, cut several more of them.

The zigzag fretwork dimensions are shown in the section drawing of the box on p. 129. You may have to slide the auxiliary fence to the left or right until you achieve the desired dimensions.

8. Once you've got the setup adjusted to your satisfaction, you can cut the real zigzag fretwork.

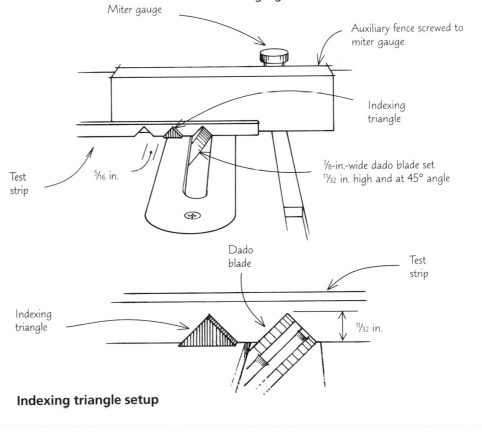

Miter gauge

Auxiliary fence screwed to miter gauge

Indexing triangle

⅜-in.-wide dado blade set ¹¹⁄₃₂ in. high and at 45° angle

Test strip

⁵⁄₁₆ in.

Dado blade

Test strip

Indexing triangle

¹¹⁄₃₂ in.

Indexing triangle setup

Southwestern Box

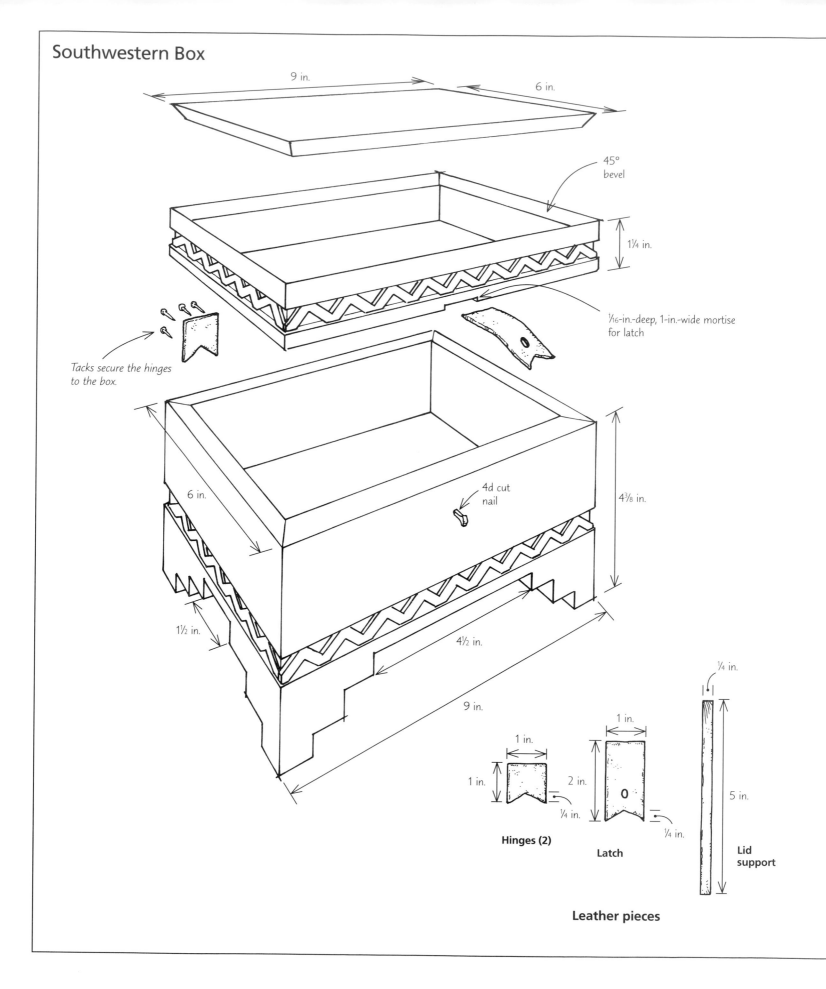

9 in.

6 in.

45°
bevel

1¼ in.

1⁄16-in.-deep, 1-in.-wide mortise
for latch

Tacks secure the hinges
to the box.

6 in.

4d cut
nail

4³⁄₈ in.

1½ in.

4½ in.

9 in.

¼ in.

1 in.

1 in.

2 in.

¼ in.

1 in.

O

¼ in.

5 in.

Hinges (2)

Latch

**Lid
support**

Leather pieces

CUTLIST

Description	Quantity	Dimensions
Front/back	2	½ x 5¾ x 9
Sides	2	½ x 5¾ x 6
Lid panel	1	½ x 6 x 9
Bottom panel	1	½ x 5³⁄₁₆ x 8¼
Fretwork blank	1	⅛ x ½ x 36

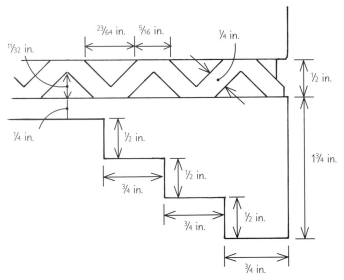

²³⁄₆₄ in. ⁵⁄₁₆ in. ¼ in. ¹¹⁄₃₂ in. ½ in. ¼ in. ½ in. 1¾ in. ¾ in. ½ in. ¾ in. ½ in. ¾ in.

Detail of stepped legs and fretwork

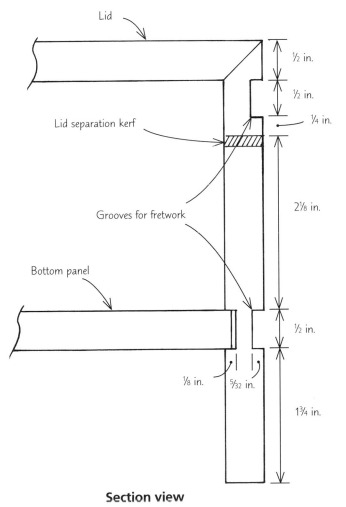

Lid

½ in.

½ in.

¼ in.

Lid separation kerf

Grooves for fretwork

2⅛ in.

Bottom panel

½ in.

⅛ in. ⁵⁄₃₂ in.

1¾ in.

Section view

Hinges, Latch, and Lid Support

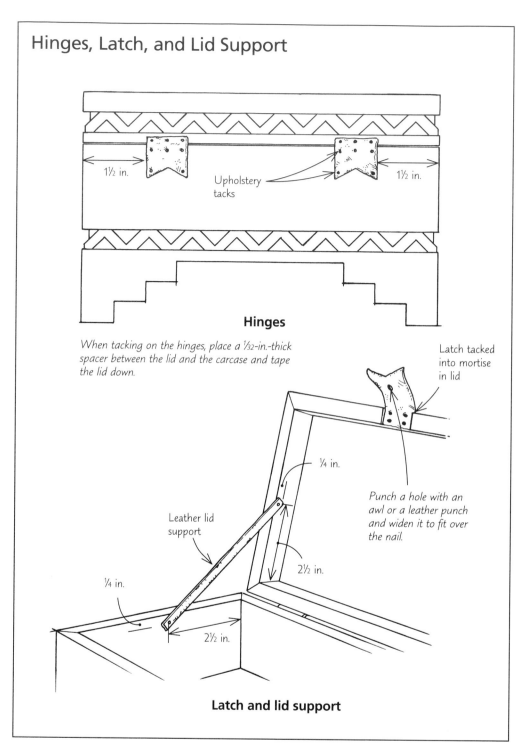

Hinges

When tacking on the hinges, place a ¹⁄₃₂-in.-thick spacer between the lid and the carcase and tape the lid down.

1½ in.

1½ in.

Upholstery tacks

¼ in.

¼ in.

2½ in.

2½ in.

Leather lid support

Latch tacked into mortise in lid

Punch a hole with an awl or a leather punch and widen it to fit over the nail.

Latch and lid support

6. When the finish dries, sand the box lightly with 220-grit sandpaper. This will prepare the box for the overcoats of sealer and lacquer. Avoid sanding the corners and sharp edges, or you'll remove much of the color.

7. Glue in the fretwork. Mike did not use clamps or tape—he just spread glue on the backs of the inlays and set them in place.

8. Sprayed on a coat of vinyl sealer for protection and two coats of lacquer for added luster.

HINGES, LATCH, AND LID SUPPORT

1. Cut the hinges, the latch, and the lid support from scrap leather (which you can obtain from an upholstery shop) to the dimensions shown in the drawing on p. 128. The leather pieces for this box were dyed, using barn-red milk paint. Since milk paint leaves a crusty powder residue on the surface of the leather after it dries, you'll need to flex the leather a few times to get rid of the residue. An alternative to milk paint is leather dye, which dries without the residue on the surface. (Leather dye is available from leather-supply stores.)

2. Drill a pilot hole for the 4d cut nail, which will serve as a catch for the leather latch. The hole's diameter should be the cut nail's thickness and should be located in the center of the carcase front, about ½ in. below the rim. Drive the nail into the pilot hole, leaving about ½ in. exposed. When driving the nail, support the inside face of the front on a corner of your bench or on another firm surface.

3. Before tacking the hinges in place, insert a ¹⁄₃₂-in.-thick spacer between the lid and carcase, which will create extra space to allow the wood to expand and the leather to shrink without restricting the lid's closing action. Also, tape the lid firmly to the carcase. (Remove the spacer and the tape after the hinges are tacked in.)

Tack the leather hinges and latch in place using #4 "gimp" upholstery tacks (see the drawing at left). These tacks have a blue, domed head similar to an escutcheon pin and are available at some hardware stores and most upholstery-supply distributors. They're ⁷⁄₁₆ in. long, and the domed head is a little less than ⅛ in. in diameter. If you can't get them locally, contact Holland Manufacturing Co. (P.O. Box 38179, Baltimore, MD 21231; 410-732-4455) for the name of the nearest distributor.

4. Pull the leather latch down and stretch it slightly over the cut nail. Mark the point where the latch hits the lower edge of the nail. At that point, punch a hole in the latch with an awl or a leather punch. Lengthen the hole upward (toward the lid) by about ¼ in. using a knife or the corner of a chisel. You should have to stretch the latch slightly when you pull it down over the nail to lock the lid closed.

5. Now install the leather lid support. The support is installed in almost the same manner as a chain support, except that the leather is attached with the gimp tacks, not screws.

METRIC EQUIVALENCE CHART

Inches	Centimeters	Millimeters	Inches	Centimeters	Millimeters	Inches	Centimeters	Millimeters
⅛	0.3	3	5	12.7	127	21	53.3	533
¼	0.6	6	6	15.2	152	22	55.9	559
⅜	1.0	10	7	17.8	178	23	58.4	584
½	1.3	13	8	20.3	203	24	61.0	610
⅝	1.6	16	9	22.9	229	25	63.5	635
¾	1.9	19	10	25.4	254	26	66.0	660
⅞	2.2	22	11	27.9	279	27	68.6	686
1	2.5	25	12	30.5	305	28	71.1	711
1¼	3.2	32	13	33.0	330	29	73.7	737
1½	3.8	38	14	35.6	356	30	76.2	762
1¾	4.4	44	15	38.1	381	31	78.7	787
2	5.1	51	16	40.6	406	32	81.3	813
2½	6.4	64	17	43.2	432	33	83.8	838
3	7.6	76	18	45.7	457	34	86.4	864
3½	8.9	89	19	48.3	483	35	88.9	889
4	10.2	102	20	50.8	508	36	91.4	914
4½	11.4	114						

Index

A

Ash, characteristics of, 6
Aspen:
    characteristics of, 6
    finish for, 19

B

Bandsaw, for lid separation, 48
Bases:
    footed, 121, 124
    raised-platform, 70
Basswood, characteristics of, 6
Beech, characteristics of, 6
Bevels, cutting, 36
Birch, characteristics of, 6
Biscuits:
    for butt joints, 78, 79
    for leg attachment, 98
    for miter joints, 81, 82
Bookmatching, technique of, 44
Bottom panels:
    grooves for, 24-25
    making, 25
    sizing, 25
Box joints. *See* Finger joints.
Boxes:
    with ball feet, 117-20
    beveled, 34-37
    with bookmatched lid, two-piece, 91-95
    carcase-and-panel construction of, 46-48
    corners of, rounding over, 18-19
    design of, 4-5
        and wood movement, 7, 8
        See also Grain pattern.
    dimensioning, 4-5
    dividers for, 86-87

with blind pin hinges, 95-98
edges of, rounding over, 18-19
with end inserts, 51-52
feet for, 71
    cutting, 73-74
with finger hole, 63
glues for, 22
grooves in, bottom-panel, 24-25
hinged vs. unhinged, 60
with inlay, 117-20
interiors of, 85-87
    lining, 85-86
with lever-action lid, 37-39
with mitered inserts, 53-56
painted, with fretwork, 126-30
with pin hinges, 75-78, 88-95
polygonal, 57-59
profiling, 120
proportions of, 4-5
with rabbeted lid, 34-37
with raised lid panels, 53-56
with slab lid, 31-34
with slot hinges, 60-63, 71
squareness of, checking, 27-28
with swivel lid, 75
    two-piece, 88-90
with tapered legs, 95-98
trays for, 74, 87
two-tiered, 57-59
See also Bases. Bottom panels. Lid panels.
    Lids. Mitered boxes.
Breadboard construction, against cup, 8
Bridle joints:
    cutting, 125
    for lid frame, 82-84
    tenoning jig for, 82-83
Bubinga, lids of, 95, 117
Buckeye burl, box of, 75

Burls:
    in box making, 9
    spalted maple, as lid material, 31
Butternut:
    characteristics of, 6
    surface preparation for, 18
Butt joints:
    for box making, 78, 79
    reinforcing, 78, 93

C

Carcase-and-panel construction, 46-48,
    53-56
Chain, for lid support, 106, 117
Chamfers, cutting, 33, 63
Cherry:
    boxes of, 65-70, 121-25
    characteristics of, 6
    finish for, 19
    lid panel of, 121
Clamps:
    for mitered frames, 82
    rubber bands as, 26, 41
Cup:
    in lid panels, avoiding, 40
    minimizing, 8

D

Danish oil, discussed, 19, 20
Dents, raising, 17
Design, elements of, 4-5
Dividers:
    making, 86-87
    micro-lumber for, 12
    recessed, 91-93, 94

PUBLISHER   James P. Chiavelli

ACQUISITIONS EDITOR   Rick Peters

PUBLISHING COORDINATOR   Joanne Renna

EDITORS   Thomas C. McKenna, Peter Chapman

LAYOUT ARTIST   Henry Roth

ILLUSTRATOR   Mike Wanke

PHOTOGRAPHER, EXCEPT WHERE NOTED   David M. Freedman

TYPEFACE   Frutiger Light

PRINTER   Quebecor Printing/Kingsport, Kingsport, Tennessee